PHARMACOLOGY - RESEARCH, SAFETY TESTING AND REGULATION SERIES

NONPRESCRIPTION DRUGS: CONSIDERING A NEW CLASS FOR BEHIND-THE-COUNTER DRUGS

PHARMACOLOGY – RESEARCH, SAFETY TESTING AND REGULATION SERIES

Antibiotic Resistance: Causes and Risk Factors, Mechanisms and Alternatives
Adriel R. Bonilla and Kaden P. Muniz (Editors)
2009. ISBN: 978-1-60741-623-4

Antibiotic Resistance: Causes and Risk Factors, Mechanisms and Alternatives
Adriel R. Bonilla and Kaden P. Muniz (Editors)
2009. ISBN: 978-1-61668-162-3

Poisons: Physiologically Active Substances
S. B. Zotov and O. I. Tuzhikov
2009. ISBN: 978-1-60741-973-0

Drug Monitoring by HPLC: Recent Developments
Victoria Samanidou and Eftichia Karageorgou
2010. ISBN: 978-1-60876-183-8

Nonprescription Drugs: Considering A New Class for Behind-the-Counter Drugs
Lars P. Eliassen (Editor)
2010. ISBN: 978-1-60741-961-7

PHARMACOLOGY - RESEARCH, SAFETY TESTING AND REGULATION SERIES

NONPRESCRIPTION DRUGS: CONSIDERING A NEW CLASS FOR BEHIND-THE-COUNTER DRUGS

LARS P. ELIASSEN

EDITOR

Nova Science Publishers, Inc.

New York

For permission to use material from this book please contact us:
Telephone 631-231-7269; Fax 631-231-8175
Web Site: http://www.novapublishers.com

LIBRARY OF CONGRESS CATALOGING-IN-PUBLICATION DATA

Nonprescription drugs : considering a new class for behind-the-counter drugs / editor, Lars P. Eliassen.
p. ; cm.
Includes bibliographical references and index.
ISBN 978-1-60741-961-7 (hardcover : alk. paper)
1. Drugs, Nonprescription--Government policy--United States. I. Eliassen, Lars P.
[DNLM: 1. Nonprescription Drugs--classification--United States. 2. Drug and Narcotic Control--legislation & jurisprudence--United States. 3. Nonprescription Drugs--supply & distribution--United States. QV 772 N814 2009]
RM671.5.U6N66 2009
615'.1--dc22

2009041020

Published by Nova Science Publishers, Inc. ✝ New York

CONTENTS

PREFACE

In the United States, most nonprescription drugs are available over-the-counter (OTC) in pharmacies and other stores. Experts have suggested that drug availability could be increased by establishing an additional class of nonprescription drugs that would be held behind the counter (BTC) but would require the intervention of a pharmacist before being dispensed; a similar class of drugs exists in many other countries. Although the Food and Drug Administration (FDA) has not developed a detailed proposal for a BTC drug class, it held a public meeting to explore the public health implications of BTC drug availability. This book explores the public health benefits of behind the counter availability of certain drugs without a prescription. In particular, the debate whether behind the counter may improve patient access to safe and effective drug products is discussed. This book looks at the pharmacist, infrastructure, and cost-related issues which would have to be addressed before a BTC drug class could be established in the United States.

Chapter 1 - In the United States, most nonprescription drugs are available over-the-counter (OTC) in pharmacies and other stores. Experts have suggested that drug availability could be increased by establishing an additional class of nonprescription drugs that would be held behind the counter (BTC) but would require the intervention of a pharmacist before being dispensed; a similar class of drugs exists in many other countries. Although the Food and Drug Administration (FDA) has not developed a detailed proposal for a BTC drug class, it held a public meeting in 2007 to explore the public health implications of BTC drug availability.

GAO was asked to update its 1995 report, *Nonprescription Drugs: Value of a Pharmacist-Controlled Class Has Yet to Be Demonstrated* (GAO/PEMD-95-12). Specifically, GAO is reporting on (1) arguments supporting and opposing a U.S.

BTC drug class, (2) changes in drug availability in five countries since 1995 and the impact of restricted nonprescription classes on availability, and (3) issues important to the establishment of a BTC drug class.

GAO reviewed documents and consulted with pharmaceutical experts. To examine drug availability across countries, GAO studied five countries it had reported on in 1995 (Australia, Italy, the Netherlands, the United Kingdom, and the United States) and determined how 86 drugs available in all five countries were classified in each country.

Chapter 2 – This is a testimony of Randall Lutter, Deputy Commissioner for policy at the Food and Drug Administration and Douglas Throckmorton, Deputy Director, Center for Drug Evaluation Research. Food and Drug Administration Behind the Counter Availability of Certain Drugs Public Meeting.

In: Nonprescription Drugs: Considering... ISBN: 978-1-60741-961-7
Editor: Lars P. Eliassen

Chapter 1

NONPRESCRIPTION DRUGS: CONSIDERATIONS REGARDING A BEHIND-THE-COUNTER DRUG CLASS*

Government Accountability Office

WHY GAO DID THIS STUDY

In the United States, most nonprescription drugs are available over-the-counter (OTC) in pharmacies and other stores. Experts have suggested that drug availability could be increased by establishing an additional class of nonprescription drugs that would be held behind the counter (BTC) but would require the intervention of a pharmacist before being dispensed; a similar class of drugs exists in many other countries. Although the Food and Drug Administration (FDA) has not developed a detailed proposal for a BTC drug class, it held a public meeting in 2007 to explore the public health implications of BTC drug availability.

GAO was asked to update its 1995 report, *Nonprescription Drugs: Value of a Pharmacist-Controlled Class Has Yet to Be Demonstrated* (GAO/PEMD-95-12). Specifically, GAO is reporting on (1) arguments supporting and opposing a U.S. BTC drug class, (2) changes in drug availability in five

* This is an edited, reformatted and augmented version of a U. S. Government Accountability Office publication dated February 2009.

countries since 1995 and the impact of restricted nonprescription classes on availability, and (3) issues important to the establishment of a BTC drug class.

GAO reviewed documents and consulted with pharmaceutical experts. To examine drug availability across countries, GAO studied five countries it had reported on in 1995 (Australia, Italy, the Netherlands, the United Kingdom, and the United States) and determined how 86 drugs available in all five countries were classified in each country.

WHAT GAO FOUND

Arguments supporting and opposing a BTC drug class in the United States have been based on public health and health care cost considerations, and reflect general disagreement on the likely consequences of establishing such a class. Proponents of a BTC drug class suggest it would lead to improved public health through increased availability of nonprescription drugs and greater use of pharmacists' expertise. Opponents are concerned that a BTC drug class might become the default for drugs switching from prescription to nonprescription status, thus reducing consumers' access to drugs that would otherwise have become available OTC, and argue that pharmacists might not be able to provide high quality BTC services. Proponents of a BTC drug class point to potentially reduced costs through a decrease in the number of physician visits and a decline in drug prices that might result from switches of drugs from prescription to nonprescription status. However, opponents argue that out-of-pocket costs for many consumers could rise if third-party payers elect not to cover BTC drugs.

All five countries GAO studied have increased nonprescription drug availability since 1995 by altering nonprescription classes or reclassifying some drugs into less restrictive classes. Italy and the Netherlands, which previously allowed nonprescription drugs to be sold only at specialized drug outlets, made some or all of these drugs available for OTC sale. Australia, the United Kingdom, and the United States switched certain drugs from more restrictive to less restrictive drug classes, increasing these drugs' availability. However, the impact of restricted nonprescription drug classes on availability is unclear. When we examined the classification of 86 selected drugs in the five countries, we found that the United States required a prescription for more of those drugs than did Australia or the United Kingdom—the study countries using a BTC drug class. However, the United States classified more of the 86 drugs as OTC—the option that provides greatest access to these drugs for consumers—than all four of the other study countries.

Pharmacist-, infrastructure-, and cost-related issues would have to be addressed before a BTC drug class could be established in the United States. For example, ensuring that pharmacists provide BTC counseling and that pharmacies have the infrastructure to protect consumer privacy would be important. Issues related to the cost of BTC drugs would also require consideration. For example, the availability of third-party coverage for BTC drugs would affect consumers' out-of-pocket expenditures and pharmacists' compensation for providing BTC services would need to be examined.

In commenting on a draft of this report, the Department of Health and Human Services (HHS) agreed that cost-related issues would have to be addressed before implementing a BTC drug class and also provided technical comments. The Department of Veterans Affairs (VA) also reviewed the report and provided technical comments. We have incorporated HHS and VA technical comments as appropriate.

ABBREVIATIONS

AIDS	acquired immunodeficiency syndrome
BTC	behind-the-counter
CMS	Centers for Medicare & Medicaid Services
EU	European Union
FDA	Food and Drug Administration
HHS	Department of Health and Human Services
IHS	Indian Health Service
MHRA	Medicines and Healthcare products Regulatory Agency (United Kingdom)
MMA	Medicare Prescription Drug, Improvement, and Modernization Act of 2003
MTM	medication therapy management
OBRA '90	Omnibus Budget Reconciliation Act of 1990
OTC	over-the-counter
VA	Department of Veterans Affairs

February 20, 2009
The Honorable Henry A. Waxman
Chairman
The Honorable John D. Dingell
Chairman Emeritus
Committee on Energy and Commerce
House of Representatives

The Honorable Bart Stupak
Chairman
Subcommittee on Oversight and Investigations
Committee on Energy and Commerce
House of Representatives

The United States has a two-tier system for the classification of drugs: prescription and nonprescription. Prescription drugs can be dispensed only with written or oral orders (i.e., a prescription) from a licensed prescriber—such as a doctor, nurse practitioner, or physician's assistant— to a pharmacist or other licensed dispenser. Most nonprescription drugs are available for sale over the counter (OTC) by self-service in pharmacies and in nonpharmacy outlets such as grocery stores, mass merchandisers, and gas stations. The two-tier system in the United States is distinct from other countries that have more or different categories of nonprescription drugs. In other countries, levels of restriction on where and by whom a nonprescription drug can be sold vary. For example, certain nonprescription drugs may be sold only under the supervision of a pharmacist.

Pharmacists, academics, and other experts have suggested that an additional class of nonprescription drugs could increase drug availability, because more drugs could be made available without the need to obtain a prescription. In the United States, the Food and Drug Administration (FDA), an agency within the Department of Health and Human Services (HHS), has authority to approve drugs prior to their marketing, to ensure that they are safe and effective, and to determine their prescription or nonprescription status. Although FDA has not developed a specific proposal, in November 2007, it held a public meeting to explore the public health implications of behind-the-counter (BTC) availability of certain drugs.[1] BTC drugs would be held behind a pharmacy counter and available without a prescription, but dispensed only after intervention by a pharmacist. The primary purpose of a BTC class would be to increase access to drugs to promote public health by making drugs available without a prescription when intervention by a pharmacist or other means can help ensure the safe and effective use of such drugs. Similar proposals have been considered in the past and, in 1995, GAO issued a report titled *Nonprescription Drugs: Value of a Pharmacist-Controlled Class Has Yet to Be Demonstrated* (GAO/PEMD-95-12).[2] In that report, we stated that there was little evidence to support the establishment of a BTC or similar class of drugs in the United States. The evidence at the time tended to show that countries with a BTC or similar drug class were not obtaining major benefits from that class.

In light of the FDA hearing on BTC drugs and the fundamental change that a BTC drug class would represent in the U.S. drug classification system, you asked us to update our 1995 report. Specifically, we are reporting on (1) the arguments that have been made supporting and opposing the creation of a BTC drug class in the United States; (2) changes in drug availability in our five study countries[3] since 1995 and the impact of restricted nonprescription drug classes on drug availability; and (3) issues that would be important to the establishment of a BTC drug class.

To describe the arguments that have been made supporting and opposing a BTC drug class in the United States, we reviewed published literature, reports, and meeting minutes of FDA hearings on prescription-to-OTC switches,[4] and the transcript of and docket submissions for the November 2007 FDA meeting on BTC drugs.[5] We interviewed officials at FDA, pharmacy associations, drug manufacturers, consumer groups, and industry associations in the United States. We also interviewed academics and other officials knowledgeable about pharmaceutical practice.

To determine the impact of restricted nonprescription drug classes on drug availability, we interviewed experts to ask them to help us identify countries that had evaluated drug classification since our 1995 report. Based on this information, we selected 5 of the 11 countries covered in our previous report.[6] We also examined drug classification in the European Union (EU), because it affects drug availability in three of our study countries. We reviewed published literature, reports, and agency documents on drug classification and prescription-to-nonprescription switches in our study countries. We also interviewed agency officials, industry representatives, and others knowledgeable about pharmaceutical practices in the United States and the other study countries. We examined changes since 1995 in the drug classification systems in two study countries (Italy and the Netherlands) that changed the number or type of nonprescription drug classes in use. We also determined the number of drugs switched from one drug class to another (e.g., prescription to BTC) between 1995 and 2008 for the three study countries (Australia, the United Kingdom, and the United States) that maintained the same number and type of nonprescription drug classes during that time. Additionally, we determined the classification of selected drugs in our study countries. We chose a sample of drugs using World Self-Medication Industry data on the classification of more than 200 drugs in 36 countries and identified 86 of these drugs as available in all five study countries.[7] We examined the survey format used to collect information on drug classification and response rates from the most recent survey, and determined that the data were sufficiently reliable for our purposes. We then used drug classification documents published by the regulatory agencies in each of the study countries and information from agency officials to determine how each of the 86 drugs was classified in each country. The data in these reference documents are standard data sources published by each country's regulatory authority and were sufficiently reliable for our purposes.

To identify issues that would be important to the establishment of a BTC drug class in the United States, we reviewed published literature and reports. We interviewed officials at FDA, the Centers for Medicare & Medicaid Services (CMS), the Department of Veterans Affairs (VA), the Indian Health Service (IHS), pharmacy associations, drug manufacturers, consumer groups, industry associations, and drug regulatory agencies in other countries. We also interviewed academics and other experts— including individuals who have testified before FDA on the possible creation of a BTC drug class in the United States—knowledgeable about pharmacists' prescribing authority. Appendix I provides a more detailed explanation of the scope and methodology for this report. We conducted our work from March 2008 through February 2009 in accordance with all sections of GAO's quality assurance framework that are relevant to our objectives. The framework requires that we plan and perform the engagement to obtain sufficient and appropriate evidence to meet our stated objectives and to discuss any limitations in our work. We believe that the information and data obtained, and the analysis conducted, provide a reasonable basis for any findings and conclusions.

Results in Brief

Arguments supporting and opposing a BTC drug class in the United States have been based on public health and health care cost considerations, and these arguments reflect general disagreement on the likely consequences of the establishment of such a class. Some who support a BTC drug class suggest that such a class would lead to improved public health through increased availability of nonprescription drugs. For example, a BTC class might allow more drugs to be switched out of the prescription class, providing increased access to these drugs for consumers. Additionally, proponents argue that pharmacists have extensive knowledge of drug use and drug interactions and could help consumers to assess their medical needs and determine whether a physician's visit would be appropriate. However, opponents are concerned about the potential for a BTC class to become a default class for all drugs switching from prescription to nonprescription status even when the additional restrictions of BTC classification are not necessary for safe use of all such drugs; BTC classification would reduce consumers' access to drugs if those drugs would otherwise have switched to OTC status. Opponents also note that pharmacists are not trained in clinical diagnosis, generally do not have access to relevant patient information (such as laboratory results), and lack the time to provide counseling to patients. Health care cost arguments in favor of a BTC drug class center on possible reduced costs through a decrease in the number of physician visits and a decline in drug prices that might result from nonprescription status. However, opponents argue that out-of-pocket costs for many consumers could rise if prescription drugs currently covered by insurance are switched to BTC status and third-party payers elect not to cover BTC drugs. Additional costs to consumers could result if pharmacists require a fee in order to provide counseling.

All five study countries have increased nonprescription drug availability since 1995; however, the impact of restricted nonprescription drug classes on drug availability is unclear. The five study countries—selected because they evaluated drug classification in their countries since 1995—have increased drug availability in two ways: by changing nonprescription drug classes or by switching some drugs into less restrictive classes. Italy—in 2006—and the Netherlands—in 2007—changed their nonprescription drug classes by making some or all of their nonprescription drugs available for OTC sale at nonpharmacy outlets, such as grocery stores. Previously, the Netherlands restricted drug sales to drugstores (operated by a licensed druggist and allowed to sell certain nonprescription drugs) or pharmacies (operated by a pharmacist and allowed to sell all prescription and nonprescription drugs); Italy also previously limited the sale of all drugs to pharmacies. Since 1995, Australia, the United Kingdom, and the United States have switched a number of drugs from more restrictive to less restrictive drug classes, again resulting in an overall increase in drug availability. When we examined the classification of 86 selected drugs in the five study countries, we found that the impact of restricted nonprescription drug classes on availability is unclear. The United States required a prescription for more of those drugs than did Australia or the United Kingdom—the study countries using a BTC drug class. However, the United States also classified more of the drugs from our sample as OTC—the option that provides greatest access to these drugs for consumers—than all four of the other study countries. Additionally, we did not find an association between the restrictions placed on the availability of particular drugs in our sample by the study countries and the presence of a BTC drug class. The United States gave more restrictive classification to some drugs and less restrictive classification to other drugs when compared to the other four study countries.

Pharmacist-, infrastructure-, and cost-related issues would have to be addressed before a BTC drug class could be established in the United States. The roles and responsibilities of pharmacists in a BTC drug class that would need to be considered include defining pharmacist responsibilities for dispensing BTC drugs, ensuring that pharmacists provide the necessary BTC counseling, and determining whether additional training would be needed for pharmacists and pharmacy staff. In addition, whether or not there is a sufficient pharmacist workforce to make such a class viable would need to be determined, and pharmacists' new role would need to be communicated to the public. Ensuring that pharmacies have the data infrastructure necessary to provide pharmacists with patient information and the physical infrastructure to protect consumer privacy would also be important. Additionally, several cost issues would be important to the implementation of a BTC drug class. For example, the availability of third-party coverage for BTC drugs would affect consumers' out-of-pocket expenditures. If BTC drugs were more expensive than prescription or OTC alternatives, it could discourage consumer use of BTC drugs. Also, pharmacists' compensation for providing BTC services would need to be considered. The level of pharmacist compensation might influence pharmacists' willingness to engage in activities required for dispensing BTC drugs, such as providing counseling, and therefore could affect their participation in a BTC drug class. Other cost issues might also affect the viability of a BTC drug class. Pharmacists' liability risk could increase as a result of their expanded role in a BTC drug class and thus deter pharmacists from participating in a BTC drug class.

In commenting on a draft of this report, HHS agreed that cost-related issues would have to be addressed before implementing a BTC drug class and also provided technical comments. VA also reviewed the report and provided technical comments. We have incorporated HHS and VA technical comments as appropriate.

BACKGROUND

In the United States, although drugs are classified as prescription or nonprescription at the federal level by FDA, the practice of pharmacy is typically regulated by states. For example, states license pharmacists and enforce pharmacists' continuing education requirements.

The 1951 Durham-Humphrey Amendments to the Federal Food, Drug, and Cosmetic Act provided the statutory basis for the two-tier drug classification system that currently exists in the United States.[8] Since that time, there have been a number of proposals to introduce a third category of drugs in the United States. This category has been called by a number of names, including pharmacist-legend, pharmacist-only, third class of drugs, and BTC. Although there is some variation between proposals, the basic idea is the same: a class of drugs would be established that would be available without a prescription, but only in pharmacies. The BTC idea that FDA sought comment on would require that these drugs be sold only in pharmacies, and that a pharmacist's intervention with a consumer occur before the drug could be dispensed.[9]

Use of a BTC Drug Class

There are two general views on how a BTC class of drugs would be used in the United States. The first is that BTC would be a permanent class. It would be similar to the current prescription and OTC classes, in that drugs would be placed in the BTC class with no expectation that they would eventually switch to the prescription or OTC class. Drugs in the BTC class would be those determined by FDA to be nonprescription but would require the intervention of a pharmacist. Drugs in the BTC class could come from the current prescription and OTC classes or new drugs could be classified as BTC, although proposals for a BTC drug class generally seek to increase access to medications by switching drugs out of the prescription class.

The second view is that the BTC drug class could function as a transition class for some drugs and a permanent class for others. A drug being switched from prescription to nonprescription would spend time in the transition class, during which the suitability of the drug for OTC status could be assessed. In addition to studies specifically designed for such an assessment, consumer use of the drug as a prescription drug and as a BTC drug could be examined.[10] The argument is that this would provide a better picture of how the drug would be used by the public if it were available as an OTC product. Information that could be gathered while the drug was in the transition class includes types and levels of misuse among the general public, incidents of adverse drug reactions, and interactions with other medications. At some point after the product has been BTC, a decision might be made based on the available data to switch the drug to OTC, return the drug to prescription status, keep the drug in the BTC class for future study, or keep the drug in the BTC class with no expectation that it would eventually be switched to the prescription or OTC class.

FDA has not indicated which drugs might be classified as BTC in the United States. However, among the drugs suggested by some proponents are certain drugs that treat chronic conditions such as high cholesterol, asthma, high blood pressure, diabetes, urinary incontinence, and osteoporosis. Vaccines; the epinephrine auto-injector used in emergency situations following insect bites, stings, or exposure to other allergens; and oseltamivir—which is used to treat influenza and might be effective in the event of an influenza pandemic—have also been suggested as possible BTC products. More generally, drugs that are subject to abuse and drugs that are to be sold only to consumers of a minimum age have been mentioned as possible candidates for a BTC class.

Nonprescription Drug Classes in Other Countries

Figure 1 defines the terms we use to describe the drug classes in the United States and other countries and how the levels of restriction vary among classes based on the conditions under which drugs are sold. As discussed in our previous report, varying levels of restriction on nonprescription drugs already exist in other countries.[11] Among the criteria foreign countries have used for switching a drug from prescription to a less restrictive nonprescription drug class are: (1) the symptoms or circumstances for use of the drug are suitable for self-medication, including self-diagnosis, with the intervention of a pharmacist; and (2) the drug has a low potential for side effects or overdose, and intervention by a pharmacist could minimize these risks. In contrast, nonprescription drugs in the United States generally have these characteristics: (1) their benefits outweigh their risks; (2) consumers can use them for self-diagnosed conditions; (3) they can be adequately labeled for self-medication; and (4) a prescription by a licensed prescriber is not needed for the consumer to safely and effectively use the drug and the conditions or symptoms are generally self-limiting. Appendix II provides details on the drug classification systems in each study country and the European Union (EU).

While Figure 1 indicates how the levels of restriction for prescription and nonprescription drug classes affect drug availability, there are other factors that can also affect availability including cost, patient participation in health decisions, and purchase site convenience. For example, the number of pharmacies in a country affects the availability of BTC drugs. The more pharmacies there are, the greater the availability of BTC drugs and the smaller the difference in availability between BTC and OTC drugs. Also, the distribution of pharmacies can affect availability. Areas without a local pharmacy but with outlets that sell OTC drugs, would be more affected by not having drugs available OTC than would areas with nearby pharmacies.

Arguments Made Supporting and Opposing a BTC Drug Class Reflect Disagreement on Its Impact on Health Care and Health Care Costs

Arguments that have been made supporting and opposing a BTC drug class are generally based on public health or cost considerations and reflect disagreement on the likely consequences of the establishment of such a class. Many of the arguments are concerned with how a BTC drug class might affect consumers' access to medications, pharmacist involvement in selecting drugs, the costs of drugs, and payment policies.

Term used in the report	Definition	Levels of restriction
Prescription drugs		
Prescription	Available only from a pharmacist or other licensed dispenser upon submission of a prescription	Most restrictive ↑
Nonprescription drugs		
BTC	Available only in pharmacies; contact with pharmacist required	
Pharmacy	Available only in pharmacies; contact with pharmacist not required	
Drugstore	Available only in pharmacies or drugstores; contact with pharmacist not required[a]	
OTC/pharmacist	Available for self-selection in pharmacies and other retail outlets, but a pharmacist must be present	
OTC	Available for self-selection in pharmacies and other retail outlets, including those without pharmacists or druggists	↓ Least restrictive

Source: GAO analysis of agency documents from the study countries.

[a] in the Netherlands, a distinction is made between pharmacies (run by pharmacists and able to sell all prescription and nonprescription drugs) and drugstores (run by druggists with less training than pharmacists and able to sell only some nonprescription drugs).

Figure 1. Definitions and Relative Levels of Restriction for Drug Classes Used in This Report

Some Proponents of a BTC Drug Class Argue It Will Improve Public Health

Some of those who support a BTC drug class, including representatives of pharmacist associations and some academics, suggest that such a class would lead to improved public health through increased availability of nonprescription drugs.[12] Proponents of a BTC drug class argue that such a class would increase access because drugs that might not otherwise be suitable for general OTC use could be available without a prescription. The switching of a drug from prescription to OTC represents a large change in the distribution of the drug, from requiring a prescription to requiring no medical intervention at all. Proponents argue that pharmacists could help bridge this gap if there were a BTC drug class. By providing a new avenue for switches from prescription to nonprescription, a BTC drug class would give consumers access to more drugs that could benefit their health. Pharmacists could counsel consumers on BTC medications and, consequently, some drugs that were unsuitable for OTC availability could be made available as BTC drugs. Proponents argue that this would be particularly important for underserved populations, such as the uninsured, underinsured, or those with limited access to a primary care provider and, thus, to prescription drugs. Moreover, an FDA official told us that many of the drugs that could be switched to OTC under the current two-tier drug classification system have already been reclassified and that a BTC drug class might allow additional drugs to be switched out of prescription status.. The convenience of acquiring BTC drugs at a pharmacy could improve consumer adherence to drug regimens by eliminating the need for a visit to a physician to obtain refill prescriptions. Additionally, FDA has noted that people are now taking a larger role in managing their health. Experts have stated that increased access to drugs through a BTC class could give them even more tools to do so, thus potentially improving their health.

Other arguments in favor of a BTC drug class focus on the expanded role of pharmacists under such a class, suggesting that greater use of pharmacist expertise would improve health outcomes. Proponents of a BTC drug class note that pharmacists are successfully engaging in activities beyond their traditional role of dispensing drugs, such as prescribing drugs under certain circumstances[13] or reviewing individuals' drug regimens if they participate as providers of medication therapy management (MTM) in programs where they are authorized to perform such reviews.[14] Proponents also point out that pharmacists are well trained in medication therapy, and a BTC drug class would make better use of pharmacists' knowledge of drug use, drug interactions, and other factors. Additionally, pharmacy schools are becoming more patient focused, integrating training on counseling, physical assessments of patients, and interpretation of lab results into their curricula. Because pharmacists might be more accessible than physicians, better health outcomes could result from the greater consumer interaction with pharmacists brought on by a BTC drug class. During such interactions, pharmacists might also refer individuals with potentially serious medical conditions to a physician; these individuals might not have otherwise entered the health care system. Moreover, proponents of a BTC class note that numerous studies have demonstrated that expanded pharmacist roles in individuals' care can result in health improvements. They note that the pharmacy practice literature generally supports the ability of community pharmacists[15] to reduce adverse reactions and improve clinical outcomes for conditions such as asthma, diabetes, hypertension, and high cholesterol.[16]

Proponents also argue that a BTC drug class would improve public health by permitting additional data to be obtained that would better indicate when a drug would be appropriate for OTC availability. For example, BTC availability might allow consumer–pharmacist interactions to be studied to determine if consumers really need the pharmacist's input. Additionally, information might be collected from pharmacists about whether consumers could understand product information and appropriately assess their suitability for a medication without pharmacist prompting. This could affect the labeling if the drug were switched to OTC availability. Depending on a drug's safety and usage profile in a BTC class, a drug could either remain permanently in the BTC class or subsequently transition to OTC.

Some Opponents of a BTC Drug Class Raise Concerns about Potential Harm to Public Health

Opponents of a BTC drug class, including some academics and representatives of drug manufacturers, raise concerns that such a class could harm public health by decreasing the availability of nonprescription drugs. Overall, opponents believe that the current two-tier drug classification system works well and provides consumers with an appropriate level of drug availability.[17] Opponents of a BTC drug class argue that such a class could become the default option for drugs being switched from prescription status due to the cautious approach of regulators. Prescription drugs that could have switched to OTC might instead be placed into a BTC drug class, resulting in decreased consumer access compared to OTC availability. Drugs might also remain in a BTC drug class even if suitable for OTC use. Concerns have also been raised that current OTC products could be moved into a BTC class, thereby reducing availability. Additionally, depending on how well information is communicated to consumers about a BTC drug class, both in public campaigns and within pharmacies, consumers could be unaware of available BTC drugs. Underserved and rural communities with few or no pharmacies might also experience barriers to accessing BTC drugs, which would only be available through pharmacies.

Opponents also raise concerns about the potential harm that might be done to consumers if pharmacists are not able to provide high-quality, reliable BTC services. Physician association representatives and others have stated that pharmacists lack adequate clinical training to properly diagnose and treat illnesses, skills which might be required when dispensing BTC drugs.[18] Opponents also raise the concern that pharmacists are very busy and might not have enough time to provide individualized counseling to consumers regarding BTC drugs. Additionally, pharmacists might not have access to relevant information (e.g., a complete medical record, laboratory results, and a complete list of medications taken by the individual) necessary to make an optimal and safe BTC drug recommendation. Opponents also argue that, currently, pharmacists counsel infrequently and sometimes incorrectly. Beyond concerns over inadequate service, opponents suggest that a lack of private confidential areas in pharmacies for consumer–pharmacist interactions could discourage individuals from seeking care for sensitive matters.

Some opponents of a BTC drug class assert that adverse health outcomes could result from improper use of BTC drugs. Individuals who use BTC drugs without consulting a physician might treat symptoms but not the underlying cause of the illness, thus delaying appropriate therapy. Readily available BTC drugs could also encourage individuals with chronic conditions to seek pharmaceutical remedies instead of lifestyle changes that could alleviate the conditions. Additionally, an individual's personal physician might not be aware when a person begins a pharmacist- recommended BTC drug regimen and thus might not be able to monitor the individual appropriately. Experts told us this uncoordinated care could further fragment the provision of health care.

Some Proponents of a BTC Drug Class Argue that It Would Reduce Costs

Proponents of a BTC class have argued that establishment of such a class would likely reduce costs. In the past, the price of a drug has decreased when it was switched from prescription to OTC. Consequently, if a BTC drug class permits increased switching of drugs and pricing follows this pattern, it could reduce costs to consumers and to the overall health care system. Cost savings could also result from a decrease in the number of physicians' visits. The availability of BTC drugs that previously had prescription status could result in fewer physician office visits for patients seeking prescriptions and, accordingly, fewer co-payments and third-party reimbursements to physicians. This would reduce costs for both consumers and insurers, as well as overall health care system expenditures. The pharmacy practice literature also supports the ability of community pharmacists to provide cost-effective interventions and reduce the cost of drug therapy.[19]

Additionally, because third-party payers do not typically reimburse consumers for nonprescription drugs and thus might not provide coverage for BTC drugs, drug expenditures for third-party payers could decrease if prescription drugs were switched to a BTC class. Cost reductions for insurers could also be realized in the area of compensation for professional services. Although pharmacist associations maintain that pharmacists would need to be compensated for health care services provided under a BTC paradigm, health services provided by pharmacists are less expensive than those provided by physicians—pharmacists are reimbursed at approximately 80 percent of physician rates for similar time- based services.[20]

Some Opponents of a BTC Drug Class Cite the Potential for Increased Costs

Many arguments against a BTC drug class are based on the potential increased costs to individuals, third-party payers, and the overall health care system that such a class might cause. For instance, because insurers do not typically reimburse consumers for OTC drugs and thus might not provide coverage for BTC drugs, out-of-pocket expenses for consumers could increase if prescription drugs were switched to a BTC drug class and if the cost of the BTC product were greater than the previous copay.[21] Opponents of a BTC drug class have argued also that costs could increase as the result of the pharmacy services required for establishing such a class. Compensation for pharmacists providing BTC services could result in greater costs for consumers and third-party payers than if the drugs had been made OTC in the current two-tier system. Furthermore, restricted competition could also increase costs. It has been noted that there would be fewer outlets for BTC drugs than for OTC products because BTC products could not be sold at retail outlets other than pharmacies. This reduced availability could adversely affect retail competition and, as a result, drive up prices.

Additionally, improper use of BTC drugs and the absence of physician consultations in the BTC process could result in expensive adverse health outcomes. For example, without a physician's diagnosis, a pharmacist might recommend a BTC drug to treat stomach pain. However, potentially serious gastrointestinal problems might underlie this symptom, and delays in obtaining appropriate treatment could have serious and expensive consequences to the consumer and the health care system as a whole.

ALL STUDY COUNTRIES HAVE INCREASED NONPRESCRIPTION DRUG AVAILABILITY, BUT THE IMPACT OF RESTRICTED NONPRESCRIPTION DRUG CLASSES ON AVAILABILITY IS UNCLEAR

All five study countries have increased nonprescription drug availability since 1995; however, the impact of restricted nonprescription drug classes on availability is unclear. The five study countries increased drug availability in two ways: by changing nonprescription drug classes or by switching some drugs into less restrictive classes. Italy and the Netherlands established new OTC classes by making some or all nonprescription drugs available for sale at nonpharmacy outlets, while Australia, the United Kingdom, and the United States switched a number of drugs from more restrictive to less restrictive drug classes. When we compared the classification of 86 selected drugs in the five study countries, we found that the impact of restricted nonprescription drug classes on availability is unclear. The United States required a prescription for more of the selected drugs than did the two study countries (Australia and the United Kingdom) with a BTC drug class but also had more of these drugs classified as OTC—the option that provides greatest availability— than the other four study countries.

All the Study Countries Have Increased Nonprescription Drug Availability Since 1995 by Changing Drug Classes or Switching Drugs

Consumers in all five study countries have experienced an increase in nonprescription drug availability compared to 1995 due to changes in drug classes or reclassification of drugs into less restrictive classes. Two countries changed their drug classes. The Netherlands added an OTC class in 2007; previously, all nonprescription drugs in the Netherlands were restricted to pharmacy or drugstore sales.[22] As a result, the Netherlands now has three nonprescription drug classes: pharmacy, drugstore, and OTC. Italy also relaxed nonprescription drug sale restrictions in 2006 by making all nonprescription drugs available in nonpharmacy outlets; previously, nonprescription drugs could be sold only in pharmacies. Italy requires that a pharmacist be on the premises in any outlet that sells nonprescription drugs. As a result, Italy's single nonprescription drug class has changed from a pharmacy class to an OTC/pharmacist class. The presence of a pharmacist is not a requirement for the OTC class in any of the other countries we examined. Due to the changes made by Italy and the Netherlands, all five of the study countries now have some form of OTC availability of drugs. The other three study countries made no changes to their drug distribution categories since 1995. Australia has three nonprescription drug classes: BTC, pharmacy, and OTC.[23] The United Kingdom has two nonprescription classes: BTC and OTC.[24] The United States has one nonprescription class: OTC. (Table 1 summarizes the drug classes in use in the study countries in 2008. Appendix II provides more details on the drug classification systems in each of the study countries.)

Australia, the United Kingdom, and the United States have increased drug availability since 1995 by switching certain drugs from more restrictive to less restrictive drug classes.[25] For example, the United States switched 31 drugs—including nonsedating antihistamines, orlistat (a weight-loss aid), and levonorgestrel (an emergency contraceptive switched for consumers aged 18 and above)—from prescription to nonprescription status during this period; there were no switches from nonprescription to prescription status. Australia approved more than six times as many drug switches as the United States—193—to less restrictive classes in the same period. Australia does not require drugs to switch in a stepwise manner; for example, 28 percent of switches approved from 1995 to 2008—54 out of 193 switches—bypassed an intermediate class in favor of a less restrictive class (e.g., bypassing BTC when switching from prescription to pharmacy status). During this same period, an additional 67 drug switches resulted in more restrictive classification (e.g., from pharmacy to prescription).

The United Kingdom also switched drugs from more restrictive to less restrictive classes, approving more than 50 switches from prescription to BTC or BTC to OTC between 1995 and 2008. Among the switches approved were two that were the first of their kind for any country: the 2004 switch of a cholesterol-lowering statin—simvastatin—from prescription to BTC status and the 2008 switch of an antibiotic—azithromycin for treatment of chlamydia—to BTC status.[26] In 2002, the United Kingdom began exploring ways to increase the number of drugs available without a prescription. As part of this process, the United Kingdom has changed its approach to nonprescription switches from a focus on switching drugs for short-term conditions to include drugs for chronic conditions. The United Kingdom uses a stepwise process in which drugs leaving prescription status are given BTC status for several years before they are considered for OTC sale. Thus the BTC drug class in the United Kingdom can serve as a transition class.

The Impact of Restricted Nonprescription Drug Classes on Drug Availability Is Unclear

It is unclear whether the presence of restricted nonprescription drug classes increases drug availability. The United States required a prescription for more of the drugs we examined than did the two study countries—Australia and the United Kingdom—using a BTC drug class in addition to other nonprescription drug classes. When we compared the classification status of 86 selected drugs in the five study countries, the United States required a prescription for 42 drugs while Australia and the United Kingdom each required a prescription for 23 of the drugs (see table 2). The United States had slightly more of the selected drugs available without a prescription than the two study countries—Italy and the Netherlands—that did not use a BTC drug class. (See app. III for further details on classification of these 86 drugs in the study countries.)

However, the United States had more of the 86 selected drugs classified as OTC—the option that provides greatest availability of these drugs for consumers—than all other study countries. With the exception of levonorgestrel (an emergency contraceptive), all nonprescription drugs (43 drugs, or 98 percent) were OTC in the United States without any restrictions. In contrast, 54 to 100 percent of nonprescription drugs in the other four study countries had conditions placed on their sale that restricted their availability. These restrictions included limiting sale to pharmacies and requiring pharmacist involvement in the sale (Australia and the United Kingdom), limiting sales to pharmacies and drugstores (the Netherlands), or requiring a pharmacist to be on the premises at any retail outlet selling nonprescription drugs (Italy).

Table 1. Drug Classes Used in the Study Countries, 2008

Drug class	Australia	Italy	Netherlands	United Kingdom	United States
Prescription drugs	X	X	X	X	X
Nonprescription drugs					
Subclasses:					
BTC	X			X	
Pharmacy	X		X		
Drugstore			X		
OTC/pharmacist		X			
OTC	X		X	X	X

Source: GAO analysis of agency data from the study countries

Table 2. Number of 86 Selected Drugs Assigned to Each Drug Class in the Study Countries

	Number of drugs assigned to each				
Drug class	Australia	Italy	Netherlan ds	United Kingdom	United States
Prescription drugs	23	43	45	23	42
Nonprescription drugs	63	43	41	63	44
Subcategories:					
BTC	11	NA[a]	NA[a]	34	NA[a]
Pharmacy	29	NA[a]	2	NAa	1b
Drugstore	NA[a]	NA[a]	26	NA[a]	NA[a]
OTC/pharmacist	NA[a]	43	NA[a]	NA[a]	NA[a]
OTC	23	NA[a]	13	29	43
Total (prescription + nonprescription)	86	86	86	86	86

Source: GAO analysis of agency data from the study countries.

[a] Class does not exist in this country.

[b] In the United States, levonorgestrel (an emergency contraceptive) may only be sold in pharmacies— as a nonprescription drug for those 18 and over, and by prescription for those under 18.

Table 3. Drugs with OTC Status in the United States but a More Restrictive Status in All Other Study Countries

Drug	Austraia	Italy	Netherlands	United Kingdom	United States
Bacitracin (*topical*)	Rx	OTC/P	Rx	Rx	OTC
Dextromethorphan	P	OTC/P	P	BTC	OTC
Insulin	Rx	Rx	Rx	Rx	OTC
Ketoprofen	BTC	OTC/P	D	BTC	OTC
Ketotifen	BTC	Rx	Rx	Rx	OTC
Miconazole (*vaginal*)	BTC	OTC/P	Rx	BTC	OTC
Naproxen	P	OTC/P	D	BTC	OTC
Nizatidine	P	Rx	Rx	BTC	OTC
Omeprazole	Rx	Rx	D	BTC	OTC
Orlistat	BTC	Rx[a]	P	Rx[b]	OTC
Polymyxin B(*topical*)	Rx	OTC/P	Rx	Rx	OTC
Tetracycline	Rx	Rx	Rx	Rx	OTC[b]

Legend: Rx = prescription; BTC = behind-the-counter; P = pharmacy; D = drugstore; OTC/P = over- the-counter (pharmacist required); OTC = over-the-counter.

Source: GAO analysis of agency data from the study countries.

Note: This table indicates the least restrictive class to which each drug was assigned regardless of pack size, dosage, or combination ingredients. Other formulations of a drug may only be available under a more restrictive class. For example, in the United States some types of insulin are available as prescription drugs and other insulin products are available OTC.

[a] On January 21, 2009, the European Commission approved orlistat (60 mg) for nonprescription use in the EU. At the time of this report, nonprescription orlistat was not yet available to consumers.

[b] In the United States, the topical dosage form of tetracycline is OTC.

Conversely, we found that seven drugs (8 percent) in the sample had prescription status in the United States and nonprescription status in all other study countries (see table 4).

Therefore, an assessment of the restrictiveness of the drug distribution system in the United States compared to the other countries studied depends on the definition of availability. If availability is defined by the number of drugs available for OTC sale, the United States appears to have the least restrictive system, because more of the 86 drugs are available for OTC sale than in any of the other countries. However, if availability is defined by the number of drugs for nonprescription sale regardless of any other restriction on their sale, the United States is more restrictive than Australia and the United Kingdom but slightly less restrictive than Italy and the Netherlands.

The classification of drugs in other countries and the existence of other classes provide little insight into the likely effect of a BTC drug class on nonprescription drug availability in the United States. It is unclear whether establishing a BTC drug class in the United States would allow more drugs to be switched out of the prescription class. We did not find a consistent association between the classification of particular drugs in our sample by a given country and the drug classification system in that country. For example, the United States gave less restrictive classification to some drugs and more restrictive classification to other drugs when compared to the other four study countries. Twelve drugs (14 percent) in the sample had OTC status in the United States but a more restrictive status in all of the other study countries, including two drugs with OTC status in the United States but prescription status in all of the other study countries (see table 3).

Table 4. Drugs with Prescription Status in the United States but Nonprescription Status in All Other Study Countries

Drug	Australia	Italy	Netherlands	United Kingdom	United States
Aciclovir (*topical*)	OTC	OTC/P	OTC	OTC	Rx
Diclofenac	P	OTC/P	D	OTC	Rx
Econazole	OTC	OTC/P	D	BTC	Rx
Hyoscine (*Scopolamine*)	P	OTC/P	D	BTC	Rx
Lactulose	OTC	OTC/P	D	BTC	Rx
Nicotine (*oral inhaler*)	P	OTC/P	D	OTC	Rx
Penciclovir	P	OTC/P	OTC	BTC	Rx

Legend: Rx = prescription; BTC = behind-the-counter; P = pharmacy; D = drugstore; OTC/P = over- the-counter (pharmacist required); OTC = over-the-counter.

Source: GAO analysis of agency data from the study countries.

Note: This table indicates the least restrictive class to which each drug was assigned regardless of pack size, dosage, or combination ingredients. Other formulations of a drug may only be available under a more restrictive class.

Table 5. Drugs with Prescription Status in Countries without a BTC Drug Class but Nonprescription Status in Countries with a BTC Drug Class

Drug	Australia	Italy	Netherlands	United Kingdom	United States
Beclometasone	P	Rx	Rx	OTC	Rx
Budesonide (*nasal*)	P	Rx	Rx	BTC	Rx
Cyproheptadine	BTC	Rx	Rx	BTC	Rx
Fluticasone	P	Rx	Rx	BTC	Rx
Nitroglycerin	P	Rx	Rx	BTC	Rx
Nystatin	P	Rx	Rx	BTC	Rx
Theophylline	BTC	Rx	Rx	BTC	Rx

Legend: Rx = prescription; BTC = behind-the-counter; P = pharmacy; D = drugstore; OTC/P = over- the-counter (pharmacist required); OTC = over-the-counter.

Source: GAO analysis of agency data from the study countries.

Note: This table indicates the least restrictive class to which each drug was assigned regardless of pack size, dosage, or combination ingredients. Other formulations of a drug may only be available under a more restrictive class.

Additionally, we found that seven drugs (8 percent) in the sample had prescription status in the United States, Italy, and the Netherlands but had nonprescription status in Australia and the United Kingdom, the two countries with a BTC drug class (see table 5). Study countries without a BTC drug class, therefore, had reduced availability of a small percentage of drugs when compared with the study countries using a BTC drug class.

Pharmacist-, Infrastructure-, and Cost-Related Issues Would Be Important Considerations if a BTC Drug Class Were Established

Pharmacist-, infrastructure-, and cost-related issues would have to be addressed before a BTC drug class could be established in the United States. Several issues involved with implementing a BTC drug class pertain to the roles and responsibilities of pharmacists, such as defining their BTC dispensing responsibilities and training needs. Infrastructure issues, such as establishing systems for the transfer of patient information and private consultation areas, would also be important if a BTC drug class were established. In addition, cost-related issues, such as the availability of third-party coverage for BTC drugs and counseling, would also be important considerations.[27]

Issues Related to Pharmacists' Roles and Responsibilities Would Be Important to Consider if a BTC Drug Class Were Established

If the United States were to establish a BTC drug class, it would be important to establish pharmacists' responsibilities for dispensing BTC drugs. According to FDA, pharmacists' responsibilities for dispensing BTC drugs could include but are not limited to reviewing or conducting an initial screening for clinical laboratory results, contraindications, or drug interactions; advising consumers on safe drug use; and monitoring for continued safe or effective use. Additionally, a pharmacist could be required to document interventions with consumers when dispensing BTC drugs. Experts told us that dispensing procedures could vary depending on the product and disease. Determining whether a standard set of BTC dispensing requirements would apply to all pharmacies and pharmacists across the country would also be important. Determining whether BTC drugs could be sold through mail-order and Internet pharmacies—where physical observation of the consumer would not be possible—would be important, as well as determining whether pharmacists in these settings would need to fulfill additional dispensing requirements, such as using screening questions designed for remote counseling to ensure appropriate drug use.

Ensuring that pharmacists meet their responsibilities for dispensing BTC drugs, including providing necessary counseling, would be an important issue to resolve. One potential purpose of classifying drugs as BTC is for pharmacists to ensure that consumers meet specified criteria for using these drugs and then to provide education on the proper use of these drugs. Failure to ensure that such counseling occurs would diminish the value of a BTC drug class. In Australia, one of our study countries with a BTC drug class, a 2000 government-sponsored review of the drug classification system found that pharmacist counseling did not occur to the intended extent and called for an enhancement of professional standards for pharmacists. Australian agency officials told us that since the time of this report, pharmacists' provision of counseling for BTC drugs has improved with the development of counseling standards and clarification of legislative controls which regulate these professional standards. Professional associations have also played a role in monitoring the quality of pharmacist counseling in Australia. A study examining the Quality Care Pharmacy Support Centre's "mystery shopper" visits—used to monitor and provide feedback on Australian pharmacies' performance since 2002—found that repeated mystery shopper visits led to notable improvement in pharmacists' handling of nonprescription drugs.[28]

FDA officials told us that, if a BTC drug class were created in the United States, FDA would need to work with the states to determine the mechanisms through which oversight would be provided. An official from the National Association of Boards of Pharmacy told us that, if a BTC drug class were created, the state boards of pharmacy would need to establish national standards for a number of issues, including the types of data systems, consumer interactions, documentation, and expertise required for a BTC practice. This official noted that it could be challenging for the state boards of pharmacy to provide oversight for a BTC drug class because of resource constraints. Pharmacy practice experts and others have also raised concerns that BTC verbal counseling requirements would need to be more stringent than the counseling requirements associated with the Omnibus Budget Reconciliation Act of 1990 (OBRA '90).[29] Under OBRA '90, consumers are allowed to waive their right to speak with a pharmacist, and according to pharmacy practice experts and others, many consumers do so. These experts told us that verbal counseling for a BTC drug class should be mandatory.

Another consideration in the establishment of a BTC drug class would be determining if additional training would be needed for pharmacists and pharmacy staff and assessing whether all pharmacists and pharmacy staff would need to undergo this training. In pharmacist education today, more emphasis is being placed on patient care and assessment than was the case in earlier years. To fulfill degree requirements, pharmacy students must now earn a Doctor of Pharmacy degree, for which they are required to complete a minimum of 4 academic years, with at least 30 percent of the program spent in clinical training in settings such as community pharmacy, hospital pharmacy, ambulatory care, and acute care general medicine to develop advanced professional practice skills.[30] However, one study found significant variation in courses used to teach patient assessment skills—which have been mentioned as potentially important for pharmacists providing BTC counseling.[31] Further, pharmacists who received their education prior to the current shift toward patient care and assessment might not have the same skills and abilities as recent graduates. Consequently, several experts told us that additional training would be necessary for at least some pharmacists in order for them to appropriately dispense BTC drugs. At VA and IHS, where some pharmacists have expanded dispensing responsibilities and have been authorized to prescribe drugs, credentialing programs are used to assess pharmacists' competencies before they are granted expanded privileges. Pharmacy associations have indicated that they could design and administer training for a BTC drug class. It would also be necessary to determine whether all pharmacists and pharmacy staff would be required to be trained in BTC-related skills. For example, one retail chain we spoke with suggested that each pharmacy should have the discretion to designate certain pharmacies or pharmacists who would be responsible for dispensing BTC drugs. However, if BTC drugs were only dispensed at certain pharmacies or by BTC-accredited pharmacists, confusion about how to access BTC drugs could result.

To implement a BTC drug class, it would be important to evaluate whether a sufficient pharmacist workforce would be available to make such a program viable. Pharmacy practice experts told us that there is currently a pharmacist shortage that will continue for some time.[32] The Health Resources and Services Administration found that pharmacists have experienced increasing demand for their time in part because of an increase in prescription volume and in part because of the increased amount of time needed to address insurance coverage problems for prescriptions. In addition, experts we interviewed raised the possibility that some pharmacists might not want to take on the additional duties associated with dispensing BTC drugs, which could further reduce the number of pharmacists available to participate. In other countries, pharmacists have been unwilling at times to dispense BTC products. For example, a survey of 1,156 community pharmacists regarding their views and early experiences with BTC simvastatin (a cholesterol-lowering drug) in Great Britain revealed that pharmacists had a number of concerns and infrequently sold simvastatin.[33] Despite feeling well prepared to counsel on BTC simvastatin, pharmacists were still reluctant to dispense the drug without cholesterol or blood pressure testing—which was not required by the drug's protocol—and therefore infrequently sold it.

Another example of this can be seen in Florida, which in 1985 authorized pharmacists to independently prescribe certain drugs.[34] Experts have stated that despite having this authority, pharmacists in Florida have rarely done so. Florida pharmacists' rare use of their prescribing authority is primarily attributable to drugs being available without a prescription that are just as effective as those they are allowed to prescribe. Pharmacists were also concerned that they would increase their liability risk if they prescribed and they considered the recordkeeping requirements associated with prescribing a drug to be excessively time consuming. Having an inadequate number of pharmacists willing to carry out BTC functions could reduce the value of such a class.

Communicating pharmacists' new role to the public could influence demand for products and services and would be an important issue for the implementation and viability of a BTC drug class. Experts have stated that consumers would need to understand protocols for obtaining BTC drugs, such as the necessity of consulting with a pharmacist before obtaining a BTC drug. Consumers would also need to be aware that, after a consultation, the pharmacist could decide that a BTC drug is not appropriate for the consumer or that a physician visit is necessary. If a BTC drug class were established in the United States, consumers might need time to adjust to pharmacists' new role under such a class. For example, in the United Kingdom, which has had a BTC drug class since 1968, pharmacists have expressed concerns that consumers have a poor understanding of the pharmacist's role. Researchers have suggested that marketing pharmacists' professional services could help to create a demand for these services. Officials with the United Kingdom Department of Health consider increasing the public's awareness of pharmacist services to be a goal. According to these officials, while some consumers are comfortable obtaining health advice through a pharmacy, very few use a pharmacy's full range of services.[35]

In implementing a BTC drug class, it would be important to determine whether restrictions on the size of a BTC drug class are necessary. Experts raised concerns that if a BTC drug class were too large or if whole categories of drugs switched to BTC at once, it could overwhelm pharmacies because of the time burden involved in dispensing these drugs and the need to train pharmacists and pharmacy staff on new procedures associated with BTC drugs. As a consequence, this situation could create unintended gaps in care by disrupting pharmacies' regular prescription dispensing duties or interfering with their ability to provide BTC drugs. For instance, pharmacists in the United Kingdom found following different dispensing procedures for multiple drugs to be burdensome. Their ability to make appropriate recommendations was hampered by the time involved in following these procedures. However, some pharmacy officials we spoke with told us that restricting the size of a BTC drug class would not be necessary because pharmacists are accustomed to managing a large number of drugs for various individuals.

Infrastructure Issues Would Be Important Considerations in the Establishment of a BTC Drug Class

An assessment of infrastructure needs would be important to the establishment of a BTC drug class in the United States. Implementing a BTC drug class could entail infrastructure changes for pharmacies so that pharmacists could have better patient information on which to base dispensing decisions. For example, data infrastructure enhancements would be necessary for some pharmacies to meet the possible record- keeping requirements of a BTC drug class and to facilitate communication between pharmacists and physicians. Other countries consider information-sharing systems important for supporting physician– pharmacist communication. For example, in the Netherlands, physicians and pharmacists communicate regularly through electronic prescribing systems, and health officials are developing a system that physicians and pharmacists can use to share patient-specific drug data. Electronic patient health information, such as laboratory results and diagnoses, could also help U.S. pharmacists make better decisions when dispensing BTC drugs. Although commentators note that most state regulations require that a patient drug profile be maintained at the pharmacy and reviewed prior to dispensing a drug, pharmacies currently have limited access to electronic patient health information.[36] For example, a study of Nebraska pharmacists found that 6 percent of surveyed pharmacists had access to electronic patient health information from other providers. Additionally, a 2003 survey of community pharmacies from across the United States found that 54 percent of the respondent pharmacies were using a paper documentation system.[37] Researchers have found several challenges associated with a paper system, all of which could impact implementation of a BTC drug class; these challenges include documentation time, retrieval of patient data, tracking consumer outcomes, and storage. Improving pharmacists' access to patient information has been shown to improve decision-making. One study found that pharmacists performing drug utilization reviews made better decisions when they had access to more complete patient information on which to base decisions.[38]

The need for private pharmacy consultation areas is another important infrastructure issue that would require consideration if a BTC drug class were implemented. Several groups have identified a need to establish private counseling areas in pharmacies to ensure consumer privacy. Consumers might be reluctant to receive counseling from pharmacists if they have concerns about privacy. A study of Dutch pharmacies indicated that if individuals are aware that a pharmacy has a separate consultation room, they might be more likely to seek a private consultation with a pharmacist.[39] Similarly, researchers have found that enclosed counseling areas in Australian pharmacies increase the likelihood that screening activities and other enhanced pharmacy services occur.[40] One pharmacy practice expert told us that the majority of Australian pharmacies are including private consultation areas when updating their infrastructure.[41] If private consultation rooms were required as part of a BTC drug class, U.S. pharmacies could incur costs to remodel their facilities. Although the National Association of Boards of Pharmacy currently recommends that U.S. pharmacies have a private area for confidential conversations, states have varied in requiring these areas.[42]

Cost-Related Issues for Drugs, Pharmacists' Services, and Drug Switches Would Be Important Considerations in Establishing a BTC Drug Class

Several cost-related issues would be important for the establishment of a BTC drug class. One consideration would be the availability of third-party coverage of BTC drugs. Pharmacy association and consumer group officials we spoke with told us that the effect of a BTC drug class on consumers' out-of-pocket drug expenses would depend on the reimbursement decisions of third-party payers such as health insurers, who often pay all or most of the cost of prescription drugs but generally do not pay for OTC products. A 1999 review of insurance plan benefits reported that less than one-third of plans covered selected OTC products and that less than one-third of plans continued to cover products switched from prescription to OTC status.[43] A 2003 study found that although 39 of 43 state Medicaid programs reporting in 2003 covered some OTC drugs when ordered by a prescriber, only 12 provided coverage for OTC drugs that switched from prescription to OTC.[44] HHS officials told us that legislative changes might be necessary to allow for Medicare Part D coverage of BTC drugs. A similar consideration concerns drugs now covered under the Medicaid program. If third-party payers do not reimburse consumers for drugs that were switched from prescription to BTC, consumers' out-of-pocket expenditures could increase.

The cost of nonreimbursable BTC drugs could also affect the extent to which consumers use BTC drugs. Evidence from other countries suggests that drug costs can be prohibitive to consumers. In the view of pharmacists in Great Britain, the high cost of BTC drugs such as omeprazole, especially relative to prescription or OTC alternatives, might deter consumers from using the drug.[45] Another expensive BTC drug in the United Kingdom is simvastatin, which is intended for use by individuals who do not qualify for National Health Service coverage of statin treatment. However, according to pharmacists, the high cost of the drug could discourage some consumers from using it. Officials with the Medicines Evaluation Board of the Netherlands told us that consumers often oppose switches of drugs from prescription to pharmacy status because they lose insurance coverage when a drug becomes nonprescription. Therefore, in the Netherlands, prescription drugs that are not already covered by insurance are more likely to be considered viable switch candidates for pharmacy class status. A survey of individuals with indigestion or hypertension found that about half of all Italian respondents—regardless of their ability to pay for drugs—had obtained prescriptions for drugs that were available OTC in order to obtain insurance coverage because they considered the OTC products too expensive.[46]

The availability of third-party coverage for BTC counseling could influence pharmacists' involvement in a BTC drug class and the quality of pharmacists' services, and third-party coverage for BTC counseling could also increase drug prices. Officials from the American Pharmacists Association have raised concerns about whether it would be financially feasible for pharmacies to carry BTC drugs unless pharmacists were able to bill and be fully paid for the clinical services that might be required for a BTC drug class. In addition to influencing pharmacists' willingness to participate in a BTC drug class, whether or not pharmacists are compensated might also affect their performance. One study of the factors that increase the prevalence of patient care services in community pharmacies found that paying pharmacists increased their detection of drug-related problems.[47] Another study found that providing pharmacists with a financial incentive was associated with significantly higher documentation levels and higher advanced service levels.[48] A counseling fee could lead to higher drug prices if pharmacist compensation were included in the price of BTC drugs. However, consumers might be willing to pay more for BTC drugs if they consider pharmacist services valuable. A survey of 2,500 adults in the United States found that the majority of respondents were willing to pay an out-of-pocket fee for pharmaceutical care services, even if they were not currently receiving such services.[49] Third-party payers might also be willing to cover pharmacist services. In one diabetes management study, self-insured employers reimbursed pharmacists for consultation services, and based on the clinical improvements and financial savings associated with the diabetes management program, decided to retain the program as a permanent component of their health plan benefit.[50]

Compensation for BTC services might be necessary to offset increased liability. Additional liability could be incurred by pharmacists and pharmacies as a result of their participation in BTC counseling. Pharmacy officials raised the possibility that pharmacists participating in the implementation of a BTC drug class could have a greater exposure to liability because they would dispense drugs without a physician's order. Concerns about liability might deter pharmacists from dispensing BTC drugs. For instance, such concerns were cited by pharmacists in Florida who were hesitant to use their prescribing authority.

Costs might also be affected by new incentives necessary to encourage drug manufacturers to invest funds in a two-stage switch process (from prescription to BTC and then from BTC to OTC). Clinical trials, including actual use studies, are often conducted to help determine whether a drug could be switched from prescription to OTC, and an FDA official indicated that these trials may also be needed to determine if a product could be switched from prescription to BTC and from BTC to OTC. Currently, drug manufacturers may receive 3 additional years of exclusive marketing rights for drugs switched from prescription to OTC status if the switch requires additional clinical trials.[51] Some FDA officials and manufacturers we spoke with believe it might be necessary to provide manufacturers with exclusive marketing rights for drugs switching from prescription to BTC status and also for BTC-to-OTC switches. It is unclear what period of exclusivity would make drug manufacturers' investment in clinical studies for prescription-to-BTC and BTC-to-OTC switches worthwhile. However, FDA noted that granting this additional period of market exclusivity could reduce competition.

AGENCY COMMENTS AND OUR EVALUATION

HHS provided comments on a draft of this report. The comments are reproduced in appendix IV. In its comments HHS agreed that cost-related issues would have to be addressed before implementing a BTC drug class.

HHS recommended that GAO add a discussion regarding the statutory authority to provide reimbursement under Medicare Part D for drugs that would be included in a BTC drug class if it were to be created. Such discussion is beyond the scope of this report, but we noted in the report that the ramifications for Medicare, as well as Medicaid, would need to be considered before establishment of a BTC drug class.

HHS also suggested that a footnote in the report could mislead the reader to believe that the Medicare Prescription Drug, Improvement, and Modernization Act of 2003 (MMA) requires pharmacists to review Medicare beneficiaries' prescription drug regimens as a component of MTM under Medicare Part D. While pharmacists are required to participate in the development of such programs, we added text to the main body of the report to clarify that MMA does not require that pharmacists furnish the services provided in MTM programs but also does not prohibit them from doing so.

HHS stated that while MMA required Part D sponsors to implement MTM programs, the Part D program does not establish any payment schedules for either physicians or pharmacists performing MTM. HHS was concerned that a footnote in the report might be read to mean that MMA specified such a payment schedule. We have revised the text to clarify that MMA does not specify a payment schedule but that CMS often uses a rate that is 80 percent of the physician rate to determine their payments under Medicare.

In addition, HHS and VA provided technical comments on the report draft, which we have incorporated as appropriate.

Marcia Crosse
Director, Health Care

Appendix I: Objectives, Scope, and Methodology

Objectives

In light of the November 2007 Food and Drug Administration (FDA) public meeting to explore the public health implications of behind-the-counter (BTC) availability of certain drugs in the United States and the fundamental change that BTC availability would represent in the U.S. drug classification system,[52] we are updating information we first presented in our 1995 report.[53] Specifically, we are reporting on (1) the arguments that have been made supporting and opposing the creation of a BTC drug class in the United States; (2) changes in drug availability in our five study countries[54] since 1995 and the impact of restricted nonprescription drug classes on drug availability; and (3) issues that would be important to the establishment of a BTC drug class.

Scope and Methodology

To describe the arguments that have been made supporting and opposing a BTC drug class in the United States, we reviewed published literature, reports, and meeting minutes of FDA hearings on prescription-to-over-thecounter (OTC) switches, and the transcript of and docket submissions for the November 2007 FDA meeting on BTC drug availability.[55] We interviewed officials at FDA, pharmacy associations, drug manufacturers, consumer groups, and industry associations in the United States. We also interviewed academics and other officials knowledgeable about pharmaceutical practice.

To determine the impact of restricted nonprescription drug classes on drug availability, we interviewed experts to ask them to help us identify countries that had evaluated drug classification in their countries since our 1995 report. Based on this information, we selected 5 of the 11 countries covered in our previous report.[56] We also examined drug classification in the European Union (EU) because these factors affect drug availability in three of our study countries. We reviewed published literature, reports, and agency documents on drug classification and prescription-to-nonprescription switches. We also interviewed agency officials, industry representatives, and others knowledgeable about pharmaceutical practices and the relevant laws and regulations in our study countries.[57] Although some countries—including the United States—place additional restrictions on certain prescription drugs, a complete analysis of prescription drug classification was beyond the scope of this report.[58] For our analysis, all prescription drugs were placed in the same class. We examined changes since 1995 in the drug classification systems in two study countries (Italy and the Netherlands) that changed the number or type of nonprescription drug classes in use. We also determined the number of drugs switched from one drug class to another (e.g., prescription to BTC) between 1995 and 2008 for the three study countries—Australia, the United Kingdom, and the United States—that maintained the same number and type of nonprescription drug classes during that time. We examined relevant documents and interviewed knowledgeable officials in those countries. We counted the first switch of a particular drug (e.g., ibuprofen) from one drug class to another that occurred after January 1, 1995, but did not count subsequent switches of additional products containing the same drug between the same two drug classes (except in the case of different nicotine dosage forms such as gum and patches) in order to achieve consistency with the World Self- Medication Industry (WSMI) data discussed below.[59] We also did not count switches that changed only the allowable dosage, pack size, or indications for a drug that had previously been switched. In some cases, a switch in one country may have involved a drug that was not approved for use in one of the other countries or was not subject to regulation as a drug in another country.

Additionally, we determined the classification of selected drugs in the United States and the other study countries. We selected a sample of drugs using the WSMI databases that describe the classification status— prescription or nonprescription—of more than 200 drugs in 36 countries.[60] We used the February 1, 2007, tables; these were the most recent tables available at the time we were conducting our study. We excluded from the list any drugs listed as "not registered" or with a blank entry for Australia, the Netherlands, the United Kingdom, or the United States; a sample of 110 drugs resulted. We examined the survey format used to collect information on drug classification and response rates from the most recent survey, and determined that the data were sufficiently reliable for our purposes. After drawing the initial sample from the WSMI tables, we added Italy to our scope. We then determined the classification status of the sample drugs in each of the study countries using agency information including information from knowledgeable agency officials and an examination of the Standard for the Uniform Scheduling of Drugs and Poisons No. 22 (Australia); the Prontuario Farmaceutico Nazionale and the Elenco indicativo dei farmaci SOP e OTC in commercio con prezzo in vigore al 31/12/2006 ai sensi del comma 802 dell'art. 1 Legge 27 dicembre 2006, n. 296 (Italy); the Medicines Evaluation Board Database Human Medicines (Netherlands); List A: Consolidated list of substances which are present in prescription only medicines (POM), with exemptions for pharmacy sale or supply (P), List B: Consolidated list of substances which are present in authorised medicines for general sale, and List C: Consolidated list of substances which are present in authorised products which have been reclassified since 1 April 2002 (United Kingdom); the list of Approved Drug Products with Therapeutic Equivalence Evaluations, 28th Edition (i.e., the Orange Book) (United States); and other agency documents. The data in these reference documents are standard data sources published by each country's regulatory authority and were sufficiently reliable for our purposes. We found that 24 of the 110 drugs in our initial sample were not approved in one or more of the five study countries and eliminated these drugs from our sample, resulting in a final sample of 86 drugs. We then compared the classification of these drugs across the five study countries in order to determine the least restrictive class to which each drug was assigned regardless of pack size, dosage, or combination ingredients.

To identify issues that would be important to the establishment of a BTC drug class in the United States, we interviewed officials at FDA, the Centers for Medicare & Medicaid Services (CMS), the Department of Veterans Affairs (VA), the Indian Health Service (IHS), pharmacist associations, drug manufacturers, consumer groups, and industry associations. We interviewed academics and other experts knowledgeable about pharmacists' prescribing authority, including individuals who have testified to FDA on the possible creation of a BTC drug class in the United States. We also interviewed agency officials, industry representatives, pharmacist association representatives, and others knowledgeable about pharmacy practices in our other study countries. We reviewed reports and the transcript of and docket submissions for the November 2007 FDA meeting on BTC drugs. We also reviewed published, peer-reviewed pharmacy practice literature, focusing on articles published since our 1995 report and relating to the United States or our other study countries. For this literature review, we searched 67 databases, including International Pharmaceutical Abstracts, EMBASE, Pharmaceutical News Index, Gale Group Health & Wellness Database, Pharm-Line, Science Citation Index, and MEDLINE. Key search terms used were pharmacy practice, pharmacist counseling, pharmacist intervention, pharmacist prescribing authority, pharmaceutical care, collaborative practice, medication therapy management, drug classification, and drug reclassification. We also reviewed literature cited in these studies and studies recommended to us by those we interviewed.

We conducted our work from March 2008 through February 2009 in accordance with all sections of GAO's quality assurance framework that are relevant to our objectives. The framework requires that we plan and perform the engagement to obtain sufficient and appropriate evidence to meet our stated objectives and to discuss any limitations in our work. We believe that the information and data obtained, and the analysis conducted, provide a reasonable basis for any findings and conclusions.

APPENDIX II: DESCRIPTION OF DRUG CLASSIFICATION SYSTEMS IN THE FIVE STUDY COUNTRIES AND THE EUROPEAN UNION

In this appendix, we describe the drug classification systems in our five study countries—Australia, Italy, the Netherlands, the United Kingdom, and the United States. We also describe drug classification in the EU because it affects drug availability in three of our study countries. Although the terms used for different drug classes are included for each country, a standardized set of terminology is also used to facilitate comparisons (see figure 2).

Term used in the report	Definition	Levels of restriction
Prescription drugs		
Prescription	Available only from a pharmacist or other licensed dispenser upon submission of a prescription	Most restrictive ↑
Nonprescription drugs		
BTC	Available only in pharmacies; contact with pharmacist required	
Pharmacy	Available only in pharmacies; contact with pharmacist not required	
Drugstore	Available only in pharmacies or drugstores; contact with pharmacist not required[a]	
OTC/pharmacist	Available for self-selection in pharmacies and other retail outlets, but a pharmacist must be present	
OTC	Available for self-selection in pharmacies and other retail outlets, including those without pharmacists or druggists	↓ Least restrictive

Source: GAO analysis of agency documents from the study countries.

[a] In the Netherlands, a distinction is made between pharmacies (run by pharmacists and able to sell all prescription and nonprescription drugs) and drugstores (run by druggists with less training than pharmacists and able to sell only some nonprescription drugs).

Figure 2. Definitions and Relative Levels of Restriction for Drug Classes Used in This Report

Australia

The Therapeutic Goods Administration within the Department of Health and Ageing is responsible for the evaluation and approval of new drugs in Australia. The National Drugs and Poisons Schedule Committee makes recommendations on the appropriate classification of drugs and is also responsible for all decisions to switch a drug from one class to another.[61] Generally, the committee requires that a drug be marketed for 2 years before it will consider allowing it to move to a less restrictive classification; applications that do not meet this requirement may be considered when sufficient evidence is presented. While each state or territory has the authority to determine drug classification independently, all states and territories agreed in 2005 to adopt the national scheduling committee's decisions in full in order to reduce barriers to commerce in Australia.[62]

Australia has a complex, multilevel classification system for drugs that includes

- Schedule 2 (equivalent to pharmacy),
- Schedule 3 (equivalent to BTC),
- Schedule 4 (equivalent to prescription),
- Schedules 5 and 6 (certain essential oils for human therapeutic use, as well as household and agricultural chemicals); available without a prescription at nonpharmacy outlets, and
- Schedule 8 (controlled substances for which restrictions on availability are necessary to reduce abuse, misuse, or dependence; e.g., opioids and amphetamines).

Additionally, if a substance does not appear in a schedule, it is referred to as unscheduled; unscheduled drugs can be supplied to the public from any retail outlet (i.e., these are OTC drugs).[63] Schedule 1 (formerly containing a number of toxic volatile oils) is not currently in use; Schedule 7 contains dangerous agricultural and industrial poisons; and Schedule 9 contains substances whose manufacture, possession, sale, or use is prohibited except under specific circumstances (e.g., heroin and cannabis).[64]

Italy

The Italian Pharmaceutical Agency (l'Agenzia Italiana del farmaco), an autonomous agency under the oversight of the Ministry of Health, authorizes the marketing of drugs in Italy. The agency is assisted by the Scientific and Technical Committee which evaluates and issues opinions on marketing applications. Italy currently has the following drug classes:

- prescription, and
- nonprescription.[65]

All nonprescription drugs in Italy are available for sale in nonpharmacy outlets such as supermarkets as long as a pharmacist is on the premises. The requirement that a pharmacist be present wherever nonprescription drugs are sold means that nonprescription drugs in Italy are in an OTC/pharmacist class. However, Italian officials are evaluating the possibility of making small packs of some drugs available in nonpharmacy outlets without the presence of a pharmacist.

The agency is also responsible for the decision to switch drugs from one classification to another. Switches from prescription to nonprescription status are generally initiated by the manufacturer; switches from nonprescription to prescription status are much less frequent. Drugs can also be switched from prescription to more restrictive classification on rare occasions for safety reasons.

Netherlands

The Medicines Evaluation Board (College ter Beoordeling van Geneesmiddelen) is responsible for drug approval and classification in the Netherlands. The Medicines Evaluation Board is also responsible for approving requests to switch a drug; requests for OTC classification must be initiated by the company holding the marketing authorization.

The drug classification system in the Netherlands includes four categories:

- prescription,
- pharmacy only (equivalent to pharmacy),
- pharmacy and drugstore (equivalent to drugstore), and
- general sale (equivalent to OTC).

The last three categories are all nonprescription and differ primarily in the locations at which the drugs are available for sale. OTC classification in the Netherlands is based, in part, on a determination of public benefit and the risk–benefit profile of the drug. The drugstore class is the default class for all nonprescription drugs that do not meet the criteria for pharmacy or OTC sale. In the Netherlands, the distinction between drugstore and OTC classification is often based on the dosage or pack size; large pack sizes or higher dosages of a drug might be restricted to pharmacies and drugstores even when smaller pack sizes or lower dosages are available for OTC sale. The pharmacy class in the Netherlands is reserved for drugs requiring interaction with pharmacy staff although not necessarily a pharmacist; agency officials told us that they do not expect to place many drugs into this class. At the time of our analysis, six drugs were assigned to the pharmacy class: domperidone (to suppress nausea), orlistat (weight loss aid), aliskiren (treatment of hypertension), clotrimazole (antifungal agent), hexamidine, and dextromethorphan (cough suppressant).

United Kingdom

The Medicines and Healthcare products Regulatory Agency (MHRA) within the Department of Health is responsible for drug approval and classification in the United Kingdom. The United Kingdom continues to use the three-tier drug classification system that was in place in 1995. This system includes

- prescription only (equivalent to prescription),
- pharmacy (equivalent to BTC),[66] and
- general sale list (equivalent to OTC).

The presumption under law is that all drugs are restricted to the BTC drug class unless they meet the criteria for prescription or OTC status.[67]

MHRA encourages wider availability of drugs as soon as there is adequate evidence of safety in use. Manufacturers or other interested parties can initiate switches, which proceed in a stepwise manner (prescription to BTC, then BTC to OTC). Experience gained at one level is used to inform the decision to switch the drug to the next level. For example, MHRA guidelines indicate that substances suitable for OTC classification will have been in widespread use in BTC products for many years. Switching to more restrictive classes can also occur when warranted; this was done for large pack sizes of paracetamol in 1998 in an attempt to reduce adverse events associated with this drug.

United States

In the United States, FDA has authority to approve drugs before they are marketed, to ensure that they are safe and effective, and to determine whether they will be available only by prescription. The United States uses a two-class drug system—prescription and nonprescription—established by the 1951 Durham-Humphrey Amendments to the Federal Food, Drug, and Cosmetic Act.[68] Prescription drugs can be dispensed only with written or oral orders (i.e., a prescription) from a licensed prescriber—such as a doctor, nurse practitioner, or physician's assistant—to a pharmacist or other licensed dispenser, while nonprescription drugs do not require a prescription. Although most nonprescription drugs in the United States are publicly available without any restrictions, a few are stored behind the counter due to refrigeration requirements (e.g., insulin), to monitor quantity of purchase (e.g., pseudoephedrine), or are restricted to pharmacy sale in order to monitor consumer age (e.g., levonorgestrel). Nonprescription drugs are often referred to in the United States as OTC drugs.

Between 1995 and 2007, FDA assigned 99.7 percent (1233 out of 1237) of newly approved drugs to the prescription class, with four new drugs—a topical herpes simplex treatment, a sunscreen product, a nicotine lozenge, and a product to block contact with poison ivy—classified as nonprescription. Drugs can be switched from prescription to OTC status in a number of ways, including through rulemaking or submission of a supplemental new drug application to FDA by the sponsor. In making switch decisions, FDA may seek advice from the Nonprescription Drugs Advisory Committee, often in conjunction with an appropriate specialty committee (e.g., the Pediatric Advisory Committee or the Gastrointestinal Drugs Advisory Committee). Although not bound by the advisory committee's advice, FDA follows the committee's recommendation most of the time.

European Union

The Pharmaceuticals Unit of the European Commission Directorate General for Enterprise and Industry is responsible for approving new drugs submitted for marketing throughout the EU, and the European Medicines Agency makes a recommendation on whether the new drug should receive prescription or nonprescription status. The EU leaves to each member state the decision on whether to use subcategories within the prescription and nonprescription classes. Pharmacy experts told us that European countries have a long tradition of restricting drug sales to pharmacies and that about 60 percent of EU countries do not have an OTC drug class.

There are four primary methods to receive marketing approval for a drug in the EU. These include national authorization procedures that allow a drug to be marketed in a specific country based on an individual application and for which the classification decision is made by the appropriate national authority, plus three methods that are handled at the EU level:

- The centralized approval procedure allows applicants to market an approved product throughout the EU with a single application.
- The mutual recognition procedure can be used to request that a drug approval from one EU country be recognized as valid in one or more other EU countries.
- The decentralized procedure allows a company to apply for simultaneous approval in multiple EU countries for a drug that is not yet approved in any EU country.

Centralized approval is required for certain categories of drugs, including all drugs developed through biotechnology; drugs for the treatment of certain diseases, including acquired immunodeficiency syndrome (AIDS), cancer, neurodegenerative diseases, diabetes, and autoimmune diseases; and orphan drugs.[69] Although most drugs currently on the market in the EU were originally approved through national authorization procedures prior to the development of a centralized approval process, about 95 percent of new drugs brought to market are now approved through the centralized procedures. The first-ever application for the centralized switch of a drug (orlistat) from prescription to nonprescription status, which will make orlistat available without a prescription in all EU countries, was recently approved.[70] Orlistat was granted centralized approval as a prescription drug in 1998.

Appendix III: Classification of 86 Drugs in Australia, Italy, the Netherlands, the United Kingdom, and the United States

Ingredient	Australia	Italy	Netherlands	United Kingdom	United States
Acetylcysteine	OTC	OTC/P	OTC	Rx	Rx
Acetylsalicylic acid	OTC	OTC/P	D	OTC	OTC
Aciclovir (*topical*)	OTC	OTC/P	OTC	OTC	Rx
Adenosine	Rx	Rx	Rx	BTC	Rx
Azelastine	P	Rx	OTC	BTC	Rx
Bacitracin (*topical*)	Rx	OTC/P	Rx	Rx	OTC
Beclometasone (*nasal*)	P	Rx	Rx	OTC	Rx
Benzoyl peroxide	OTC	OTC/P	D	OTC	OTC
Bisacodyl	OTC	OTC/P	D	OTC	OTC
Budesonide (*nasal*)	P	Rx	Rx	BTC	Rx
Calcium carbonate	OTC	OTC/P	D	OTC	OTC
Cetirizine	P	OTC/P	OTC	OTC	OTC
Chloramphenicol	Rx	Rx	Rx	BTC	Rx
Cimetidine	BTC	OTC/P	Rx	BTC	OTC
Clindamycin	Rx	Rx	Rx	Rx	Rx
Clotrimazole (*topical*)	OTC	OTC/P	D	OTC	OTC
Clotrimazole (*vaginal*)	BTC	OTC/P	Rx	OTC	OTC
Colestyramine	Rx	Rx	Rx	Rx	Rx
Cromoglicic acid	P	Rx	OTC	BTC	OTC
Cyproheptadine	BTC	Rx	Rx	BTC	Rx
Dextromethorphan	P	OTC/P	P	BTC	OTC
Diclofenac	P	OTC/P	D	OTC	Rx
Dimeticone	OTC	OTC/P	Rx	OTC	OTC
Econazole	OTC	OTC/P	D	BTC	Rx
Epinephrine (*not for asthma*) (*adrenaline*)	OTC	Rx	Rx	BTC	OTC
Erythromycin (*topical*)	Rx	Rx	Rx	Rx	Rx
Famotidine	P	Rx	D	OTC	OTC
Fexofenadine	P	Rx	Rx	Rx	Rx

Flunisolide (*nasal*)	Rx	Rx	Rx	BTC	Rx
Fluoride (sodium)	OTC	OTC/P	D	OTC	OTC
Flurbiprofen (*lozenges*)	P	OTC/P	Rx	BTC	Rx
Fluticasone	P	Rx	Rx	BTC	Rx
Hydrocortisone (*topical*)	P	OTC/P	Rx	OTC	OTC
Hydroxyzine	Rx	Rx	Rx	BTC	Rx
Hyoscine (scopolamine)	P	OTC/P	D	BTC	Rx
Ibuprofen (*oral*)	OTC	OTC/P	D	OTC	OTC
Insulin	Rx	Rx	Rx	Rx	OTC
Itraconazole	Rx	Rx	Rx	Rx	Rx
Ketoconazole (*topical*)	OTC	OTC/P	Rx	OTC	OTC
Ketoprofen	BTC	OTC/P	D	BTC	OTC
Ketotifen	BTC	Rx	Rx	Rx	OTC
Lactulose	OTC	OTC/P	D	BTC	Rx
Levonorgestrel	BTC	Rx	D	BTC	Pa
Lidocaine (*topical/oral topical*)	OTC	OTC/P	OTC	OTC	OTC
Loperamide	P	OTC/P	OTC	OTC	OTC
Loratadine	P	OTC/P	OTC	OTC	OTC
Mebendazole	P	Rx	D	BTC	Rx
Metoclopramide	BTC	Rx	Rx	Rx	Rx
Miconazole (*topical*)	OTC	OTC/P	D	BTC	OTC
Miconazole (*vaginal*)	BTC	OTC/P	Rx	BTC	OTC
Minoxidil (*topical*)	P	OTC/P	D	OTC	OTC
Mometasone (*nasal*)	P	Rx	Rx	Rx	Rx
Mupirocin (*topical*)	Rx	Rx	Rx	Rx	Rx
Naproxen	P	OTC/P	D	BTC	OTC
Nicotine (*gum*)	OTC	OTC/P	OTC	OTC	OTC
Nicotine (*oral inhaler*)	P	OTC/P	D	OTC	Rx
Nicotine (*patch*)	OTC	OTC/P	D	OTC	OTC
Nitroglycerin	P	Rx	Rx	BTC	Rx
Nizatidine	P	Rx	Rx	BTC	OTC
Nystatin	P	Rx	Rx	BTC	Rx
Omeprazole	Rx	Rx	D	BTC	OTC
Orlistat	BTC	Rx[b]	P	Rx[b]	OTC
Orphenadrine	Rx	Rx	Rx	Rx	Rx
Oxymetazoline	P	OTC/P	D	OTC	OTC
Pantoprazole	Rx	Rx	Rx	Rx	Rx

Table. (Continued)

Ingredient	Australia	Italy	Netherlands	United Kingdom	United States
Paracetamol	OTC	OTC/P	OTC	OTC	OTC
Penciclovir	P	OTC/P	OTC	BTC	Rx
Phenylephrine	OTC	OTC/P	Rx	OTC	OTC
Polymyxin B (*topical*)	Rx	OTC/P	Rx	Rx	OTC
Povidone iodine	OTC	OTC/P	OTC	OTC	OTC
Pravastatin	Rx	Rx	Rx	Rx	Rx
Prednisolone	Rx	Rx	Rx	Rx	Rx
Prilocaine	P	Rx	D	BTC	Rx
Promethazine	P	OTC/P	Rx	BTC	Rx
Ranitidine	P	Rx	D	OTC	OTC
Salbutamol	BTC	Rx	Rx	Rx	Rx
Selenium sulfide	OTC	OTC/P	D	BTC	OTC
Silver sulfadiazine 1%	Rx	OTC/P	Rx	Rx	Rx
Simvastatin	Rx	Rx	Rx	BTC	Rx
Sumatriptan	Rx	Rx	Rx	BTC	Rx
Terbinafine	OTC	Rx	OTC	BTC	OTC
Tetracycline	Rx	Rx	Rx	Rx	OTC[c]
Theophylline	BTC	Rx	Rx	BTC	Rx
Tretinoin	Rx	Rx	Rx	Rx	Rx
Xylometazoline (*nasal*)	P	OTC/P	D	OTC	OTC
Zolmitriptan	Rx	Rx	Rx	Rx	Rx

Legend: Rx = prescription; BTC = behind-the-counter; P = pharmacy; D = drugstore; OTC/P = over- the-counter (pharmacist required); OTC = over-the-counter.

Source: GAO analysis of agency data.

Note: This table indicates the least restrictive class to which each drug was assigned regardless of pack size, dosage, or combination ingredients. Other formulations of a drug may only be available under a more restrictive class. For example, in the United States some types of insulin are available as prescription drugs and other insulin products are available OTC.

[a] In the United States, levonorgestrel (an emergency contraceptive) may only be sold in pharmacies— as a nonprescription drug for those 18 and over, and by prescription for those under 18.

[b] On January 21, 2009, the European Commission approved orlistat (60 mg) for nonprescription use in the EU. At the time of this report, nonprescription orlistat was not yet available to consumers.

[c] in the United States, the topical dosage form of tetracycline is OTC.

Appendix IV: Comments from the Department of Health and Human Services

DEPARTMENT OF HEALTH & HUMAN SERVICES — OFFICE OF THE SECRETARY

Assistant Secretary for Legislation
Washington, DC 20201

FEB 2 2009

Marcia G. Crosse
Director, Health Care
U.S. Government Accountability Office
441 G Street N.W.
Washington, DC 20548

Dear Ms. Crosse:

Enclosed are comments on the U.S. Government Accountability Office's (GAO) report entitled: "NONPRESCRIPTION DRUGS: Considerations Regarding a Behind-the-Counter Drug Class (GAO-09-245).

The Department appreciates the opportunity to review this report before its publication.

Sincerely,

Barbara Pisaro Clark

Barbara Pisaro Clark
Acting Assistant Secretary for Legislation

Attachment

DEPARTMENT OF HEALTH & HUMAN SERVICES

Centers for Medicare & Medicaid Services

200 Independence Avenue SW
Washington, DC 20201

DATE: JAN 29 2009

TO: Barbara Pisaro Clark
Acting Assistant Secretary for Legislation
Office of the Secretary

FROM: Charlene M. Frizzera
Acting Administrator

SUBJECT: Government Accountability Office (GAO) Draft Report: "NONPRESCRIPTION DRUGS: Considerations Regarding a Behind-the-Counter Drug Class" (GAO-09-245)

Thank you for the opportunity to review and comment on the GAO's draft report entitled, "NONPRESCRIPTION DRUGS: Considerations Regarding a Behind-the-Counter Drug Class." The Centers for Medicare & Medicaid Services (CMS) agrees with GAO's finding that cost-related issues would have to be addressed before implementation of a behind-the-counter (BTC) drug class. We also offer these specific comments:

1. The CMS recommends GAO include some discussion about statutory authority to provide reimbursement under Medicare Part D for a potential BTC class. The statutory definition of "covered part D drug" includes drugs that may be dispensed only upon a prescription. CMS currently interprets the phrase "dispensed only upon a prescription," to mean a drug that is recognized by the Food and Drug Administration (FDA) as a prescribed drug requiring "Rx only" on the label as set forth in section 503(b)(4) of the Federal Food Drug and Cosmetic Act. Depending upon FDA implementation of a BTC provision, a BTC drug class may not meet the existing statutory definition and subsequently would not be covered under Part D. Lack of Medicare payment for BTC drugs may result in a shift by Medicare beneficiaries to alternative and more costly prescription drugs, which could, in turn, result in additional Federal expenditures. As a result, we believe GAO should address the potential lack of Medicare Part D payment for a BTC class in its report to Congress.

2. Page 13, footnote 14: This footnote references the Medicare Prescription Drug, Improvement, and Modernization Act of 2003 (MMA) in support of pharmacist review of individuals' drug regimens. We believe this may mislead the reader to thinking that the MMA requires pharmacists to review Medicare beneficiaries' prescription drug regimens as a component of medication therapy management (MTM) under Part D. The MMA only specified that licensed pharmacists and physicians be involved in the development

Page 2 -

of Part D sponsors' MTM programs, not that they provide any corresponding interventions. Given the larger body of evidence supporting pharmacists' efforts in this area, we believe this reference to the MMA should be deleted and replaced with current pharmacy practice literature.

3. Page 17, footnote 20: This footnote references the MMA in support of paying pharmacists 80 percent of the physician reimbursement rate. While the MMA required Part D sponsors to implement MTM programs, the Part D program does not establish any payment schedules for either physicians or pharmacists performing MTM. Thus, we recommend the first and second sentence of this footnote be deleted.

We appreciate the effort that went into this report. Again, we thank you for the opportunity to review and comment.

End Notes

[1] A transcript of this meeting, *Behind the Counter Availability of Certain Drugs: Public Meeting*, is available at http://www.fda.gov/oc/op/btc/transcripts11_14_07.html.

[2] GAO, *Nonprescription Drugs: Value of a Pharmacist-Controlled Class Has Yet to Be Demonstrated*, GAO/PEMD-95-12 (Washington, D.C.: Aug. 24, 1995).

[3] In addition to the United States, the study countries are Australia, Italy, the Netherlands, and the United Kingdom. We also describe drug classification in the European Union (EU).

[4] The reclassification of drugs from one class to another is referred to as switching.

[5] One issue that has been raised, but is beyond the scope of this report, is whether FDA has authority to create such a class without a legislative change.

[6] In addition to the United States, in our previous report we examined the drug classification systems in Australia, Canada, Denmark, France, Germany, Italy, the Netherlands, Sweden, Switzerland, the United Kingdom, and the EU (GAO/PEMD-95-12, pp. 85-10). In this report, the study countries are Australia, Italy, the Netherlands, the United Kingdom, and the United States.

[7] The World Self-Medication Industry is a federation of more than 50 member associations representing manufacturers and distributors of nonprescription medicines. Methodology adapted from A. Gilbert, D. Rao, and N. Quintrell, "A Review of Pharmaceutical Scheduling Processes in Six Countries and the Effect on Consumer Access to Medicines," *International Journal of Pharmacy Practice*, vol. 14, no. 2 (2006).

[8] Pub. L. No. 82-215, 65 Stat. 648 (1951).

[9] Since FDA has not issued a detailed BTC proposal, it is unknown if mail-order or Internet pharmacies would be permitted to dispense BTC drugs. At the November 2007 public meeting, one FDA official stated that the specific role of the pharmacist would need to be determined. See FDA, *Behind the Counter Availability of Certain Drugs: Public Meeting*, p. 1. A pharmacist's intervention with a consumer might include reviewing drug interactions and reading and interpreting laboratory results.

[10] Currently, label comprehension, self-selection, and actual use studies are conducted to help support a request to switch a drug from prescription to OTC status. For some drugs, clinical safety and efficacy trials are also needed. Label comprehension studies are used to

determine whether the label clearly communicates the uses, directions, and warnings to diverse populations and enables the consumer to make appropriate judgments about self-selection. Self-selection studies are used to evaluate whether consumers can appropriately select a product based on the product label and their unique medical histories. Actual use studies are clinical studies designed to simulate the OTC use of a drug. They are meant to assess drug selection, compliance with labeling, and safe use of the drug.

[11] In addition to the United States, in our previous report we examined the drug classification systems in Australia, Canada, Denmark, France, Germany, Italy, the Netherlands, Sweden, Switzerland, the United Kingdom, and the EU. GAO/PEMD-95-12, 85-103.

[12] Academics, pharmacy association officials, manufacturer representatives, and others presented many arguments supporting and opposing a BTC drug class at FDA's November 2007 public meeting. See FDA, *Behind the Counter Availability of Certain Drugs*.

[13] VA and IHS allow some specially trained VA and IHS pharmacists to prescribe drugs. Additionally, according to the American College of Clinical Pharmacy, 44 states now allow some form of collaborative drug therapy management, in which pharmacists enter into collaborative practice agreements with physicians and other prescribers. Under these agreements, pharmacists can be authorized to select appropriate drug therapies and regimens for patients who have a confirmed diagnosis by a physician and adjust them on the basis of patients' responses.

[14] Under the Medicare Prescription Drug, Improvement, and Modernization Act of 2003 (MMA), for example, drug plan sponsors participating in Medicare Part D—a voluntary insurance program for outpatient prescription drug benefits—must offer MTM programs to improve prescription drug use and outcomes among individuals with multiple chronic diseases and taking multiple drugs covered under Part D. (Individuals targeted for MTM programs must also be identified as likely to incur annual costs for covered Part D drugs that exceed a level specified by the Secretary of Health and Human Services.) See Pub. L. No. 108-173, § 101(a), 117 Stat. 2066, 2085-87 (2003). MTM services are designed to optimize therapeutic outcomes through improved drug use and to reduce the risk of adverse events. Examples of MTM services might include performing assessments of the individual's health status; initiating, modifying, or administering drug therapy; monitoring and evaluating the response to therapy; and providing verbal education and training designed to enhance individuals' appropriate use of their drugs.

[15] Community pharmacy settings include independent, chain, mass merchandiser, and supermarket pharmacies. This term excludes pharmacists who practice in hospitals and other institutional settings.

[16] For example, see B. A. Bunting and C. W. Cranor, "The Asheville Project: Long-Term Clinical, Humanistic, and Economic Outcomes of a Community-Based Medication Therapy Management Program for Asthma," *Journal of the American Pharmacists Association,* vol. 46, no. 2 (2006); T. Fera, et al., "The Diabetes Ten City Challenge: Interim Clinical and Humanistic Outcomes of a Multisite Community Pharmacy Diabetes Care Program," *Journal of the American Pharmacists Association,* vol. 48, no. 2 (2008); D. G. Garrett and B. M. Bluml, "Patient Self-Management Program for Diabetes: First-Year Clinical, Humanistic, and Economic Outcomes," *Journal of the American Pharmacists Association,* vol. 45, no. 2 (2005); B. J. Isetts, et al., "Clinical and Economic Outcomes of Medication Therapy Management Services: The Minnesota Experience," *Journal of the American Pharmacists Association,* vol. 48, no. 2 (2008); and B. A. Bunting, et al., "The Asheville Project: Clinical and Economic Outcomes of a Community-based Long-term Medication Therapy Management Program for Hypertension and Dyslipidemia," *Journal of the American Pharmacists Association,* vol. 48, no. 1 (2008).

[17] Opponents argue that if a drug is not suitable for OTC use, it should be available only by prescription. Consequently, they believe that a BTC class is inappropriate.

[18] Although some pharmacists are engaging in expanded roles, such as providing MTM services or participating in collaborative practice agreements, some experts we interviewed do not

consider these experiences adequate preparation for the role pharmacists would be expected to assume for a BTC drug class. Whereas physicians and prescription drug plans can initiate the provision of MTM services, BTC counseling would be initiated by a pharmacist. Additionally, MTM programs primarily focus on managing consumers' current drug therapy, not initiating new therapy, as pharmacists would for BTC drugs. Collaborative practice agreements involve physicians delegating some responsibilities to pharmacists, whereas a BTC drug class would give pharmacists independent decision-making authority. Physician–pharmacist interaction is also formalized through collaborative practice agreements, but physician involvement would likely not be a requirement of a BTC drug class.

[19] For example, pharmacists participating in a diabetes care program in Asheville, North Carolina helped individuals set and monitor treatment goals, performed physical assessments, and provided physician referrals, as needed. Pharmacists also provided individuals with diabetes education training, home glucose monitor training, and information about adherence to their treatment regimens. Individuals in the study maintained clinically meaningful improvements in their levels of glycosylated hemoglobin—a diabetes-related indicator—over time, and third-party payers experienced an overall decline in mean total direct medical costs during each year of follow-up. Pharmacists were reimbursed for their services by employers' health plans. Based on the clinical improvements and financial savings associated with this diabetes management program, the participating employers made the program a permanent component of their health plan benefit. See C. W. Cranor, et al., "The Asheville Project: Long-Term Clinical and Economic Outcomes of a Community Pharmacy Diabetes Care Program," *Journal of the American Pharmaceutical Association,* vol. 43, no. 2 (2003).

[20] Under MMA, plans offering Part D prescription drug coverage must include a MTM program for certain plan enrollees which may be provided by a pharmacist and may include elements to promote the appropriate use of medications by enrollees and adherence with prescription medication regimens. Pharmacists are eligible to be compensated for the services they provide under such plans. Pub. L. No. 108-173, 117 Stat. 2086-7 (2003). Although MMA does not specify a payment schedule, the rate often used by CMS to pay for pharmacists' services under the Medicare program is 80 percent of the physician rate.

[21] Additionally, lack of third-party payment for BTC drugs may result in a shift by consumers to alternative and more costly prescription drugs, which could, in turn, result in additional expenditures.

[22] In the Netherlands, a distinction is made between pharmacies (run by pharmacists and able to sell all prescription and nonprescription medicines) and drugstores (run by druggists with less training than pharmacists and able to sell only some nonprescription drugs). Although the Netherlands has both pharmacy and drugstore classes for nonprescription drugs, contact with the pharmacist or druggist is not required. Therefore, the Netherlands does not have a BTC drug class.

[23] Although Australia has not changed its drug classification system since 1995, research is currently being undertaken to determine whether there is benefit in retaining separate BTC and pharmacy drug classes. These studies were prompted by the Galbally Review, which made a number of recommendations related to achieving uniformity of regulations between Australian states, territories, and the national government through legislative reforms. The review noted that the goals of the BTC and pharmacy drug classes (e.g., ensuring that consumers have sufficient information for the safe and appropriate use of drugs) were valid but concluded that use of these restricted classes resulted in reduced competition and higher costs to consumers, industry, and the government. As a result, the review recommended that standards be developed to facilitate a risk-based approach to pharmacist intervention in the supply of drugs to individual consumers and that research be conducted to determine the benefits obtained from such pharmacist intervention. See Galbally, Rhonda, *National Competition Review of Drugs, Poisons and Controlled Substances Legislation, Final Report*

Part A, a special report prepared at the request of the State, Territory, and Commonwealth governments of Australia, December 2000. A report on the results of this research will be presented in 2011; the BTC and pharmacy drug classes will be retained if the report provides evidence to support doing so.

[24] The BTC drug class in the United Kingdom (called pharmacy medicines) has some characteristics of both the BTC and pharmacy classes as defined in figure 1. The United Kingdom makes these drugs available only in pharmacies under the supervision of a pharmacist and requires that they be stored behind the counter. The pharmacist establishes procedures so that all staff involved in the supply of these drugs should know when to refer a customer to the pharmacist. Although direct pharmacist–consumer contact is necessary for only some of these drugs, the requirement that pharmacists supervise the sale of all drugs in this class and store them behind the counter makes this class most similar to a BTC class.

[25] In some cases, a switch in one country may have involved a drug that was not approved for use in one of the other countries or was not subject to regulation as a drug in another country.

[26] Chlamydia is a sexually transmitted disease that can damage a woman's reproductive organs. BTC azithromycin will be available only after a consumer purchases a chlamydia test kit from a pharmacy, sends a urine sample to an approved laboratory, and receives a positive result. The consumer can then visit a pharmacy where the test results will be confirmed via computer and azithromycin will be dispensed to the consumer and his or her partners.

[27] In addition to these issues, it would also have to be determined whether a BTC drug class could be established administratively by FDA or whether legislation would be necessary; however, this issue is beyond the scope of this report.

[28] Australia's Quality Care Pharmacy Support Centre, a joint effort of the Pharmacy Guild of Australia and the University of Sydney, has monitored the application of practice standards in community pharmacies since 2002. Mystery shopping involves researchers acting as consumers or potential consumers in order to monitor the quality of service delivery.

[29] See Pub. L. No. 101-508, § 4401(a)(3), 104 Stat. 1388, 1388-143 to 1388-161 (1990). As a result of OBRA '90, states participating in the Medicaid program must require pharmacists to offer to counsel Medicaid beneficiaries on matters which the pharmacist, in his or her professional judgment, deems significant, including special directions for preparation and administration, common severe side effects that may occur, and techniques for self-monitoring drug therapy. In addition, 45 states extended these counseling requirements to cover all individuals receiving prescriptions. J. C. Vivian and J. L. Fink III, "OBRA '90 at Sweet Sixteen: A Retrospective Review," *U.S. Pharmacist*, vol. 33, no. 3 (2008).

[30] The Accreditation Council for Pharmacy Education adopted the Doctor of Pharmacy degree as the sole professional practice degree offered by schools of pharmacy in the United States in 1997. The deadline for implementing the new standards for entering professional classes was in academic year 2000-2001, and the last student graduated from an accredited baccalaureate in pharmacy program in the academic year 2004-2005.

[31] J. W. Spray and S. A. Parnapy, "Teaching Patient Assessment Skills to Doctor of Pharmacy Students: The TOPAS Study," *American Journal of Pharmaceutical Education,* vol. 71, no. 4 (2007).

[32] The duration of the pharmacist shortage is uncertain. The supply of pharmacists is affected by factors such as the number of new graduates entering the workforce, the creation of new schools of pharmacy, annual hours of employment, and losses through death and retirement. K. K. Knapp and J. M. Cultice, "New Pharmacist Supply Projections: Lower Separation Rates and Increased Graduates Boost Supply Estimates," *Journal of the American Pharmacists Association,* vol. 47, no. 4 (2007).

[33] BTC simvastatin is indicated to reduce the risk of a first major coronary event in individuals who are likely to be at moderate risk of such events.

[34] See 1985 Fla. Laws ch. 85-35.

[35] United Kingdom Department of Health, *Pharmacy in England: Building on Strengths—Delivering the Future* (Norwich, 2008). Also available online at http://www. official-documents.gov.uk/document/cm73/7341/7341.asp (accessed Oct. 8, 2008).

[36] D.B. Christensen and K.B. Farris, "Pharmaceutical Care in Community Pharmacies: Practice and Research in the US," *The Annals of Pharmacotherapy*, vol. 40, no. 7 (2006). Pharmacists may also have difficulty transferring patient information to physicians electronically. In a national survey, 4 percent of physicians reported having an extensive, fully functioning electronic health records system—13 percent of physicians reported having a basic system. See C. M. DesRoches, et al., "Electronic Health Records in Ambulatory Care—A National Survey of Physicians," *New England Journal of Medicine,* vol. 359, no.1 (2008).

[37] This is the most recent survey that we identified of community pharmacies that examined pharmacies' use of paper and electronic documentation systems. It is likely that the percentage of pharmacies using electronic documentation systems has increased since 2003.

[38] T. Warholak-Juarez, et al., "Effect of Patient Information on the Quality of Pharmacists' Drug Use Review Decisions," *Journal of the American Pharmacists Association,* vol. 40, no. 4, 2000.

[39] M. P. Mobach, "The Counter and Consultation Room Work Explored in the Netherlands," *Pharmacy World & Science,* vol. 30 (2008).

[40] C. G. Berbatis, et al., "Enhanced Pharmacy Services, Barriers and Facilitators in Australia's Community Pharmacies: Australia's National Pharmacy Database Project," *International Journal of Pharmacy Practice,* vol. 15 (2007); and Andrew Joyce, et al., "Analysis of Primary Prevention Service for Cardiovascular Disease in Australia's Community Pharmacies," *Australian and New Zealand Journal of Public Health,* vol. 31, no. 6 (2007).

[41] Australia's Quality Care Pharmacy Program Standards require that community pharmacies maintain a Professional Services Area that, among other requirements, is easily identifiable by consumers as the area of the pharmacy from which therapeutic products are available and that will accommodate privacy and confidentiality requirements.

[42] Regulations implementing title II of the Health Insurance Portability and Accountability Act of 1996, Pub. L. No. 104-191, 110 Stat. 1936, require most health providers, including pharmacists, to have in place appropriate physical safeguards to protect the privacy of health information. See 45 C.F.R. §164.530(c)(2008).

[43] Novartis Pharmaceuticals Corporation, "Novartis Pharmacy Benefit Report, Facts & Figures, 2001 ed.," (East Hanover, N.J., 2001).

[44] J. S. Crowley, et al., "Medicaid Outpatient Prescription Drug Benefits: Findings from a National Survey, 2003," Kaiser Commission on Medicaid and the Uninsured (Washington, D.C., 2003).

[45] Great Britain includes England, Scotland, and Wales, while the United Kingdom includes Great Britain and Northern Ireland.

[46] V. Atella, et al., "Affordability of Medicines and Patients' Cost-Reducing Behaviour: Empirical Evidence Based on SUR Estimates from Italy and the UK," *Applied Health Economics and Health Policy,* vol. 4, no. 1 (2005).

[47] D. B. Christensen and R. W. Hansen, "Characteristics of Pharmacies and Pharmacists Associated with the Provision of Cognitive Services in the Community Setting," *Journal of the American Pharmaceutical Association,* vol. 39, no. 5 (1999).

[48] D. B. Christensen, et al., "Frequency and Characteristics of Cognitive Services Provided in Response to a Financial Incentive," *Journal of the American Pharmaceutical Association,* vol. 40, no. 5 (2000).

[49] Pharmaceutical care services were described in the survey as pharmacists consistently providing detailed counseling, monitoring outcomes, determining the appropriateness of drugs based on individual medical history, and consulting with physicians on prescriptions. See R. A. Larson, "Patients' Willingness to Pay for Pharmaceutical Care," *Journal of the American Pharmaceutical Association,* vol. 40, no. 5 (2000).

[50] C. W. Cranor, et al., "The Asheville Project: Long-Term Clinical and Economic Outcomes of a Community Pharmacy Diabetes Care Program," *Journal of the American Pharmaceutical Association,* vol. 43, no. 2 (2003).

[51] 21 U.S.C. § 355(c)(3)(E)(iv).

[52] While our study defined BTC drugs as those that require the intervention of a pharmacist, FDA noted that there may be other models for providing access to these drugs. They stated that these may include other health care personnel (e.g., nurse practitioners or physician assistants) providing access to BTC drugs in various professional settings.

[53] GAO, *Nonprescription Drugs: Value of a Pharmacist-Controlled Class Has Yet to Be Demonstrated,* GAO/PEMD-95-12 (Washington, D.C.: Aug. 24, 1995), www.gao.gov/archive/1995/pe95012.pdf.

[54] In addition to the United States, the study countries are Australia, Italy, the Netherlands, and the United Kingdom. We also describe drug classification in the European Union (EU).

[55] One issue that has been raised, but is beyond the scope of this report, is whether FDA has the regulatory authority to create such a class without a legislative change.

[56] In addition to the United States, in our previous report we examined the drug classification systems in Australia, Canada, Denmark, France, Germany, Italy, the Netherlands, Sweden, Switzerland, the United Kingdom, and the EU (GAO/PEMD-95-12, 85-103). In this report, the study countries are Australia, Italy, the Netherlands, the United Kingdom, and the United States.

[57] We did not perform the legal analysis of any laws and regulations of foreign jurisdictions, but relied on summaries provided by those jurisdictions.

[58] For example, some prescription drugs classified in the United States as controlled substances cannot be refilled and have stricter documentation requirements than ordinary prescription drugs.

[59] WSMI is a federation of more than 50 member associations representing manufacturers and distributors of nonprescription medicines.

[60] Methodology adapted from A. Gilbert, D. Rao, and N. Quintrell, "A Review of Pharmaceutical Scheduling Processes in Six Countries and the Effect on Consumer Access to Medicines," *International Journal of Pharmacy Practice*, vol. 14, no. 2 (2006).

[61] The National Drugs and Poisons Schedule Committee also determines the classification of agricultural, veterinary, and household chemicals.

[62] Rhonda Galbally, *National Competition Review of Drugs, Poisons and Controlled Substances Legislation, Final Report Part A*, a special report prepared at the request of the State, Territory, and Commonwealth governments of Australia, December 2000, 27.

[63] Except in Queensland and South Australia, where an unscheduled new drug or poison is deemed to be a prescription drug until the classification is determined by the National Drugs and Poisons Schedule Committee.

[64] The specific circumstances are when use of the substance is required for medical and scientific research, or for analytical, teaching, or training purposes with the approval of the Australian government and/or state or territory health authorities.

[65] Italy subdivides its nonprescription drugs into two categories based on whether they can be advertised to the public; there is no other difference between the two categories.

[66] The BTC drug class in the United Kingdom (called pharmacy medicines) has some characteristics of both the BTC and pharmacy classes as defined in figure 2. The United Kingdom makes these drugs available only in pharmacies under the supervision of a pharmacist and requires that they be stored behind the counter. The pharmacist establishes procedures so that all staff involved in the supply of these drugs should know when to refer a customer to the pharmacist. Although direct pharmacist–consumer contact is necessary for only some of these drugs, the requirement that pharmacists supervise the sale of all drugs in this class and store them behind the counter makes this class most similar to a BTC class.

[67] The Medicines Act 1968 and EU Directive 200 1/83/EC.

[68] Pub. L. No. 82-215, 65 Stat. 648 (1951).

[69] In the EU, orphan drugs are defined as those intended for the diagnosis, prevention, or treatment of life-threatening or chronically debilitating conditions that affect no more than 5 in 10,000 people in the EU, or are drugs which, for economic reasons, would be unlikely to be developed without incentives.

[70] On January 21, 2009, the European Commission approved orlistat (60 mg) for nonprescription use in the EU. At the time of this report, nonprescription orlistat was not yet available to consumers.

In: Nonprescription Drugs: Considering…
Editor: Lars P. Eliassen
ISBN: 978-1-60741-961-7

Chapter 2

Food and Drug Administration Behind the Counter Availability of Certain Drugs, Public Meeting*

United States Department of Health and Human Services

RANDALL LUTTER: Good morning, everyone. Welcome to FDA's public meeting on behind the counter drugs. We're very pleased today to see so such a great interest in this issue, and we're looking forward to the presentations and discussions that will occur throughout the day. I'm Randall Lutter, deputy commissioner for policy at the Food and Drug Administration, and on behalf of the Commissioner Dr. Andrew von Eschenbach, I'd like to welcome everybody today to this meeting on behind the counter access.

We're here to explore the public health benefits of behind the counter availability of certain drugs without a prescription, but after an interaction with a pharmacist, and in some countries this is called third class, pharmacists only, pharmacy only or behind the counter. We're particularly interested today in whether behind the counter may improve patient access to safe and effective drug products. If a patient (monitor?) can't go to a doctor because of limits to time or money, there may be a health benefit if they can get safe and effective medicines by going to a pharmacy, consulting with their pharmacist and getting a drug without a prescription.

* This is an edited, reformatted and augmented version of a U. S. Department of Health and Human Services publication dated November 2007.

Currently, drugs products are available with prescription or nonprescription. Nonprescription products are often referred to as over the counter or OTC products. OTC products typically have a large margin of safety, low incidence of side effects and low potential for misuse and abuse and the labeling provides adequate directions for safe and effective use by consumer. For a drug to switch from prescription to nonprescription often referred to as a OTC switch process, FDA conducts a review of the post-marketing safety data and determines whether the consumer can use a product safely without supervision of the healthcare provider.

We want to be clear at this point that FDA has not and is not putting forth a specific proposal for you to consider while we would want to hear your suggestions about how behind the counter access can be structured and implemented in such a way as to increase access, benefit patients and improve public health. I'm here with several other senior officials and representatives of the Food and Drug Administration, and at this point, I'd like to turn the microphone over to my colleague, Dr. Doug Throckmorton who is deputy director of the Center for Drug Evaluation Research. Doug.

DOUGLAS THROCKMORTON: Thanks, Randy very much. And I'd echo your interests in having a good discussion to this morning. I think it's terribly important that we hear from all of the stakeholders to really understand where to take this. There are a couple of items just to go through.

First, at today's meeting, we really hope to obtain information about what if any appropriate mechanisms and measures need to be put into place to assure that behind the counter availability would be efficient and effective. Specific criteria would need to be developed for determining the role that a pharmacist or healthcare professional might play and we hope to hear some ideas from you about that this morning. In the Federal Register notice we offered up some suggestions for comments such as reviewing or conducting initial screening, reviewing clinical laboratory testing, contraindications or drug interactions. Again, we hope that you're able to give us some feedback on those ideas.

A second area that we hope we'll be able to obtain some information from you this morning is with regards to the experience in the foreign areas, in other places in the world where systems similar to this have been put into place, important information is available and I hope that people are able to share that with us.

Finally, we are here to ask – to hear and listen to you and ask questions as we need you to clarify. We ask for information from you about whether there should be behind the counter availability, what criteria should be used to consider drugs for behind the counter availability, how this might impact healthcare including drug prices, logistical issues that pharmacies would face – effects on patient compliance and impacts on pharmacy in the practice of medicine in general. We're sincerely interested in having your input on all of those areas and any other areas that you feel we need to fully understand to move to the next step here.

We're doing this in part because of the changes that have occurred recently in regards to healthcare, both with regards to the technology and the promise that additional data sharing has for making it possible for patients to understand and use the medicines more effectively themselves. And additionally, the increased interest in patients in their own healthcare and their own engagement in that process. Both those things make it at least promising to consider the possibility of this third path. We have had a wonderful response. Very broad audience. Look forward to all of the conversation today. We're very pleased to have representative from Health Canada's Therapeutics Products Directorate to share the Canadian experience for instance.

Randy, like you I know that Dr. von Eschenbach is very interested in this and I'm looking forward to this conversation. Thank you very much.

MR. LUTTER: Thank you. We've broken the presentations into six groups. Each individual presentation will last no longer than 10 minutes. After all presenters in the groups present, there will be a time for questions from the FDA panel. Presenters will be given a – (unintelligible) – when they have about two minutes remaining and we ask that each presenter finish promptly in fairness to others. I've given a gavel here and it sounds like this and I'll try not to be too intimidating with respect to messages about use of the clock, but I think it will be in everybody's best interest if we try and respect everybody's time here. With such a great turnout, we want to make sure that the presenters are on time to fit everyone into the limited time available.

The docket will remain open until November 28th, 2007 to receive comments. Comments can be mailed or emailed information can be found at the behind the counter meeting web page on FDA's website at www.fda.gov. A transcript and all presentations will be made available after the meeting on the docket in within the next two to three weeks. The docket numbers 2007n-0356.

At this point, I'd like to turn to my colleagues from FDA so that they have an opportunity to introduce themselves. Please. Maybe we could start on the right, Diane.

DIANE MALONEY: Okay. Good morning. I'm Diane Maloney. I'm the associate director for policy in the Center for Biologics.

JANE AXELRAD: I'm Jane Axelrad. I'm the associate director for policy in the Center for Drug Evaluation and Research.

LISA BERNSTEIN: I'm Lisa Bernstein. I'm director of Pharmacy Affairs – (off mike).

SCOTT DANZAS (PH): I'm Scott Danzas. I'm an attorney with the Food and Drug and Administration in the Office of the Chief Counsel.

CHARLES GANLEY: I'm Charlie Ganley. I'm the director of the Office of Nonprescription Products in the Center for Drugs.

SUSAN JOHNSON: Susan Johnson, associate director, Office of Nonprescription Products.

MS. : (Unintelligible) – with the management team in the Office of Surveillance and Epidemiology.

DENNIS BASHAW: I'm Dennis Bashaw, division director, division of Clinical Pharmacology III, CDER.

CLARK MARTINELLI (PH): I'm Clark Martinelli, director of the economic staff, Office of the Commissioner.

CONNIE JOHN (PH): Good morning. I'm Connie John in the Office of Policy, Office of the Commissioner.

MR. LUTTER: Thank you very much. At this point, we're ready to begin group one. We have one, two, three, four, five six speakers. Our first speaker is Mr. William Zellmer of the American Society of Health System Pharmacists. Welcome.

WILLIAM ZELLMER: Dr. Lutter, Dr. Throckmorton, distinguished members of the FDA panel, good morning. My name is William Zellmer. I'm deputy executive vice president of the American Society of Health-System Pharmacists, ASHP. ASHP represents pharmacists who practice in hospitals and in health system settings including outpatient pharmacies and ambulatory care clinics. Pharmacy practice in these institutional environments is characterized by collaboration with multidisciplinary healthcare teams, with pharmacist access to patient health records and by compliance with quality enhancing practice standards, such as those of the Joint Commission.

Pharmacists in hospital and health systems use pharmacy technicians and computer technology extensively to increase their productivity and give them more time for patient care. Pharmacists in this setting are in a good position to contribute to the public health success of a behind the counter category of medicines, and we appreciate this opportunity to share our views with you this morning.

As you probably know, outpatient care is a major part of what hospitals do today. There were nearly 700,000 outpatient visits in hospitals in 2006.

Nationwide about 28 percent of general and children's medical surgical hospitals have an outpatient pharmacy. Among hospitals with more than 400 beds, 55 percent have an outpatient pharmacy. Many of these pharmacies serve a large number of patients. For example, the outpatient pharmacies of one large health system in the southeast have 500 patient visits and dispense 1.6 million prescriptions per year.

I will discuss four topics. First of all, ASHP's official policy on behind the counter category of medicines, secondly, our views on the optimal features of pharmacists' enabled access to behind the counter medicines, third, our emerging policy on criteria for selecting medicines for behind the counter status, and then finally a suggestion for moving this public policy discussion forward.

My first topic: ASHP policy. Since 1985, ASHP official policy has supported the establishment of an intermediate or behind the counter class of drug products that would not require a prescription, but would be available only from a pharmacist or a licensed healthcare professional authorized to prescribe medications. ASHP believes that behind the counter availability of certain medications that are currently prescription only and that have unmet potential for improving health status would be in the public interest. It has been shown that reclassification of some prescription medications to nonprescription status resulted in improved patient autonomy and healthcare knowledge as well as improvements in self-care behavior.

However, from a safety perspective, some medications that may be potential candidates for nonprescription status may not be ready for widespread sale in any retail outlet, and for such medications, consumers should be able to draw on the education, training and experience of pharmacists to help them assess their need for the medication and if use of the medication is appropriate, to learn how to take it and monitor its effects. Additional points in our policy specify that drug products appropriate for this intermediate category would be identified through the advice of physicians, pharmacists and other healthcare professionals on the basis of the medical conditions to be treated and potential adverse effects, also that data from post marketing surveillance, epidemiologic studies and adverse drug reaction reporting would be collected to help determine a product's eventual movement to nonprescription status or return to prescription-only status or continuation in the intermediate category.

In 2005, ASHP opposed the proposed transition of a statin to nonprescription status. Although the estimated public benefit of increased patient access to this medication was immense, ASHP did not support the switch because of the lack of safeguards and oversight that would have prevailed if the medication were a nonprescription product. However ASHP supports statin availability in an intermediate category that is designed consistent with our policy.

Let me turn to my second topic, the optimal features of pharmacist practice related to behind the counter medications. Based on best practices in hospitals and health systems, we believe that the pharmacists' practice when providing these therapies should optimally include the following six features: first of all, an initial assessment of the patient using a standardized protocol such as might be developed by professional pharmacy associations to determine appropriateness of the medication; second, obtaining required patient health information such as laboratory data to aide in the assessment; third, counseling the patient about proper medication use at the patient's literacy and comprehension level; fourth, maintaining a standardized record of behind the counter medication and the accompanying professional services that have been provided; fifth, with the consent of the patient, informing his or her primary care provider of any behind the counter medication provided, and finally, ongoing monitoring and effectiveness of safety.

The overall role of the pharmacist here is one of clinical interventions and consultation and that role should be recognized by appropriate payment for the service beyond the retail price of the medication.

Now, my third topic. ASHP is currently developing a policy statement under the direction of our counsel on therapeutics that will outline detailed criteria for determining if a medication is appropriate for behind the counter availability. We are seeking public comment on this document and the policy will be finalized early next year. The current draft says that medications for behind the counter status should, first of all, have a well established benefit to risk ratio and a high safety margin. Secondly, have been marketed as a prescription product for sufficient length of time and been used in sufficient numbers of patients. Third, have evidence of effectiveness and safety at the dose and regimen recommended for the specific formulation of the behind the counter product. Fourth, be used to treat a disease, symptom or condition that can be readily detected or diagnosed by the patient or pharmacist. Fifth, have a means of assessing the effectiveness of the medication and have a means of detecting symptoms of potential toxicity. And finally, not be an anti-infective agent to which emergence of resistance is a concern.

Finally, let me make a suggestion. It is entirely possible that after everything is said today some important questions about the appropriateness and practicality of a behind the counter category may go unanswered. The

United States has no experience base to answer some of these questions. For that reason, we suggest that there may be merit in behind the counter demonstration projects for one or more medications in selected markets with FDA oversight and systematic data collection. The experiences documented in such projects would help answer the public policy questions in the context of conditions here in the United States. Among the settings selected for such demonstration projects, in addition to community pharmacies should be some outpatient pharmacies in hospitals and health systems that are well integrated with patients overall healthcare services, and ASHP would welcome the opportunity to help design such a study.

In conclusion, ASHP believes that a behind the counter class of medications would be in the public interest. It would give the public greater access to medications that have potential for yielding large gains in health status. It would allow manufactures and the FDA to assess the safety of moving such medications to even more widespread access as nonprescription products, and it would tap the expertise of a health professional who is well prepared to help people make the best use of medications in this category. Thank you very much.

MR. LUTTER: Thank you very much, Mr. Zellmer. Do we have questions from the FDA panel? We'll move to Dr. Webb of the American College of Clinical Pharmacy, please.

EDWIN WEBB: Good morning, ladies and gentlemen. My name is Ed Webb. I'm director of government and professional affairs for the American College of Clinical Pharmacy, and I am a pharmacist. ACCP is a national professional and scientific society representing almost 10,000 clinical pharmacist practitioners who practice in essentially the full range of healthcare settings in which medication use and patient care is delivered.

ACCP supports the availability of certain medications without a prescription following consultation with an appropriate patient assessment and education by a pharmacist. We believe in improvements in both overall public health and enhanced patient specific medication use outcomes and quality of life would result from greater availability of appropriate medications through the establishment of a system like this when linked with clinical care and supervision of a pharmacist. We commend the agency for exploring this issue as a means to improve public health and facilitate greater access to these medications.

Studies in both the institutional and community settings have clearly demonstrated that pharmacists' involvement in patient care in collaboration with other healthcare professionals can indeed improve patient care and outcomes. One of the most successful and frequently cited examples in the U.S. is commonly known as the Asheville Project which demonstrated that the clinical services and interventions of pharmacists in collaboration with other healthcare providers substantially improve the clinical, economic and humanistic outcomes associated with patients with diabetes, asthma and lipid disorders.

What's in a name? We believe it's obvious, but we want to emphasize that the benefit to patients and the healthcare system of implementing such an approach will not derive from segregation of the product within a facility, nor from a minimalist expectation of the pharmacist as a gatekeeper of these products as seen with the recent approaches with the pseudo-ephedrine or with emergency contraception. Rather the value will be achieved from an expectation of and policy support for active patient interaction between pharmacists and consumers to enhance their understanding of use of such medication. Evidence from other countries that utilize pharmacist only systems for access to certain medications suggest that these benefits are substantial and that they are valued by consumers and patients.

Therefore, we urge the FDA in subsequent notices and rulemaking activities to use the terms pharmacist-supervised medications or similar terminology to describe the framework being considered by the agency. We believe this terminology would also encourage patients and consumers to seek the clinical guidance and expertise of pharmacists for other health, wellness and disease prevention needs that they may have. Of the 25 or so areas that were raised in the notice, obviously, 10 minutes doesn't allow us to comment on 25 issues, we've chosen at this point in time to comment in four particular areas anticipating that this will be the first of many discussions going forward on this issue among all the stakeholders. And these key areas for us are the criteria for medication availability, documentation and medication record issues, professional services and payment and patient safety and pharmaco vigilance.

In terms of criteria for medication and availability, we believe that pharmacists supervise medications approval should strike a logical and appropriate balance between the existing criteria categorization prescription-only and nonprescription drugs at the current time. A key element of that balance would be that the medication can be more appropriately and safely used by patients and consumers with the active involvement of a pharmacist rather than without. Such a determination should be based on sound clinical evidence and information supported by the input of health professionals, consumers, policy analysts and pharmaceutical companies. Existing methods to identify such medications such as a citizen's petition may also be appropriate to consider.

ACCP supports what we interpret to be based on introductory comments in the October 4th notice the perspective of the agency that these medications would usually be medications that require a prescription but which could be made available without a prescription with the appropriate intervention and services of a pharmacist.

In addition, we recommend consideration of these criteria as noted in the slide above. The medication is used for a treatment of a disease on condition that can be accurately detected and monitored by the patient caregiver, pharmacist or other care providers. The medication has a demonstrated and highly positive benefit to risk profile, the medication has undergone appropriate clinical testing sufficient post marketing surveillance as a prescription medication to have identified the true rate of occurrence of serious adverse effects.

Evidence of effectiveness or ineffectiveness of the treatment clinically should be able to be assessed by the patient and or pharmacist during monitoring and follow up of therapy. Any laboratory test that might be needed to effectively monitor the patient's disease and the therapeutic –(unintelligible) – should either be available to or performable by the pharmacist, and evidence exists to demonstrate that availability of the medication only by prescription unnecessarily restricts access to the medication due to economic or sociologic barriers.

With regard to documentation and medication records issues, the successful implementation of a system of pharmacist-supervised medications must include a requirement for consistent and accurate documentation of both the patient-pharmacist clinical encounter and a record of the dispensing of the medication to that patient. In that regard, the documentation procedures for dispensing of a pharmacist-supervised medication should generally be of the same order of rigor as for prescription-only medications. Adaptation of existing medication profile systems to include documentation of the dispensed medication should be relatively straight forward requiring perhaps some minor adaptation of a few selected data elements such as the prescriber's name, numbering and tracking systems to accurately document the transfer of the medication to the patient.

Documentation of the clinical encounter should generally meet established standards for healthcare provider services, concise notations in the patient's medication record that documents subjective and objective data, assessment of the patient and the suggested plan from the pharmacist perspective, the analogy being SOAP notes in the medical record relative to the pharmacist's supervised medication should be consistently recorded and retrievable to facilitate follow-up and referral activities that might be required. Such an approach is essential to adequately serve patients and drive maximum benefit from such a system. The current procedures employed for the limited number of existing products that are sometimes characterized as behind the counter such as emergency contraceptions and pseudo-ephedrine require currently only proof of age from a government issued photo ID. ACCP believes that this technique is clearly insufficient for a system of pharmacist-supervised medications.

In terms of professional services and payment, we believe that the scope and intensity of services will vary substantially from patient to patient and from medication to medication depending on the particular medication being used. We believe that all of the areas of pharmacist professional practice that are outlined in the October 4th notice are part of the picture but there's more to it probably than that even because patients do vary and service needs of patients will vary. ACCP does believe strongly that the professional services that would accompany the provision of a pharmacist-supervised medication are just that; they are professional services. What we envision and what the healthcare system should expect with this approach is a pharmacist-patient clinical encounter rather than a policed commercial transaction. Therefore, these services are clearly appropriate for payment by patients and by public and private payers of healthcare services. The recent approval of AMA category 1CPT codes for pharmacists face to face medication therapy services for patients provide a standardized and HIPAA-compliant framework for building and documentation of these services.

With regard to patient safety and pharmaco vigilance, any decision to develop and implement a system of pharmacist-supervised medications must have as a central tenant a firm commitment to patient safety and enhanced and targeted pharmaco vigilance activities that support examination of both the positive and negative clinical outcomes associated with the use of these medications. We therefore urge an expanded profile of the activities of the MedWatch program to include not only adverse effect reporting but successful clinical outcome reporting as well.

In summary, ACCP supports this approach to pharmacist access to prescription medications and believes that the creation of this system will substantially improve public health and access and we look forward to working with the agency and other stakeholders in moving this issue forward. Thank you very much.

MR. LUTTER: Thank you very much, Dr. Webb. Our next speaker is Dr. Moné of the American Pharmacist Association.

MICHAEL MONÉ: Good morning, and thank you for the opportunity to provide pharmacists' perspectives on various issues related to the FDA's interest in behind the counter availability of certain drugs.

I am Michael Moné, a pharmacist and a lawyer, and currently service the director of regulatory compliance for the Medicine Shop International. I'm here today as a representative of the American Pharmacist Association, the first established and oldest professional organization for pharmacists that represents more than 60,000 members in all practice settings.

Improving the public health and safety with respect to medication use is APhA's highest priority. Let me restate that, please: improving the public's health and safety with respect to medication use is APhA's highest priority. Pharmacists, the medication experts on the healthcare team are the most accessible healthcare providers and the only healthcare provider available to interact and communicate with patients at the point of sale for prescription and OTC medications.

As such, pharmacists have demonstrated that we successfully assist patients to manage and improve their medication use. APhA applauds the FDA's recognition that pharmacists are in an unique position to proved the oversight needed to improve medication use outcomes of certain medications used to treat patients identified conditions or symptoms. BTC medications that require a pharmacist's clinical intervention would facilitate more pharmacist-patient communication that would ultimately lead to improved medication use outcomes and improved public health.

APhA receive feedback from more than 600 responders to a recent poll about the questions posed in the Federal Register meeting notice. More than 80 percent indicated that they support the concept of BTC status for certain drugs and would be willing to provide additional information to patients related to BTC medications. APhA supports FDA classification of certain drugs being available without a prescription but only after intervention by a pharmacist. This public health initiative will be successful only if it designed around a collaborative pharmacist-patient healthcare encounter not solely a retail transaction. The patient and the pharmacist will jointly assess the patient's condition to determine if the BTC medication is appropriate or whether the patient requires a referral. This pharmacist-patient encounter will result in improved public health, enhance patient access to medications and will facilitate safe and appropriate use of medications.

APhA relies on the FDA to determine drug status and to establish those market factors that would ensure viability of this initiative. APhA's support of certain drugs being available without a prescription but only after an intervention by a pharmacist is based upon four key principles: principle one, a pharmacist-patient clinical intervention is essential; principle two, the FDA must base its BTC categorization decisions on science; principle three, the processes for drug availability without a prescription must be uniform, and principle four, pharmacists must be able to bill and be paid for the clinical services provided.

Principle one: the pharmacist-patient clinical intervention is essential. BTC will be successful when a BTC medication is only available after a patient receives assessment, consultation and clinical evaluation by a pharmacist, and patients may not waive this requirement by signing an opt- out form. BTC will be successful when a BTC medication is identified as appropriate for treatment based upon a patient's self-identified condition or symptoms for which the patient is seeking care and the pharmacist's clinical assessment confirms that the conditions for which the patient is seeking care can be addressed appropriately with an available BTC medication.

Pharmacist interventions to determine the clinical appropriateness of BTC medication has the potential to increase appropriate patient access to medications that would otherwise be available only by prescription. This pharmacist-patient interaction is particularly relevant to patients with no health insurance and for other underserved populations who do not have ready access to healthcare providers. A benefit of certain drugs being available without a prescription but only after intervention by a pharmacist may offer an opportunity for the FDA to preserve access to certain medications in the rare case when the primary concern with that medication is preventing inappropriate use or misuse. In such a case, transition of a production from OCT to BTC could allow the medication to remain available in the marketplace with the patient care oversight provided by a pharmacist that would be required for its safe and effective use.

Pharmacists' clinical intervention in providing a BTC medication would also serve to increase compliance with medication therapy. An additional value to the healthcare system of certain medications being available without a prescription but only after intervention with a pharmacist would be the identification of patients that require either no treatment, those that can be treated with a BTC medication, or those that require referral to a physician. In all cases, more patients would receive higher quality healthcare. Studies such as the Asheville Project that have been described earlier have demonstrated that referrals to physicians increase when pharmacists are actively engaged in clinical interventions with the patient. These studies further document that pharmacists assist patients to manage their prescription medication, increase patient compliance, improve patient safety, and the patient's overall health outcome improves significantly.

Principle two: the FDA must base its BTC decisions on science. BTC will be successful when FDA realize on clinical evidence of medication safety and efficacy when determining which products to include as BTC medications. BTC will be successful when FDA designates a product as BTC when clinical evidence exists that a particular drug product can be used safely with the intervention of a pharmacist. And BTC will be successful when a defined standardized process is created by the FDA for BTC product designation and for movement among prescription-only BTC and OTC classes.

Opportunities for increased pharmacist-patient interaction will improve safe medication use and outcomes. A pharmacist's intervention will include an assessment of the patient's symptoms to confirm that a BTC medication is an appropriate therapy option for the patient. A pharmacist may review, conduct, and/or assess patient screening outcomes which may include laboratory testing data and provide patient risk assessment, counseling and education on the safe and effective use of BTC medication.

Principle three: the processes for drug availability without a prescription must be uniform. BTC will be successful when standardized, administrative and clinical processes are created to ensure an effective pharmacist-patient clinical interaction. And BTC will be successful when pharmacists are able to access and share as appropriate required patient medical information in a timely and efficient manner. The pharmacist- patient interaction would also mean that when appropriate, the pharmacist and patient could arrange for follow-up monitoring. The pharmacist would maintain a standardized electronic patient record to document the intervention and upon consent to communicate relevant data and information to a known primary care provider.

Principle four: pharmacists must be able to bill and be paid for the clinical services provided. BTC will be successful when a standardized mechanism is established and in place for pharmacists to bill and be paid for the services provided either by the patient, a third-party payer or others. And BTC will be successful when payment for related clinical services is separate from payment for the BTC product.

In conclusion, we are pleased that the FDA is recognizing the value of pharmacists and their ability to address a growing healthcare concern related to medication use. APhA firmly believes that pharmacists are a valuable and readily accessible resource to help meet patients' healthcare needs regarding access to and the safe and appropriate use of medications. As consumers become more aware of product risks and benefits, pharmacists can play a valuable role in patient self-care decisions. Providing patients with safe and appropriate medications after consultation in clinical interventions by a pharmacist will increase patient access to medications, enhance patient education and improve medication use.

As the agency moves ahead with this concept, APhA recommends that the agency incorporate these four key principles: principle one, the pharmacist-patient clinical interaction; principle two, science based decision making; principle three, uniform administrative and clinical processes and principle four, the ability for pharmacists to bill and be paid for the clinical services provided.

APhA offers its support in this instance to the agency in future discussions and meetings about this important public health initiative. Thank you for the opportunity to present the views of the nation's pharmacists.

MR. LUTTER: Thank you very much, Dr. Moné. Our next speaker is Ms. Eileen Harley from the Food Marketing Institute.

EILEEN HARLEY: Good morning. The Food Marketing Institute appreciates the opportunity to comment on the Food and Drug Administration's request for input on the availability of behind the counter drugs. We applaud the FDA's desire to study the public health implications of certain drugs being available without a prescription after intervention by a pharmacist.

There are several issues surrounding the possible creation of a BTC class of drugs that are of particular concern to FMI, specifically how products will be evaluated for inclusion in the BTC class, what protections pharmacists will receive from claims of liability, how pharmacists will be reimbursed for their time, services and expertise and the logistical issues that will arise with this new class? Given the complexity of the issues involved, FMI requests that the FDA extend the comment period to ensure that all stakeholders are given the opportunity to express their concerns.

FMI conducts programs and research education industry relations and public affairs on behalf on its 1,500 member companies, food retailers and whole sellers in the United States and around the world. FMI's U.S. members operate approximately 26,000 retail food stores with a combined annual sales volume of 340 billion which is three-quarters of all retail food store sales in the United States. FMI's retail membership is composed of large multi-store chains, regional firms and independent supermarkets. Its international membership includes 200 companies in 50 countries.

FMI's retail members operate over 19,000 in-store pharmacy departments. Based on current industry trends towards larger store formats and the convenience of one-stop-shopping, we anticipate that the number of pharmacies located in supermarkets will continue to increase in the coming years as will the number of prescriptions that are dispensed on an outpatient basis from these community settings. Earlier this year, FMI committed significant resources to develop the Pharmacy Services Department to provide our members with a clinical perspective in identifying and developing federal policy impacting retail pharmacy.

First, I'd like to address patient access to pharmaceuticals. As noted by the FDA in the October 4th Federal Register notice, some groups have asserted that a BTC category could increase patient access to medications, particularly those patients without health insurance. FMI believes strongly in affordable access to medications and actively works to ensure that its members' customers have convenient access to needed healthcare products and medication. However, FMI cautions that if product selection criteria are not narrowly defined and strictly applied, a BTC category may actually decrease patient access to needed medications especially in rural and underserved markets.

Many individuals living in rural areas do not have convenient access to a pharmacy and instead rely on FMI member stores not all of which have pharmacies as their only convenience store is a pharmaceutical and healthcare products. Classifying certain over-the-counter medications as BTC would limit the products available in these stores which would necessarily limit the access these individuals have to the products they depend on for their health and wellbeing. We support maintaining consumer access to those medications that can be taken safely and effectively without a prescription. Such products should remain over-the-counter medications available to consumers through various retail outlets.

As the FDA explores the possibility of behind the counter availability of drugs, we remind the agency that criteria used to identify products for inclusion in this potential category should address the concern associated with the substantial self-diagnosis and/or self-medication role of the patients. The approval process should be carefully developed and they're early defined and should allow for input from drug manufacturers, pharmacists and other health professionals, citizens and the FDA. Likewise, the criteria used to determine acceptability in the BT class must be based upon sound scientific evidence with a strong emphasis on safety concerns. FMI believes strongly in increasing consumers' access to the products and medications but not at the expense of patient safety.

We also caution the FDA to only use the BTC category as a means to increase patient access to drugs that require intervention from the pharmacist but that do not have the safety concerns that warrant physician supervision. The BTC category must not be used as a means to enforce age limits, quantity of product purchase or other drug enforcement concerns. Pharmacists are trained as healthcare professionals with the expertise, education and experience to assist patients with their healthcare and pharmaceuticals needs. As has been shown with pseudo-ephedrine, pharmacists are not needed to enforce quantity limits and ensure that patients' purchasing particular products meet minimum age requirements. FMI urges the FDA to limit the scope of any BTC class to those situations where the intervention of a pharmacist can expand access to pharmaceuticals that would otherwise only be available by prescription.

Next, I would like to address the pharmacists' liability concerns. Every day, pharmacists help patients self-manage the medication therapy and improve the medication through appropriate drug selection monitoring and education. While our pharmacists are eager to help patients access the pharmaceutical care they need, the medications must be safe and effective for their intended use and they must be properly labeled for their intended audience. Drugs should not be placed behind the counter simply to transfer liability from manufacturers to pharmacists or pharmacies because the products themselves are not properly labeled for consumers to purchase in an OTC setting or because manufacturers have not adequately established the safety or efficacy of the drug. If FDA decides to proceed in the development of a BTC class of drugs, it might be appropriate to seek legislation to ensure that liability is fairly apportioned.

With regards to a pharmacist's reimbursement for services, the creation of a BTC class of drugs will means that the pharmacist will have to spend greater amounts of time on patient assessment, counseling and dispensing and documentation services for these new drugs. FMI strongly believes that pharmacists must be compensated for these cognitive services. In designing a BTC class it will be important to consider how payers respond. For instance, will BTC drugs be treated as analogous to prescription drugs which they are typically covered by insurance, or as OTCs which generally are cash and carry products? Given the products currently being discussed for BTC status, FMI would argue that treatment closer to prescription status would be more appropriate. The status could provide a mechanism for pharmacists to be compensated for their services, the legislation might be required to accomplish this goal particularly in the case of Medicare.

Depending of the number and type of drugs placed in the BTC category, pharmacies may face considerable logistical challenges in transitioning to this new class of drugs. Behind the counter shelves space already at a premium in most stores will become even more cramped and sought after. As pharmacists take a more active role in patient diagnosis and care, they will need to communicate and coordinate care with labs, physicians and other healthcare providers. This increased level of communication will also present new challenges, and if pharmacists are required to interview and examine patients, pharmacies will need to rethink and redesign their space in order to provide a private space for the pharmacists to consult with the patient, draw blood, et cetera.

A standardized documentation system will be required beyond the simple registry of the sale to include the BTC medication dispense and the related services. Communication back to the patient's primary care provider, if known, with patient consent must also be addressed. Given the considerable logistical challenge, changes that will be required, FDA should continue to include the pharmacy community and discussions about the possible creations of the BTC class.

Finally, given the complexity of this issue and the wide array of stakeholders affected, we ask that the agency consider extending the comment period to ensure all stakeholders have the opportunity to be heard. Again, FMI credits FDA for accepting public comment on the possible creation of a BTC class. We look forward to working with the FDA as they continue to explore behind the counter availability of certain drugs. Thank you.

MR. LUTTER: Thank you very much, Ms. Harley. Our next speaker is Dr. Joseph Cranston from the American Medical Association. Welcome.

JOSEPH CRANSTON: Good morning. My name is Joseph Cranston. I'm a pharmacologist by training, and I currently serve as the director of science research and technology at the American Medical Association. I'm speaking on behalf of the AMA at this FDA public meeting on behind the counter or BTC availability of drugs.

The first question posed by the FDA in its Federal Registry Notice was should there be BTC availability of certain drug products? The focus of my comments today is to express the AMA opposition to the establishment of a BTC class of drugs in the United States. The BTC class also has been referred to third class, transitional class or pharmacy or pharmacists' only class of drugs and for the purpose of this presentation, the terms should be considered interchangeable.

The AMA has a number of reasons for opposing a BTC class of drugs. First, the AMA does not believe the FDA has the statutory authority to establish a BTC class. The Durham-Humphrey amendments to the Federal Food Drug and Cosmetic Act clearly establish two classes of drugs in the United States: prescription and over the counter. For the past half century no one, including a number of past FDA commissioners has argued that the FDA has the authority to establish additional classes of drugs such as the BTC class by regulation or guidance. Thus, it is somewhat perplexing for the AMA that this meeting is even being held today.

We are aware of at least one former high level FDA official who's publicly commented that restricted distribution provisions on the FDA Amendments Act of 2007 or FDAAA provides the authority for FDA to establish a BTC class of drugs. The AMA strongly disagrees with that interpretation of this provision of the new law. If you read the title of the section in restricted distribution in FDAAA states and I quote, "providing safe access for patients to drugs with no serious risk that would otherwise be unavailable." The purpose of the restricted distribution provision is to allow drugs with really serious risks such as thalidiomide and isotretionin to remain on the market as prescription drugs.

However, if an over-the-counter drug is found to have significant new risks, it could be moved to the current prescription-only class and would still be available. There's no need to establish a new BTC classification. There's not a scintilla of support in the statutory literature FDAAA or in the congressional record that confers the FDA the dramatic new authorities to create a whole new class of drugs. Furthermore, the AMA is unaware of any discussions within Congress about a BTC class of drugs during its deliberations on the restricted distribution or for that matter any other provision of FDAAA. If Congress wanted to establish a BTC class regarding this major new law that so profoundly affects FDA, Congress would have clearly, unequivocally done so.

Even if the FDA could make a case that it has a legal authority to establish a BTC class of drugs, the AMA is unaware of any good evidence that supports the need for such a new classification. To the contrary, the most definitive report on this subject published the U.S. General Accountability Office in 1995 concluded and I quote, "little evidence supports the establishment of a pharmacy or pharmacist class of drug in the United States as either a fixed or transitional class. The evidence that is available tends to undermine the contention that major benefits are being obtained in the countries that have such a class." Although the GAO report was written over a decade ago, there is little or no evidence to suggest that its inclusion should be disregarded today.

Many questions about the impact of a BTC class of drugs remain unanswered. For example, it is unclear what the impact of a BTC class would have on access to drugs or on their cost. If a drug that is currently available over the counter will move to a BTC class, access to the drug undoubtedly would decrease because the number of retail settings that sell the product would be lowered by at least an order of magnitude. Furthermore, the cost of the drug most likely would increase substantially because of reduced competition in the market place.

On the other hand, for drugs currently available by prescription only to move to a BTC class access to the product probably would increase. However, the cost of the patient also could increase if a third-party payer refuses provide coverage for nonprescription drugs. Currently, this is a relatively common practice among third-party payers. Of greater concern, what if a third-party payer force the patients to use a BTC class drug before paying for a visit to the patient's physician in some form of step therapy program where is the cost of removing physician oversight from the process, and I'm going to address that issue in greater detail later in the presentation.

Also, what would be the added cost to patients for pharmacist services if a BTC class of drugs is established? Pharmacists have had the authority to counsel patients about their prescription medicines since the early 1990s. And the AMA generally has been supportive of pharmacist counseling. However, pharmacists really counsel patients and overall it is routine for the pharmacy to ask you to sign a waiver that you declined counseling. The reason most likely is that pharmacists are not paid for this service. So what would be the added cost to the healthcare system for pharmacist related services that would be associated with the dispensing of BTC drugs?

The last question in the Federal Register notice for this meeting was what impact would BTC availability of drugs have on the practice of medicine? I'd like to spend the remainder of my time addressing this question. The AMA's position is that when a drug is not safe for use by consumers without supervision whether due to its toxicity, its method of use or the quality (?) measures necessary for its use, then a physician who is adequately trained to evaluate and diagnose disease and is licensed to prescribe drugs should be responsible for supervising the use of that drug. This is our interpretation of current federal law and it should not be changed by adding new BTC class of drugs. While pharmacists are very knowledgeable about drugs, they lack the necessary education and experience in patient evaluation, clinical diagnosis and prescribing for individual patients to make the types of patient management decisions that physicians do on a routine basis every day.

The AMA is especially concerned that the FDA might consider moving a number of prescription drugs used to treat various chronic conditions to BTC status. In the 2000 Federal Registry Notice seeking comments on the regulation of OTC drug products, the FDA listed antihypertensive drugs, cholesterol lowering drugs, anti-diabetic drugs, treatments for osteoporosis, treatments for asthma and contraceptives as possible candidates for Rx-to-OTC switch. One can only presume that some of these classes of drugs might be considered seriously for Rx-to-BTC switch.

For example, the manufacture of lovastatin, the cholesterol lowering medication in the statin class submitted an NVA for OTC status about three years ago for the sale of the product could only be in pharmacies. That application was rejected, but as I understand that this drug would be considered for OTC status by an FDA advisory committee next month.

The AMA opposes switching these types of products from prescription only to a BTC class. The benefits of a physician doing a thorough history and clinical examination, including for other preexisting conditions as well as performing the necessary laboratory tests to make the correct differential diagnosis and direct them in the best treatment strategy to monitor the patient for clinical response is critically important for patient with chronic diseases. Some of these diseases have poorly recognizable symptoms that only a physician can evaluate it appropriately. Also many patients have multiple chronic conditions and they require a number of drugs. Only a physician is capable of managing these complex cases. Pharmacists certainly do not have the necessary education and training to perform these critical functions. The patients lose these benefits of physician supervision by switching drug products to a BTC class that in the AMA's view will be detrimental to the health of many individuals and for the public.

In conclusion, the AMA opposes the establishment of a BTC class of drugs. We do not believe the FDA has a statutory authority to create a third class of drugs by either regulation or guidance. If this question needs to be addressed, it should be done so legislatively at the level of Congress. However, even if the FDA disagrees in that point, the AMA has identified a number of reasons why the FDA should not move forward. The need for a BTC class has not been clearly shown, and in the fact, most thorough evaluation of this subject reaches the opposite conclusion. Many questions remain unanswered about the impact of a BTC class including issues of access to drugs and cost of drugs.

Finally, removing the physician to the patient takes away an important step in determining whether the patient is properly diagnosed and being treated optimally and this can negatively impact the patient's outcome. The AMA appreciates the opportunity to presents its views on this important issue. I'd be happy to entertain any questions.

MR. LUTTER: Dr. Cranston, thank you very much for your comments. Our next speaker is Dr. Daniel Hussar from the Philadelphia College of Pharmacy, the University of the Sciences in Philadelphia.

DANIEL HUSSAR: Thank you very much. I wish to commend the FDA for convening this meeting of what I consider to be a very important opportunity that will have multiple benefits. The perspectives and the opinions that I share are based on my responsibilities as a faculty member. One of my responsibilities is the nonprescription drug therapy course. What I would like to do in my comments is to address some of the general issues that were identified in the FDA notification announcement in the Federal Register, and then I'll also mention several specific examples of medications that I consider to be excellent candidates to be transferred from prescription only to behind the counter availability in pharmacies.

The first FDA general issue identified in the Federal Register reads: should there be BTC availability of certain drug products? If so why? If not, why? My response to that question is an unequivocal yes, that certain drug products should be available without prescription behind the counter in pharmacies. I recognize that over the years there have been questions as to whether the FDA has the authority to establish such a groups or medications. I feel that that question was conclusively answered in late 2006 when the Food and Drug Administration approved the transfer of levonorgestrel or plan B to over the counter – I'm sorry – nonprescription availability behind the counter. That decision was made without any additional legislative authority or any other measure of authority that was granted to the FDA at that time.

I'll address some of the specific reason in support of my "yes" response to this question when I discuss the individual drugs. The second question that I would like to address, what might the impact of BTC be on patient access? The access of patients to medications from which they can benefit will be markedly increased by such decisions.

For various reasons, many individuals rarely, if ever, see a physician unless there is some emergency for which they need treatment. The BTC availability of certain medications from a pharmacist will not only be of value in the treatment of conditions for which physician consultation is not necessary, but it will also facilitate and increase the referral by pharmacist of patients with potentially serious problems to physicians. Those individuals may not otherwise have gotten into the healthcare system.

Indeed, the interaction with the pharmacist regarding a BTC medication will, for many individuals, represent the first step into the healthcare system and their subsequent evaluation and appropriate treatment.

General issue five that the FDA listed: please comment on the following criteria for what roles the pharmacists or rather health professionals might play. Pharmacists are well prepared and strategically positioned to review clinical laboratory test results, identify contraindications, drug interactions and other drug-related problems, counsel patients on the appropriate and safe use of medications and monitor for the continued safe and effective use. Some pharmacists have additional credentials and authorization to prepare them for added responsibilities.

General issue 11 that the FDA identified: would BTC availability be cost effective to patients? Please explain. The increase in the number of nonprescription BTC pharmacy available medications will make them available on a more cost effective basis than if they were only available on prescription. The nonprescription marketplace is very competitive, whether it's OTC or BTC. Although it is available over the counter rather than BTC, one example would be the Prilosec OTC. The cost of Prilosec OTC is a small fraction of what the other proton pump inhibitors cost on a prescription-only basis.

At the present time, most insurance company drug benefit programs provide coverage only for prescription medications and not for nonprescription medications. As medications are transferred from prescription only to BTC status, the employers and other organizations that pay the insurance companies to provide these programs should not only expect, but should insist, on continued coverage of these medications.

In my opinion, there are numerous medications that are excellent candidates for a transfer to BTC availability in pharmacies. I've selected four particular examples to illustrate different reasons for which I consider it to be in the interest of patients, society and the healthcare system in general to transfer these agents from prescription only to BTC status.

The first group that I would mention are medications that will help individuals stop smoking. Varenicline, also known by the brand name Chantix, nicotine nasal spray, also known by the brand name Nicotrol, a nicotine inhalation system. These three products now are only available on prescription. We don't need to recite the statistics of the number of deaths due to smoking related causes each year. Some individuals have not been successful with the use of the nonprescription products available to help them stop smoking, and other strategies are not readily available to them.

Some of these individuals will not take the next step and go to a physician so that the prescription options for helping them to stop smoking can be considered. There are many smokers who want to quit. but don't take that step to see a physician. For these individuals, the nonprescription availability of varenicline, nicotine nasal spray and nicotine inhalation system will provide a pharmacist-monitored opportunity for a successful effort to stop smoking.

I realize that there have been some recent reports of some occasional adverse events with varenicline and some will say that there has not been enough experience yet with this relatively new drug. However, of all the medications that have been approved in recent years for prescription use, varenicline has one of, if not the, cleanest safety profile with regard to its labeling.

It is an unacceptable irony that the only – that proof of age is the only requirement for which individuals can purchase a dangerous product like cigarettes, whereas a prescription is required to obtain the products that will help the individuals to stop smoking. Effective and safe smoking cessation age should be conveniently accessible for individuals, for smokers who choose not to visit a physician and barriers to such access must be reduced.

The second medication I would mention is the epinephrine auto-injector. Some individuals experience very serious and even life-threatening reactions following insect bites or stings or exposure to other allergens. Epinephrine is the drug of choice for these emergency situations and the administration of a product like Epipen can be a life-saving intervention. Epipen requires a prescription. Many individuals who have had that experience of a serious allergic reaction carry an Epipen with them, but they may not have it on every occasion. They may not have had occasions to use it and when the time arises, when it is needed, they'd note that it's well passed the expiration date.

Emergencies such as anaphylactic reactions seldom occur in a convenient location such as a block away from a hospital in which needed treatment can be quickly provided. Often these events occur in an area and/or at a time in which the local pharmacy is more quickly accessible than a physician or a hospital. The nonprescription BTC pharmacy availability of Epipen, or a similar product, can be lifesaving.

The third drug I would mention is oseltamivir, Tamiflu. In recent years, there has been considerable publicity about the possibility of an influenza pandemic. Osiltamivir or Tamiflu is one of a very small number of antiviral agents that is effective in the treatment of influenza. However, for this drug to be optimally effective, it is very important that treatment be initiated as soon as possible designated as within two days following the onset of symptoms. Patients who experience influenza symptoms should be provided the fastest access possible to medications that might be of significant benefit, and even the delay in seeing a physician who can be expected to be even busier than usual during the flu season, waiting that delay or for the delay in receiving the prescription, may compromise the effectiveness of therapy.

And the last group of agents that I would mention are the statins. The statins are among the most widely prescribed of all therapeutic agents. They are the most effective medications in lowering cholesterol concentrations and are well tolerated by most patients, notwithstanding the potential for musculo-skeletal adverse events. You heard earlier about request to transfer Lovastatin and also Pravastatin to nonprescription status.

The primary concern voiced by those who oppose nonprescription status for the statins is that patients will have difficulty determining their need for a medication and subsequent monitoring of a statin, particularly because hypercholesterolemia is not associated with symptoms. Although this is a valid concern, it must also be recognized that many individuals, rather than seeing a physician and receiving prescribed medications, are purchasing herbal products and dietary and nutritional supplements for the purpose of decreasing their cholesterol and deriving the suggested accompanying benefits. Just the other night, I was half listening to a television advertisement for new, Centrum Cardio; it lowers cholesterol. This is made by one of the major pharmaceutical companies that contains phytosterols. Now, to what extent have they been tested?

These products, such as the herbal products and so forth, have not been evaluated in clinical studies and I think in this context, a strong case can be made for the nonprescription BTC pharmacy availability of statins that have been extensively studied, have a known safety profile and can be monitored by a pharmacist. There are also other examples. Time does not permit me to address these individually.

The increase in number of nonprescription BTC pharmacy available medications will not only result in increased patient access to helpful medications, but will also make them available on a more cost-effective basis. The opportunity that the FDA is providing is one in which all participants can win, individual patients, society in general, the healthcare system, pharmacists, pharmaceutical companies and the FDA. Thank you for this opportunity to participate in this forum.

MR. LUTTER: Thank you very much, Dr. Hussar. At this point, we have approximately 10 minutes for questions from the FDA panel, and the questions may be posed to the most recent speakers collectively or individually. It might be beneficial if they were identified with respect to who they're aimed at and – are there questions? Yes. Jane?

MS. AXELRAD: Yes. I have some questions. The first question I'd like to address to the pharmacy members of the panel, pharmacist members of the panel. I was wondering if you could address what type of training you think pharmacists would need to be able to conduct the clinical assessments that you have all, I think, indicated are a key part of being able to dispense a drug safely behind-the-counter? Anyone, I guess can address it.

MR. HUSSAR: At the Philadelphia College of Pharmacy, and I am confident that this is the experience at all colleges of pharmacy, we provide comprehensive didactic training that includes a review of case studies in which individuals, students, meet in small groups with their clinical instructors. And then there is one entire year of experience in which – in different practice sites and rotations, students are given the responsibilities in a setting in which their performance and recommendations are monitored by the pharmacist, by physicians and other members of the healthcare team.

There is a primary focus in many of the educational programs on chronic disease, conditions like hypercholesterolemia, conditions like diabetes and asthma, so that the pharmacist, the pharmacy students, are prepared to recognize the symptoms. They know what questions to ask to distinguish between one condition and another. They are also strongly encouraged, as I do in my nonprescription drug therapy course, in the discussion of every topic, we identify the types of symptoms and situations and patients that can be appropriately treated with nonprescription drugs. We also identify the circumstances in which the best advice the pharmacist will give is to refer that individual to a physician or to an emergency department.

I don't think there is a concern about pharmacists overstepping their expertise or the boundaries. Indeed, earlier, a question was raised about liability and that shouldn't be the primary parameter by which we fulfill responsibilities to the patients, but I think pharmacists are well prepared, I think that the FDA will be discrete in determining what medications they will switch into such a category and that they will have the confidence that pharmacists will be well prepared to provide the appropriate assessment and guidance.

MS. AXELRAD: Thank you.

MR. LUTTER: Is there another response to that same question?

MR. WEBB: Yes. I think it's fair to say that a pharmacist is not a pharmacist is not a pharmacist, and I think there is – you need to appreciate the substantial changes in curriculum and education that have occurred in the last decade in terms of the movement to the doctor of pharmacy degree as the sole professional degree. And I think, clearly, the current curriculum prepares our new graduates to be very effective in this role. There are pharmacists in practice now who have graduated 15, 20, 25 years ago for whom this set of activities and skills will not necessarily be second nature, but that doesn't mean that they can't be prepared and educated to assist in this process.

We believe that – I agree with Dan. I think the greater challenge for the public and for the profession sometimes is getting pharmacists to step up to these responsibilities, not be overanxious to do things for which they are not prepared. So we believe that pharmacists are well prepared to do this and those who seek to do this will be more than prepared to accomplish it.

MR. LUTTER: Other questions from the panel?

MS. MALONEY: I had a question for Dr. Moné with regard to the survey. I think you said 80 percent supported BTC. I would be interested in knowing what the 20 percent, if there were big issues that they were raising, why they were not in support of it.

MR. MONÉ: Actually, the 20 percent that didn't show support – it was not a question of not showing support for it. They just said that there were so many more questions that they needed to see answered, which is essentially the 25 or so items that were in the notice. They said, well, we need to see what it looks like before we can say that we're in support of it. So it wasn't really a rejection of the concept. It probably would be more accurate to say that 100 percent of them were okay with the concept, 80 perçent showed significant favorability toward what was already existent in the fact that FDA was talking about doing this initiative.

MR. LUTTER: Thank you, Dr. Moné. Other questions?

MS. MALONEY: I had another question for Dr. Webb. I'm really not that familiar with the category CPT codes, and are these payment codes that you talked about the initial 15 minute consultation for new and established patient? And where I'm going with this is trying to understand more what is happening out there in the real world. Right now, if you go to the pharmacist and pick up a prescription it says, do you want to consult a pharmacist? You can do that and there's no fee. So I didn't know if this involves a charge and if you see a difference between people getting consultation or not when there's a fee involved.

MR. WEBB: I'm not sure we have data to answer that question necessarily. The newly approved CPT codes, which are now category one, go into effect in January of 2008. The CPT editorial panel approved category three temporary codes two and a half years ago for the purpose of evaluating the approach and possibility of using codes such as this for pharmacist intervention with patients. And the data presented to the CPT panel earlier this year from the profession to document more than three million patient encounters using the temporary codes convinced the AMA to move forward with changing the category to category one status.

Clearly, having a CPT code available doesn't mean payment occurs. Payment policy is a different issue than the availability and the structure of a payment code, that the code system exists and now, particularly for medication therapy management services under Part D as a Medicare benefit, for example, many of the PBMs are beginning to use this code structure for purposes of payment for medication therapy management services under Part D. We're clearly a generation or two behind medicine in its coding and billing capabilities, but that doesn't mean the structure shouldn't be there to accomplish it and we believe it's the perfect model and venue reflective of the interaction of pharmacists face-to-face with patients.

MR. LUTTER: Thank you. Other questions, Jane?

MS. AXELRAD: Yes. I believe a number of members of the panel discussed the need for substantially increased access to patient records to be able to effectively implement a behind-the-counter system. And I was wondering how the community would address concerns about patient privacy if sensitive health records beyond just the list of the medications that the patient was taking, laboratory results and other parts of the record would become more widely available outside of the controlled system of their physician.

MR. LUTTER: Who would like to volunteer to take that?

MR. HUSSAR: I'll make one comment. One of my responsibilities is to provide the ethics topics and the confidentiality of the patient information, as well as other information that should remain confidential, is one of the specific topics to which we give a strong emphasis. The pharmacists, to practice optimally, should have access to pertinent information. Indeed, there's a lot of information available to pharmacists. In fact, sometimes, pharmacists have a more complete medication history for patients than some of the prescribing physicians do, when individuals are seeing an internal medicine physician or a family practitioner and also seeing a number of specialists.

And usually, at least in many situations, those patients will go to the same pharmacies and pharmacists are in a position to identify those problems, but I can assure you that this is a responsibility that pharmacists take very seriously. I guess, in large chain store operations, where databases, information bases are huge, there are added security precautions that would need to be taken. My understanding is that those organizations have done that in a way that does protect patient confidentiality.

MR. LUTTER: Mr. Zellmer, would you like to (ever in it also?

MR. ZELLMER: Yes. Just to add briefly to Dr. Hussar's comments. You know, in the hospital outpatient pharmacy setting, ambulatory care setting, this commonly happens, where the pharmacist has complete access to the patient's health record in that institution. And I think it's well ingrained in our profession to respect that information and to use it for healthcare purposes. So there's at least one model out there in that environment where this has been going on for a long time and has done quite successfully.

MR. LUTTER: Thank you. Question from Lisa Bernstein?

MS. BERNSTEIN: Many of the pharmacy speakers talked about how it's important for the record keeping and to document the patient encounter, and then we heard from Dr. Cranston a concern that the pharmacist may not know the full background of the patient and that pharmacists aren't diagnosticians. I'm just wondering if you could elaborate a little bit about the opportunities that pharmacists have for accessing patient information and medical records or history, and the collaborations that pharmacists might have with doctors to make this more of a partnership to address some of the concerns that Dr. Cranston had.

MR. WEBB: I think access to the patients' other healthcare records is obviously, very practice site-specific in terms of pharmacy practice sites and the availability, the extremes, but it runs the gamut. In 41 or 42 states, collaborative practice agreements between pharmacists and physicians allow essentially, full information exchange and access back and forth between pharmacists and physician in the collaborative care of patients.

In other settings, that access would have to be more reengineered and structured than it is in those kinds of settings, but clearly, there are practice models where that kind of information and exchange is doable and possible. I would just reemphasize what Dr. Hussar and Mr. Zellmer said. This access to patient medical records issues, in terms of privacy issues, is really – HIPAA is about – treatment approaches under HIPAA essentially require that patient privacy be maintained. And the interaction between physicians and pharmacists in the collaboration and care of patient is basically a HIPAA covered transaction, so I think the rules and regulations in most pharmacy practice settings clearly adhere to those standards.

MR. HUSSAR: There's no question that there are many situations now in which pharmacists do not have access to as much information as would be desirable for them to practice optimally, but I look at what we're considering today as an opportunity for the pharmacists to take a more active role and be more accessible with regard to these medications for those individuals who are not served at all by the healthcare system now. I look at this as an opportunity to – I don't feel this will be one that will have pharmacists and physicians in conflict or working against each other. Indeed, I feel that there are synergies to be achieved.

And one of the comments I had made earlier was that I think that there will be some individuals who will take the initiative to speak with the pharmacist about a product they hear is available from a pharmacist, and that can be the first step in which an individuals gets into the healthcare system, often with the next step being a referral to a physician who can provide the more comprehensive evaluation. But the individuals, the patients, who are well served now by the physicians and other individuals within the healthcare community, these are the individuals who will probably need the least attention, the least follow-up from pharmacists.

MR. LUTTER: Thank you very much. I think I've benefited greatly from the comments from this first group of speakers, and please join me in giving them a round of applause for their contributions. (Applause.)

Our next group of speaker consists of six representatives of boards of pharmacies, schools of pharmacy, the Medical Center and the Consumer Healthcare Products Association. And our first speaker in this group will be Dr. Carmen Catizone from the National Association of Boards of Pharmacy.

CARMEN CATIZONE: Good morning, Randy, and others of the FDA and stakeholders. Thank you very much for the opportunity to allow the National Association of Boards of Pharmacy to share our view on the consideration of behind-the-counter availability of drugs. NABP commends the Food and Drug Administration for opening a dialogue on this issue and bringing together key stakeholders.

Since 1993, NABP has advocated for a change in the Food, Drug and Cosmetic Act to establish a new third class of drugs. A resolution adopted by all member boards of NABP called for the establishment of a third class of drugs to be dispensed by a pharmacist and address patient safety issues that occur when some prescription-only drugs are reclassified into over-the-counter status. The resolution explained that drugs classified in this third class would require appropriate patient counseling and monitoring by the pharmacist.

Continuing to push for the a third class of drugs, NABP's member state boards of pharmacy adopted a similar resolution in 1995 and again emphasized the critical patient need that exists, when drugs with serious side effects or special monitoring requirements, are allowed to move to over-the-counter status and bypass patient counseling and monitoring.

It is NABP's position that such a class, that is a transitional class of drugs, would provide significant benefits to patients without decreasing access to such medications. A transitional class of drugs would allow the FDA and manufacturers to collect additional data on drugs similar to phase four clinical trials and provide valuable data about the side effects and safety of the drug, what the long-term risk and benefits are and how well the drug works when it's used more widely than at clinical trials.

A transitional class of drugs could also be used to provide medications to those patients for when a drug is not safe to be dispensed over the counter without supervision, but does not warrant prescription-only status, or requires special monitoring such as routine blood tests. With such a third class in place, drugs that might not be brought to patients because of risk management concerns would now be available to patients who could benefit from them.

In both instances, NABP believes that pharmacists should be central to the transitional class of drugs as part of the effective provision of medication therapy management and patient care. The decision on whether a drug is categorized into the transitional class would rest with the FDA and the manufacturer, based upon the evaluation of critical data. National standards would need to be established, but the dispensing of the medication and delivery of medication therapy management would rest with, and be regulated by, the state boards of pharmacy.

Again, NABP appreciates the opportunity to present our view on this important topic. We'll be submitting more detailed comments in response to the notice and we offer any assistance we can provide to the FDA as you move through this issue. Thank you.

MR. LUTTER: Thank you. Our next speaker is Dr. William Soller from UCSF School of Pharmacy.

WILLIAM SOLLER: Thank you, Mr. Chairman, members of the panel. I'm Bill Soller. I'm professor at the University of California, San Francisco School of Pharmacy and the executive director for the Center for Consumer Self-Care. And I'm here to provide our support for a behind-the¬counter status for selected prescription drugs based on several significant health trends that I'll talk about, as well as provide recommendations on criteria for BTCness.

In 1974 in the Federal Register, FDA provided comment administrative aspects of the OTC review and stated no controlled studies, rather, adequate research data had been supplied to support a third class of drugs, and that essentially set forth FDA's policy that a public health need must be demonstrated before such a class would be formed. In that same Federal Register, FDA said that the Food, Drug, Cosmetic Act permits imposition of whatever limitations or restrictions are necessary to assure the safe use of any drug, including restrictions on channels of distribution.

Since that time, most recently in fact, BTC access of nonprescription medicines exists. It focuses mainly on potential risks, managing age restrictions, for example, in Plan B, or managing distribution to avoid misuse, and we think that BTC access should be expanded to enhance potential benefits of intended use. Our reasons for this focus on major public health needs relating to gaps in consumer use and understanding of essential drug information, as well as medication non-adherence.

Many consumers do not read the OTC or Rx drug information when they get their medicines. From two recent surveys, one at Harris Interactive online survey through NCPI, and supported by industry and about 1,000 people and studies that we've undertaken at the center, label comprehension studies funded by target pharmacy at about the same number of individuals.

In the Harris Interactive study, when asked what do you read when buying or taking a new OTC medicine the first time, you see the numbers there, all of the label, none of it about 5 percent, translates to a lot of people, side effects, warnings and alcohol interactions. People are not looking at these when they buy their OTC meds. From our studies on target clear Rx system, we ask, do you read the retail drug monograph, which is the information that is stapled to the dispensing bag before using a prescription drug the first time, or do you keep this information?

And this slide showing all study participants, about 45 percent, read or keep Rx drug information 50 percent or less of the time. This is similar across ethnic, socio-economic and age groups, and here, a category of recent interest to FDA mothers of children two to nine-years-old showing about the same pattern of distribution.

Now, in physician communication, when prescribing new medications, (TARN?) looked at audio-taped patient-physician encounters in terms of scripts for new Rx meds in 185 outpatient visits, 44 physicians covering 243 new meds, and what physicians conveyed about drugs that they prescribed, over 75 percent or so on medication name and purpose of meds, but as you get to adverse effects, and how long to take the med, the amount of information that's conveyed drops off significantly. Physicians fulfill the mean of 3.1 of five expected elements of drug information. So I think we have a national risk communication gap on medicines, OTC drug, Rx drug and health professional counseling information.

The second major trend is medication non-adherence, and I only bring up one study, but this, as I'm sure you know, is an area that has been amply studied and lots and lots of publications in this area. This was a study by Ho et al on the effect of medication non-adherence and hospitalization and mortality among patients with diabetes meletis, a retrospective cohort study from Kaiser, Colorado, in about 11,000 patients, where non-adherence was less than 80 percent of days covered.

And just to give a summary, although they found that the non-adherent patients' category was about 20 to 25 percent, which is about half of what most studies show about 50 percent after a year and a half on therapy, medication non-adherence increases the risk of all caused hospitalization, all caused mortality and is a consistent across hypoglycemics, oral hypoglycemics and the hypertensives and statins.

This is a general phenomenon across a number of disease cases and I've listed them in my bibliography to these slides but diabetes, statin therapy and our hypertensives and so on. So along with this significant gap in risk communication, we have a significant gap in medication adherence.

And the third general trend is what is something that is beyond the tipping point. We are an event cascade in relation to pharmacist care services. This was initiated in clinical pharmacy curriculum at UCSF in the '70s and then with an evolution of the pharmacy education curriculum and the Pharm.D. degree has expanded to all schools. This expansion of community pharmacy services as a result has occurred with medication therapy management, disease state management, screening, preventive care reminders and providing education that is seen routinely in the community setting. And in the box to the right, I just show some of the things that pharmacists are involved in today.

Looking back at one of the early demonstration projects here, the Asheville experiment, which was an employer-based diabetes disease management program by pharmacists, you'll see the claims data here. And if you look at the blue, which is the lower set of boxes, the insurance claims for hospitalizations and ER visits, you see that the costs go down dramatically; diabetes prescriptions and other prescriptions go up because there's more adherence and actually, physician visits go up. In fact, the pharmacist is a coach, a facilitator of the health team in the community and this is something that physicians should actually support as opposed to oppose.

The Medicare Modernization Act 2003 really put, I think, a boost in the arm in this particular area. It identified the pharmacist as a provider of medication therapy management, particularly for benefits in this area for seniors under Part D and these are basically medication reviews, doses, side effects, other essential information and adherence counseling, which is what you might expect for a statin that would go behind-the-counter. This is national in scope and must be provided by insurance providers.

So an interim summary here, we think the time is right to consider BTCness to improve the transfer of essential drug information to consumers at the time of drug product selection, to help medication adherence and to help improve disease outcomes.

I'd like to turn to the second topic here on Rx to BTC switch criteria, and in 2002, I published a study called "Rx to OTC Switch" in the *Drug Information Journal.* It was developed from presentations to the industry by past CDER director Carl Peck and OTC office Director Robert DeLap, and essentially, represented the collective wisdom of over 15 years of Rx to OTC switching, and it was published with the approval of the Consumer Healthcare Products Association Scientific Affairs Committee.

In that, I list 12 questions that provide the conceptual framework for switch, and I think with very limited addition, that the same kind of framing can be put together to really frame the discussion around what kind of research you would like to see, what kind of evidence you would like to see in terms of demonstrating safe and effective BTC status. As an example, can the condition be adequately self-diagnosed with the help of a pharmacist in a retail setting? Can the condition be successfully self-treated under BTC conditions of use?

The yellow font there shows the additions, the white font shows what was published in the study. And then as you get into consumer understanding of expected benefit or other consumer understanding of the use of the product, the general rubric, after pharmacist counseling, these same questions apply as were applied for a well proven program in Rx to OTC switch.

So other criteria. Well, criteria for – (unintelligible) – grey for the OTC review obviously don't apply here, but we think that the OTC drug facts, labeling requirement, should apply since BTC is essentially a form of nonprescription status. And as to material time and extent, considering the kinds of side effects, the unexpected side effects, that appear within the year and a half to two year post-marketing of a new drug, probably something in the range of three to five years, that is, you need a sufficient material time and extent on the Rx market before you can consider either OTC or BTC.

So main conclusions. The time is right to consider BTC access to nonprescription medicines. Risk communication gap and drug information exist; there's a gap in medication adherence, and we are in the midst of an event cascade of rapidly growing pharmacist care services throughout the country.

We have the scientific tools for demonstrating BTCness, actual use studies, label comprehensions, selection studies, as well as the studies that are emerging on pharmacist care services that, for example, we're doing in the Northern California region. And we're not the only center or school that is engaging in these kinds of demonstration projects.

BTCness should be viewed as a testable hypothesis undertaken on a case-by-case evidence basis, using modest refinements to Rx to OTC switch criteria. We don't advocate legislation, we don't advocate wholesale creation of a category and switching of many, many drugs, but to do this in an incremental basis, so that there is experience gained. Each one will likely be very different than the other one if Rx to OTC switch is anything to take lessons from. FDA has the authority to impose limitations on OTCness through BTC access and should expand this approach to selected Rx drugs incrementally. Thank you very much.

MR. LUTTER: Thank you very much for the presentation. Our next speaker is Dr. Maria Marzella Sulli. Welcome.

MS. MARIA MARZELLA SULLI: Good morning. Thank you for this opportunity to address the panel. I'm Dr. Sulli. I'm a faculty member at St. John's University College of Pharmacy and I'm here today to represent myself and three of my colleagues from the Department of Clinical Pharmacy Practice.

We're here really to highlight the education of a pharmacist, to highlight the facts that pharmacists are trained to meet this need for behind-the¬counter access of certain medications. We'd like to first address the question posed: should there be behind-the-counter availability of certain drug products? And we'd like to say we are in favor of behind-the-counter availability of certain medications. This class should be available without a prescription, only upon discussion with the registered pharmacist or by prescription from a prescriber, as several of the presenters this morning have already discussed.

We do believe the discussion should include an assessment of the patient's condition for appropriateness of therapy and counseling on the proper use of medication, and I'll highlight later how pharmacists are trained and prepared to do this. We think the discussion could be patient or pharmacist-initiated, and that a system for compensation for these services needs to be explored in order to ensure adequate participation and quality. We believe this behind-the-counter class should not just serve as a transitional stage for medications moving from Rx to OTC status, but may serve as a permanent status for certain medications where deemed appropriate.

We'd also like to highlight just briefly some of the criteria or standards for a drug to be treated as behind the counter, and many of these have already been presented this morning. Medications with overall safety, but complicated dosing instructions and administration, would likely benefit patients to be in this behind-the-counter class, so that pharmacists would be able to adequately counsel them on appropriate use and this would in turn improve patient safety. Medications with acute need in chronic previously diagnosed conditions and medications where the outcome of the treatment is dependent on prompt administration, and this also has been discussed previously.

We also feel that certain over-the-counter medications may benefit from moving into this behind-the-counter class, over-the-counter medications that have significant drug-drug interactions, drug-food interactions or drug-supplement interactions that again, moving to behind-the-counter would add a layer of patient safety.

Over-the-counter medications with a high incidence of reported abuse or misuse, serious adverse drug events or deaths, and we also support that this class would not simply serve as a class that the pharmacists would need to simply check age, identification and so forth, not be a policing of a commodity, more of a class that would involve clinical interaction between the pharmacist and the patient for use.

We also point out the recent controversies with over-the-counter medications for cough and cold in children, and believe that over-the-counter products currently approved for the use in children under the age of six should be required to have some pharmacist consultation and intervention prior to dispensing these medications to ensure that the parents are capable of administering the medication safely to a child.

Any drug for a condition that does not require extensive physical examination or laboratory monitoring that is not clear waived in many states under collaborative drug therapy management agreements, pharmacists are able to perform clear waive laboratory testing and are trained appropriately to do so. Also current prescription medications for symptomatic treatment of common and previously diagnosed conditions and the examples are there for you.

As I said earlier, we want to focus our presentation on the training because the question number seven under the logistics portion of the document was, would special training be needed for pharmacists to participate in dispensing behind-the-counter medications? We'd like to say that pharmacist graduates are trained and equipped to meet the public's need for this behind-the-counter class. I'm going to reference the standards for the Pharm.D. program put forth by the Accreditation Council for Pharmacy Education, which is the national agency responsible for the accreditation of professional degree programs in pharmacy.

I want to highlight several standards that I believe reinforce what I'm about to say about pharmacists receiving the training and the education necessary in order to provide this crucial service to the public. ACPE standard number 10 involves development of the curriculum and the delivery and the improvement, continuous quality improvement, of curriculum in colleges of pharmacy. Quoted right out of this standard, the professional portion of the degree program must be a minimum of four academic years or the equivalent, 30 percent of the curriculum of which is dedicated to professional practice experiences.

Standard number 14, which outlines the composition of those practice experiences, states that the pharmacy practice experiences must include direct interaction with the diverse patient population and involve collaboration with healthcare professionals. And as my colleagues before me have stated, we do feel that this behind-the-counter class of medications would only serve to improve communication between pharmacists and other healthcare providers that prescribe medications and maintain patient records. Our pharmacists, during their training, do receive adequate training in order to communicate with other healthcare professionals, and do strongly feel that it is important and necessary in order to provide the best care for patients.

ACPE standard number 12 mandates that graduates of a doctor of pharmacy program be competent to provide patient-centered care by being able to design, implement, monitor and evaluate patient medication use, again, in cooperation with patients, prescribers and other members of the healthcare team. It also states that pharmacists should be competent to promote health, provide, assess and coordinate safe, accurate and time-sensitive medication distribution to improve the therapeutic outcomes of medication use, and pharmacists, of course, we believe, are trained to do so.

I would like to comment here, as the question was brought up earlier regarding training of pharmacists who have not graduated recently under the standards and under the new doctor of pharmacy program that was required as of 2004. Pharmacists in all states require continuing education in order to maintain licensure and there are many certificate programs and credentialing programs available for currently practicing pharmacists who want to expand their knowledge and enhance their skills, and kind of keep up with the times in order to be able to interact with patients and perform these services. So we believe from the educational standpoint, that the current graduates are prepared and the pharmacists out there who would be interested in performing these services have adequate resources in order to gain the training required to do this well.

And just lastly, the expanding roles of the pharmacists that we have seen, since the implementation of these new guidelines, have also been highlighted today, medication therapy management under the Medicare Part D program, pharmacists are now recognized as providers under Medicare. And I think that's a testament to the training and expertise that pharmacists can provide in terms of medication management.

Collaborative drug therapy agreements, pharmacists providing immunizations, pharmacists participating in the institutional setting on committees such as the Pharmacy and Therapeutics Committee and institutional review boards also highlight how pharmacists are viewed by their colleagues, other healthcare professionals and recognized widely in the healthcare market as the medication experts.

So in conclusion, my colleagues and I support the creation of this behind-the-counter class of medications. We feel it would enhance the current system for the delivery of medications, and believe it would improve the quality and care that patients receive by improving safety, improving communication between pharmacists and other healthcare providers and improving patient satisfaction. Thank you.

MR. LUTTER: Thank you very much, Dr. Sulli. Our next speaker is Dr. Michael Hogue from the Institute for Public Health and Pharmacy.

MICHAEL HOGUE: Good morning. My name is Michael Hogue and I am the assistant director for the Institute for Public Health and Pharmacy, or IPHP. IPHP is a part of the McWhorter School of Pharmacy at Samford University in Birmingham, Alabama, where I hold the appointment of assistant professor of pharmacy practice. I am also the coordinator and primary instructor in our self-care therapeutics course.

In addition to being an academic pharmacist, I also practice clinical pharmacy in an outpatient adult medicine indigent clinic of the Jefferson County Alabama Department of Public Health. The role of our Institute of Public Health and Pharmacy is to study and teach about the relationship between the professions of pharmacy and public health and specifically, how this relationship impacts the health status of our communities.

Thank you for allowing the Institute of Public Health and Pharmacy the opportunity to comment on the proposed creation of a behind-the-counter category of drugs. Our comments are focused on the public health implications of the creation of a BTC category of drugs, and this may be a somewhat unique perspective that you hear today. I am going to focus on what we think are the most central questions that have been asked by the agency, and I have provided a more extensive comment list to you in advance.

The first question was: should there be BTC availability of certain drug products? We support the creation of a BTC category of drugs, but we issue such support with an important caveat. The BTC category, in our view, will improve access by underserved populations to important pharmacotherapy preventative services and treatments, access the poorest and most vulnerable in our population desperately need. However, making products available in a BTC category must be accompanied by the availability of professional pharmacist services to help ensure that patients will be able to use those drugs appropriately.

It may sound strange to suggest that even though a pharmacist must be available to dispense the BTC medicine, that the professional services of the pharmacist might not be available. We believe that this could, in reality, be the case. It is very important to recognize that the creation of a BTC drug category should create substantial changes, could create substantial changes, in the current practice of pharmacy. Of course, the reason to place certain drugs in the BTC category is to require interaction between a pharmacist and a patient for that drug to be dispensed.

However, simply creating a category of drug that requires that interaction does not ensure adequate care. The current economic incentives in community pharmacy practice appear to strongly favor the dispensing portion of pharmacy practice, and hence, may limit the time available for assessing and advising a patient in relation to the dispensing judgment and BTC selection.

A study published in 2002 entitled "Pharmacist Time Requirements for Counseling in an Outpatient Pharmacy," the authors came to a simple and very straightforward conclusion, and I quote, "Patient counseling in the community pharmacy setting will suffer unless community pharmacies and managed care organizations develop a method for reimbursing pharmacists for this service."

Thankfully, managed care organizations, employers, Medicare Part D and a few Medicaid agencies are beginning to realize the importance of compensating pharmacists for their medication therapy interventions. As a result, we're beginning to see some practice changes happen with regard to prescription product interventions, and there's a higher value being placed on assisting patients with ensuring appropriate medication therapy outcomes.

These remuneration changes are beginning to also change the number of pharmacists who are actively engaging in direct patient care services. Prescription medication misuse is among the greatest public health issues of our time, and we are hopeful that this trend of pharmacists being more engaged in a patient assessment and drug therapy outcome monitoring will continue, as it's in the best interest of our nation's health.

Second question that we're addressing is: what might the impact of BTC be on patient access? Patient access to care is also a major public health issue. Many would say that we have an access to care crisis in this country. Patient access to drugs themselves is a similar but separate issue. The nation's uninsured population has been estimated at over 40 million individuals. Health disparities among minorities, immigrants, children and the elderly persist, despite what seems to be very good efforts in many communities.

Even though drug therapy often represents the most cost effective disease process intervention, the cost of these life-saving therapies are often out of reach of many in our population. Thus, in our opinion, the real question is two-fold: what might the impact of BTC be on patient access to patient care, and then secondly, what might the impact of BTC be on patient access to pharmaceuticals?

First, from a public health perspective, the most vulnerable in our population tend to have the greatest difficulty with access to healthcare services. The availability and cost of transportation alone severely restrict access to even basic primary care. Faced with limited financial resources, lack of transportation and lack of educational resources, many of our most vulnerable find themselves in their inner city and rural communities with few or no available healthcare resources, except for their local community pharmacist.

Pharmacists are well trained to perform patient interview and limited physical assessment, and help many of our nation's underserved through recommendation for use of available over-the-counter products. It is for all these reasons that we believe the availability of a broader group of products and a BTC category could greatly enhance the access to care for our most vulnerable citizens.

Secondly, related to access to pharmaceuticals, many of the issues are the same. For many of the 40-million-plus uninsured in our population, access to pharmaceuticals is a choice between putting food on the table or paying rent and having the availability of medicines. The first step in having access to medicines is the ability to afford to be seen by a physician or other provider legally permitted to provide medications. The cost of a visit to one of these professionals can be significant and cost can escalate rapidly with laboratory testing. Sometimes, this is necessary.

However, a BTC category of drugs will not resolve the situation entirely and there will be a need for some compensation of the pharmacists' services at this time. We do know that data published in the American Pharmacist Association and gathered by the Lewin Group show that pharmacists are reimbursed at a rate of approximately 80 percent of the physician compensation rate for similar time-based services.

So therefore, we believe that while there will be some costs associated with BTC provided services, we believe that these costs will be much more manageable. We also agree with the previous speakers that the average cost of the medication is likely to decrease substantially, as we've seen the move of Rx to OTC products have cost reductions as much as 90 percent after coming to the OTC market.

Finally, related to access, perhaps the most extensive data on access to pharmaceutical product exist in the area of vaccines. Access to vaccines in some parts of our country is abysmal at best, particularly for adults. Vaccines represent one of the most cost effective interventions available for prevention of disease and are vital to protection of the health of the entire community, not just the individual who receives the vaccine.

Pharmacists in 46 states have the authority to administer medications including, vaccines, and do so under prescription standing orders with physicians. We would argue, from a public health perspective, that should the FDA decide to create a BTC category of pharmaceuticals, that vaccines should become the very first group of Rx-only products granted the status, so that these life-saving products are more readily available to susceptible patients.

The last thing I will comment on is, what should the criteria or standards be for a drug to be treated as BTC? The public health profession serves, in part, as a social safety network. Issues of safety which affect the health of the population are monitored on the local level by state and county departments of health. Any standards which are created for a BTC category must consider the public health implications of such actions. We believe that at least one of the following two criteria must be met for any drug to be given BTC status.

The first criteria: drugs to treat a condition which can be easily accessed and diagnosed using primarily patient interview with limited physical assessment and only point-of-care laboratory testing. Exampled conditions here could include allergic rhinitis, contact dermatitis, head lice, scabies, otitis media, and hyperlipidemia.

Our second criteria suggestion is drugs to treat or prevent conditions which have the potential to impact the health or well being of the community or a population; for example: vaccines, malaria prophylaxis, antidiarrheal preparations, topical antiinfectives and oral antivirals when used for secondary prophylaxis during influenza outbreaks.

As time is running short, I will move straight to my summary. We believe that the creation of this BTC category is in the best interest and health and welfare of the public. We believe that the category can improve access to both needed pharmaceuticals and to the patient care services of a pharmacist. Today's doctorally trained pharmacists are fully prepared to deliver the services required to successfully implement this new and very important BTC drug category.

The creation of this category will likely have significant impact on the overall practice of pharmacy and will have impact on employers and insurers. However, we believe these impacts will overall be very positive and again will be in the best interest of the health of the population broadly.

We have one final recommendation to make. We would urge the FDA to carefully word the media-related messaging put forth by the agency, should this category be decided to move forward, and also require manufacturers who have drugs approved into this category to carefully word their promotional advertising and consumer material to emphasize the fact that an assessment by a pharmacist is necessary. We do not want the public to have inappropriate expectations.

Again, thank you for allowing our institute at Samford University to testify at the hearing. I look forward to opportunity to answer your questions.

MR. LUTTER: Thank you very much, Dr. Hogue. Our next speaker is Dr. Eric Brass from the Harbor-UCLA Medical Center.

ERIC BRASS: Thank you. I am Eric Brass, director of the Harbor-UCLA Center for Clinical Pharmacology and professor of medicine at UCLA School of Medicine. I am past chair of the Nonprescription Drugs Advisory Committee and have served as a consultant to industry on issues related to OTC drug development. Expenses for my appearance today have been partially paid by the Consumer Healthcare Products Association.

It is clear that we all share the goal of improving public health by increasing access to safe and effective medicines. It is deciding where the balance lies between imposing barriers designed to protect consumers, versus limiting access to safe and effective medicines that provide the challenge. The factors that influence this balance create a natural tension and vary for each individual drug considered.

I appreciate this opportunity to share my thoughts on when additional barriers to access might be appropriate for nonprescription drugs and how we can continue to make decisions on OTC drug access in an evidence-based way.

I believe it is important to understand where we are today in the evolution of clinical research with respect to moving drugs from prescription to OTC status. As regulators have made explicit the requirement that sponsors demonstrate that consumers themselves manage the condition using only the OTC label, the research community has responded with increasingly sophisticated research tools for assessing consumer behaviors. These include iterative label comprehension testing to develop a label that could be understood by the typical U.S. consumer.

Self-selection and actual use studies are designed to assess consumer behaviors, when they are provided the opportunity to use the proposed OTC drug in an unsupervised setting. These research programs define whether the consumer can use the drug safely and effectively in an unsupervised setting and also define any limitations in consumer decision making with respect to the drugs use.

These specific limitations can then be addressed with supplemental methods, such as non-display package labeling tools or marketing restrictions. Using this approach, we have seen the ability of industry and regulators to use research and making evidence-based, case-specific regulatory decisions.

Data made clear that barriers to access in the marketplace may be substantial, even within the universe of nonprescription drugs. We have seen this in the United States in the response of consumers, to moving pseudo-ephedrine containing drugs to behind-the-counter status.

Data on this transition were recently presented by Steve Johnson of IRI. Prior to being moved behind the counter, pseudo-ephedrine-containing products accounted for 49 percent of sales in the OTC respiratory drug category. However, once pseudo-ephedrine was moved behind the counter in 2004, sales fell rapidly. By March of 2007, sales of pseudo-ephedrine containing products were only approximately 40 percent of their pre-transition sales, despite continued growth in the overall respiratory drug category.

This fall in sales cannot be accounted for by decreased diversion of pseudo-ephedrine containing products. Consumer studies of users of one specific branded pseudo-ephedrine containing product indicated that only 30 percent continued to use this product post-transition to behind-the-counter status. The barrier of behind-the-counter status was sufficient for consumers to disrupt their established normal self-treatment paradigms.

I believe Dr. Shiffman will share with you this afternoon the experience in other countries where behind-the-counter status of nicotine replacement products limited access to these drugs. Also this afternoon, Dr. Mann will share with you how pharmacist-consumer interactions in the U.K. create artificial barriers to how – to accessing statins for consumers interested in lowering the cardiovascular risk and for whom statins were appropriate.

Thus, it is evident to me that the decision to restrict a drug to behind-the-counter status must not be a default, but must be justified on the basis of data demonstrating that it is the optimal strategy to achieve the balance between access and proper use.

What data do we need to make a generalized conclusion that behind-the-counter status is optimal for any drug, much less as a rigid component of a tripartite drug access model? It has always been of interest to me that for prescription drugs, we write drug labels based on research data, and assume that prescribers will use these labels to optimize therapeutic decision making, despite considerable evidence that the label is quite ineffective in modifying prescriber behavior. In contrast, for OTC drugs, we write labels and assume that consumers cannot use the drug until we provide research data establishing that, in fact, they can.

It is unclear to me what standard would be used to assess behind-the-counter access during drug development and regulatory review.

Making the assumption that the U.S. pharmacy environment, the typical U.S. pharmacy environment, will result in an idealized consumer- pharmacist interactions, where the pharmacist precisely follows decision algorithms, is not only without experimental foundation, but also, quite frankly, defies common sense.

Based on what we have seen, a default behind-the-counter status for new prescription to OTC switches will inevitably result in barriers to access. But as we sit here today, we cannot cite any offsetting improvement in outcome in public health. Thus, we have demonstrable cost, both financial, which has been well established this morning, and in terms of decreased access without demonstrable benefit, meaning that some consumers may not have access to new safe and effective OTC drugs, potentially using inferior products in their place.

Having served on the Nonprescription Drugs Advisory Committee, it is easy to visualize the committee retreating to behind-the-counter option as the safe option, and avoiding the perceived risk of endorsing a more expanded access decision, even when the expanded access may improve public health. Thus, in any behind-the-counter consideration, we must ask explicitly what the role of the pharmacist will be, provide data that the proposed pharmacist role can, in fact, be achieved in a typical pharmacy environment and demonstrate the incremental value of the pharmacist over consumer self management.

Addressing these issues will require entirely new research methodologies. How well we can model the behavior and skill sets of the typical U.S. pharmacist working in a typical U.S. pharmacy environment to conclude that any higher order decision-making role can be completed with sufficient quality. For a specific proposed OTC drug, how do we quantify the public health value of a required pharmacist-consumer interaction, as compared with consumer self-management in order to justify the added restriction to access?

I know of no data which supports any conclusion to these questions, nor of validated research models to even address these questions.

As noted, research methodologies to ensure the effectiveness of OTC labels have evolved tremendously over the past 15 years and increasingly support a spectrum of evidence-based drug-specific marketing restrictions. This decisionmaking, based on research data along a spectrum of marketing models, has worked successfully in the current OTC environment, and has the highest potential to ensure that the balance between access and proper consumer use is optimized.

While some form of marketing restriction similar to behind-the-counter status may be the right solution for some drugs, both available data and the law of unintentional consequences suggest that creating three discrete bins of marketing classes will result in many drugs that can be used safely and effectively by consumers, in fact, being made less available to them.

In conclusion, I believe that meeting our goal of improving public health by maximizing consumer access to safe and effective medicines is dependent on evidence-based decision-making. Each potential prescription to OTC switch presents unique challenges and raises unique questions. Clinical research is, and should be, required to inform regulatory decision-making on OTC switches. Our regulatory mechanisms can function best when they use the learnings from this research to create drug-specific approvals across a spectrum of post-approval marketing restrictions.

I thank you for the opportunity to share my thoughts on these important issues.

MR. LUTTER: Thank you very much, Dr. Brass. Our next speaker is Mr. David Spangler from the Consumer Healthcare Products Association.

DAVID SPANGLER: Good morning. I'm David Spangler with the Consumer Healthcare Products Association. We represent manufacturers of OTC medicines and dietary supplements.

OTC access empowers consumers and allows them to take control of their health. It provides them a choice with convenience, and in a competitive environment that keeps cost down. The existing system provides sufficient flexibility to handle specific challenges to specific switches through a range of mechanisms and methods. This might include pharmacists. It could include distribution restrictions. It could include post- approval study commitments or other measures.

Fed by innovations and prescription to OTC switch, the existing system works and it works well. It works well for consumers; it works well for the public health. As a result, we don't need the law to change to expand access and we don't need a new class of medicines.

Before we get into the existing two-class system, let's step back for a moment and talk about some of the things that Dr. Throckmorton addressed earlier, and that's consumer interest. As you can see on the slide, about three out of four consumers agreed that they prefer to treat conditions themselves, rather than having to go to see a doctor. Roughly three out of five say that in the future, they want to diagnose and treat more of their conditions, rather than going to see a doctor. Another example of this consumer interest, roughly four out of five Americans turn to the Internet for health information.

Now, one way they take action on this interest, just one way, is through the use of OTC medicines. Access to OTC medicines provides an important cost effective, convenient benefit to consumers. Let's look at three examples around the power of access.

Thanks to the prescription to OTC switch of a number of antihistamines and decongestants through the mid to late 1970s and into the 1980s, we saw a decrease in doctor visits for the common cold of roughly 100,000 a year according to a study done by MIT economist Peter Temin. Dr. Temin also calculated roughly a three quarter billion dollar gain to society, thanks to the switches through this period.

Second example. Medical school dean Dr. Martin Lipsky found a 15 percent decline in doctor visits for vaginitis in the first four years after the switch of these proven safe and effective medicines for this condition. And we should add that the sponsors of these switches conducted studies that found that women were just as good as their doctors in recognizing the recurrence of this condition, recurrence in the OTC indication.

A final example. A number of authors have looked at nicotine replacement therapies. In one study, there was somewhere between 150 to 200 percent increase in their use in the first year following their switch to OTC status. That's because consumers had access to them. That access results in tens of thousands of new former smokers every year. That's longer, healthier lives. That's a $2 billion social benefit every year. Access provides tremendous power to consumers and that's why we continue to advocate for the switch of safe and effective medicines for direct consumer use.

Now, let's switch gears. Let's think about OTC approvals kind of with a blank slate. Every switch has its challenge, but in thinking about those challenges, you can't walk into it saying, you can't switch a medicine for reason X; you can't switch for condition Y. That's not the question. The question is, are there data, are there tools to address the specific challenges to that application?

Let's look at just a couple of examples of where if we think of OTCs with a pinched, narrow view, they're not going to fit into the existing way we think about OTCs.

First example is probably the oldest example: fluoride. Sometimes you hear people say, "You can't do a switch if it's going to be for a chronic use or if it's going to prevent something that's not readily recognizable by the consumer." Fluorides are a great example where that's emphatically wrong. That's not the case. Here you have something that we use for our lifetime, a chronic use. The conditions that it's trying to prevent are not readily recognizable by the consumer. Another example would be monoxodyl for hair loss, where again, the use is indefinite. It could be chronic; it could be episodic, depending on how successful you are in trying to re-grow your hair. I'm failing. (Laughter.)

Second example. Sometimes you hear people say that you can't switch something if there is a concern about masking. Again, that might be true, but if you have the data to show that you can address that concern, it doesn't have to be true. So we have the H2s and omeprazole, which were switched in the late '90s and in 2003, where the sponsors overcame concerns around the potential for masking through label comprehension studies and through actually use trials.

Again, each switch has its challenges. If we think about kind of the categories or clusters of challenges, there're really three basic challenges. Those are self-selection concerns, emergent signs or symptoms, and how to add value through enhanced targeted information. What the switch sponsor needs to do is figure out a way to empower consumers with more tools or information, which could include consultation with pharmacists, to help consumers make appropriate decisions on their OTC medicines around these issues.

So let's start with the first, self-selection concerns. What we're talking about here is do consumers, for whom the product is indicated, appropriately choose it and do consumers for whom the product is not indicated – are they discouraged from using it? For example, the emergency contraceptive or the advisory committee's discussion of Lovastatin in January 2005, just a couple of examples of where self-selection was really highlighted.

Second cluster of concerns. What is it about a particular medicine that needs to be addressed to fix concerns around identification of emergent signs or symptoms that a consumer might otherwise miss on their own? Examples here again would be the label comprehension work and actual use trials for the H2s and for Prisolec.

Finally, adding value through enhanced targeted information. In other words, what are the tools and information that we need to develop, well beyond the physical product itself to support optimal outcomes that include the use of medicine? They might not even be limited to the use of medicine, but include. So we're really talking here about a product-plus-program concept, and two examples here would be nicotine replacement therapy and oral statin (?).

So let's put those challenges into practice and see how companies have addressed, sponsors have addressed, with the agency, the challenges for that specific switch.

First, we already talked about the H2s and omeprazole, where they conducted label comprehension studies and actual use trials to address an emergent sign or symptom concern.

Second example, the emergency contraceptive Plan B. Here, the sponsor worked with the agency and proposed distribution limitations, pharmacist intervention for age verification, since it would be illegal to dispense the under 18 product because it bears the prescription legend, and third, packaging requirements. And they did this to address a self-selection concern, a woman's age.

Nicotine replacement therapy, another great example. Here, the sponsor developed a wealth of information beyond traditional labeling. Second, distribution limitations; third, age verification with monitoring; and fourth, phase four commitments to verify the age monitoring. Oops, sorry.

These safeguards and enhanced information addressed a couple of types of concern. One again, we had a self-selection concern since the product is indicated for those 18 and over. Second, the example demonstrates the power of using enhanced information to improve the odds of successfully quitting smoking.

So you – again, you had the wealth of information well beyond the traditional label, the product-plus-program concept. And in this NRT example, even beyond that, at least one of the sponsors has gone on to develop even more information that could be personalized through the web to help further increase the odds of quitting smoking, and I think you'll hear about that from Dr. Shiffman a little later today.

Looking ahead, we can anticipate switch sponsors can choose to develop still other innovative methods to add value and safeguards. For example, we might envision a sponsor coming forward with a health check before the use of an OTC medicine, including consultation with a pharmacist or another healthcare provider. We could envision using an automated kiosk to verify some key piece of information, or we could envision online, or other information components, well beyond the drug facts label before purchase or during use of a medicine.

We continue to advocate for wider access to nonprescription medicines through switch, but a change in law or regulation is not needed to expand access to nonprescription medicines. The two-class system works, and it works well, to the benefit of consumers and in advancing and serving public health. Consumer choice, convenience, and a competitive system that drives cost down are the drivers in our system and our system demonstrates the power of access.

Most importantly, flexibility is built into the existing framework, with sponsors having the opportunity to work with you to design the appropriate tools, including pharmacist consultation or intervention to address the challenges to that particular medicine. What needs to drive the ultimate switch decision is an assessment of the data targeted to that specific challenges in that application.

Finally, innovation and prescription on nonprescription switch is proving the power of access today.

MR. LUTTER: Thank you very much, Mr. Spangler. We have, I think, about 15 minutes for questions from FDA folks to the members of the most recent panel. Diane, would you like to start?

MS. MALONEY: Okay. I have a question for Dr. Hogue. I just wanted to – a little more clarity for me, at least, on the point about the vaccines. If it's now currently being administered by pharmacists in 46 states, can you help me to understand what a BTC change would do?

MR. HOGUE: Sure, absolutely, and currently, in order for pharmacists in those states to be able to administer the medication, there still has to be a valid prescription order from a physician for that to occur. So that occurs in many different ways, depending upon the state in which the practice is occurring. In some states, a standing order is established between a physician and a pharmacist for care of that physician's patients and administration of vaccines to that particular physician's patients.

In some states it's more broad, whereby – for instance, in Oregon, pharmacists serve under the Public Health Act and they actually can administer the vaccines under the order of the chief health officer of the state. But in other states it's much more restrictive and includes perhaps only flu vaccine by protocol with a physician.

So in – what the state laws allow currently is, they allow for the pharmacist to administer medications. What they don't allow is for the pharmacist to actually prescribe those vaccines. And so we believe that in the case of vaccines, having a behind-the-counter category status for vaccines will improve the access in communities to important adult vaccines necessary for adult protection.

MS. MALONEY: So just to follow up, in the states that have more restricted – do you know the reasons why they are more restricted?

MS. HOGUE: Yes, actually, I've been involved in some of those discussions over the years, and a lot of it has to do with the comfortability that some have had with pharmacists being able to assess the patient for appropriateness of receipt of the vaccine. However, I can say now that we have a good 12 years of experience and strong data to support that pharmacists are very capable of making decisions on who needs to be vaccinated and who does not need to be vaccinated due to contraindications.

And there's absolutely no evidence to indicate that pharmacists have been making bad decisions, that those decisions have actually been improving patients' health and improving patients' lives. And there're even some data that shows that pharmacists who have the ability to provide vaccines at the point of care readily, when a patient has made the decision to be vaccinated, have increased usage of physician services because many adult patients fall out of our healthcare system and the pharmacist is able to use that encounter to advocate for a more comprehensive physical assessment by their physician for chronic conditions.

MR. LUTTER: Thank you, Dr. Hogue. Jane?

MS. AXELRAD: Yes, I'd like – I'm interested in a concept that was expressed by Mr. Spangler and I think another speaker about the fact that creating a behind-the-counter class of drugs could actually decrease access because it could become the default category, and that people would be reluctant to put things directly into over-the-counter status. And I was wondering if any of the other panelists would like to comment on that, people who are proponents of the behind-the-counter option.

MR. SOLLER: Yes, I'm Bill Soller. Do we have the microphone to get on? Yes, I'm Bill Soller. Yes, I think it's a – I don't agree with that presumption. I think if we're arguing that it should be evidence-based, and if we know from our OTC switch experience, that each one of these individual entities has a sort of – is case-specific and is unique in terms of the provisions that might be instituted to protect patients and consumers, then the same criteria of evidence should be applied to OTCness.

So if you – for example, if you were in a situation where there was an Rx to OTC switch that was being proposed, and the sponsor came in with evidence that was questionable to the panel about OTCness, the advisory committee might vote for a BTC status, but I can't imagine the agency would go forward with that without substantial evidence that would show that moving from Rx to a new category would actually be evidence- based. So I don't see that it's default. I think that's more of a scare tactic than a real kind of issue, and I think it's one that if we are going to hold our OTC switch to evidence-based, case by case, the same would be true for BTCness and however the switch is.

MS. AXELDRAD: Thank you. I have one other question for Dr. Catizone. One of the questions that we asked, and the Federal Register noticed that no one has addressed is, what would the impact of behind-the-counter status have on the states and what would be the role in overseeing that of the state points of pharmacy?

MR. CATIZONE: If the change is effectuated through the FDA as the panelists have said, the change would be – the impact on the states would be minimal and the states could work together with the FDA to put in place the appropriate regulations or guidelines for pharmacists.

Just in response to some comments that were made earlier and a differentiating point here, the example given by Dr. Brass with all due respect for pseudo-ephedrine products is an entirely different move and an impact that the states – an impact on the states in regard to restriction of a product. The issues with behind the counter are not the same issues with pseudo-ephedrine products.

And the pseudo-ephedrine products were moved behind the counter because it was a clear and documented danger to the public health, and there's an organization involved in every single state where legislation was passed restricting the distribution of pseudo-ephedrine products. That's something that had a significant impact on state laws and state regulations.

Behind-the-counter, and the issues we are discussing today, patient comprehension, patient monitoring, patient compliance, pharmacist care would not be impacted to a significant extent by this class of drugs, and actually would probably supplement or complement existing state laws.

MS. AXELRAD: Could I follow up on that real quickly? I'd just like – do you think that because pharmacists would actually be engaged in more clinical evaluations of patients – do you feel that the expertise on the state boards of pharmacy to oversee the adequacy of the care that's being provided by pharmacists would be sufficient?

MR. CATIZONE: The boards of pharmacy may be, if you would look at this as being possible if a couple of provisions were met; first of all, the counseling and monitoring that would need to occur, and that would distinguish this class of drugs from over-the-counter status to prescription-only status must take place. It could not be executed by a signature in a logbook. Second, the states put significant bearing on that license to say to the public that this pharmacist is competent to practice and it's the pharmacist's individual responsibility to maintain their competency and currency in practice.

NABP would also ask that the profession take on, as whole, a voluntary, continuing professional development program because of some of the changes these new therapies might enact and some of the changes that might stretch beyond existing licensure. If the profession didn't take it on voluntarily, then it would be pushed for mandated, continuing professional development program to ensure to the public that the pharmacist was qualified and was maintaining the competency in this area.

MR. LUTTER: I'd like to exercise my prerogatives as chair to ask Dr. Brass if he has a comment that he'd like to make in one minute. Thank you.

MR. BRASS: Thank you. I just want to make clear that my purpose in showing the pseudo-ephedrine example was not as a prototypic example of what might merit restriction from a pharmacy class, but to emphasize that where we do have data, it is that moving something behind-the¬counter represents a barrier to consumer access. And we'll see other examples of that as well.

And with respect to Dr. Soller's observation, having seen the dynamics of the committee without a behind-the-counter option available, their predilection to – without any evidence – assume its superiority, I think, is evidenced in many transcripts of their meetings.

MR. LUTTER: Other questions from our panel?

MR. GANLEY: There's been mentioned several of the talks on the panel about the concept of benefit. I guess I want to understand what is the burden on the agency to – if they move forward with this behind-the-counter class, what is the burden on the agency to demonstrate some sort of benefit to the public prior to even considering it because I get the – I can't distinguish between the benefit that would be derived for an individual drug product versus this whole global concept of behind-the-counter class benefit.

Someone in the previous panel had mentioned the GAO report. The GAO report merely said that we don't have data that shows benefit. It didn't say that it's not a benefit. It said there was really no studies done. So is there a burden on the agency to conduct some sort of study to demonstrate that this is going to be beneficial to the public?

MR. SOLLER: Bill Soller again. Dr. Ganley, I think the – it's the same burden that the FDA has now in terms of requiring the kind of drug submission that would provide sufficient evidence that the public safety, as defined specifically for that drug, that would likely occur during discussions with your group and others at the agency and the sponsor, prior to engaging in the actual use studies, the label comprehension, and self selection.

And as I pointed out in the 12 or so questions that came out of presentations from FDA directors to industry, the conceptual basis for forming those research questions, I think, has well worked out within switch. And studies have been designed against those questions and then presented to the advisory committee and therefore, FDA.

So for example, in a self-selection type of situation, there is – in a label comprehension study, for example, the agency doesn't look for a 100 percent comprehension, but depending on the key communication objectives, might look at 90 or 95 percent, and that's been variable. There's not one set cutoff point.

But similarly, there might be a different expectation, after counseling with the pharmacists in terms of what the individual's takeaway is about the knowledge base for that drug. So I think the same – it will be different, but the same sorts of tools that we have for assessing OTCness and assessing behind-the-counter, can be met, where there might be an expectation that there is a more complex drug that's being used, a need for additional monitoring or laboratory test. There might even be an engagement of the pharmacist in providing reminders, which we all know they do, in terms of getting our next prescription.

So I think we need to look broadly. We need to be flexible. We need to see that these things are different and that there are – there is an infrastructure within pharmacy to handle this kind of documentation and there's an infrastructure at the board level to ensure that happens, the state board level.

MR. CATIZONE: Something is probably left better to legal analysts within the FDA, but in our opinion, the burden on the FDA is to ensure that products are delivered safely and effectively. And the FDA has stepped in in those instances and put black-box warnings on products, or required special monitoring or restrictions on those products.

The studies that would document the benefit to the public by the pharmacist being involved already exist, were all published in the literature. And the challenge is that pharmacists haven't engaged in higher-order thinking or there hasn't been documented is not something that pharmacy believes. It's something that has been documented and occurs everyday in practice when pharmacists recommend over-the-counter products to their patients, when they work with prescribers to select the appropriate medication for the patients, and when they educate prescribers about what medication should be used for their patients. So the documents – the documentation, the evidence is there. The burden on the FDA is to place a system that makes those products safe and effective for the public.

MR. LUTTER: Thank you. Other questions from the FDA panel?

MR. DANZAS (?): I'd like to direct this question to Dr. Soller. You presented a lot of data that looked to present a pretty compelling picture of what you call the communication gap. Given the realistic demands on pharmacist time in an average retail pharmacy, what data do we have that would give us comfort that that communication gap would be overcome if we go to a BTC type of system?

MR. SOLLER: Well, I can only comment on the study that we're engaged in now with Raleigh's chain pharmacy, as well as other partners. This covers a 30,000 square mile area in Northern California related to diabetes medication, therapy management and disease management. And it involves about 45 stores and 60 pharmacists. Not every one of the pharmacists in this particular phase of the program, as we're scaling up, is actually involved in disease management. That – what has – what the pharmacy service department at Raleigh's has done, is to identify pharmacists that will be available during store hours to provide this service. There are other pharmacists that are not engaged in that disease management.

My own view, having numerous discussions with different pharmacy service departments, and trying to think through how this would be done in a scale-up basis as we go to a 100,000 square miles and larger, and collaborations between pharmacies, is that the management is going to figure out a way in order to have coverage on that.

In the store, there are separate areas for that counseling, and in this case, it's 40 minutes for a first visit and about 15 to 20 minutes, sometimes a half hour, for follow-up visits, which as I look at a statin, I think is well beyond where you would go with a behind-the-counter kind of situation in counseling.

So that said, depending upon the particular behind-the-counter candidate, it might well be that there is a broad selection of pharmacists, all the pharmacists that are either defined by the company as being capable to engage in that kind of counseling. I believe all pharmacists are as they use CE, but what I found is that the chain pharmacies have a strong interest in ensuring CE and present these programs as mandatory CE to their pharmacists.

So in another situation, where it might be more complex – and I don't think you would pick the more complex ones first for something like this – as I said, I think it should be incremental. It might well be that there are selected pharmacists that are engaged by the store to provide that kind of coverage and then ensure also that the broader dispensing responsibilities are met. That's how it seems to be playing out today.

MR. LUTTER: Thank you, Dr. Soller. Other questions from the panel?

MS. BERNSTEIN: My question is to Dr. Hogue. You mentioned that the FDA and manufacturers would need to carefully word the promotional and advertising information related to any BTC product. I'm wondering if you gave any thought – further thought in the type of educational type programs that might be necessary to educate patients, the public or even pharmacists generally.

MR. HOGUE: That's a great question. I think that consumers currently expect an immediate ready access to their pharmacist. And the truth of the matter is that time pressures that are placed on all members of our healthcare profession – professions, not just pharmacists – are making immediate access less and less of a reality.

However, with that said, pharmacists are still pretty darn accessible compared to a number of other healthcare professionals. And we have experience from the Asheville project, which has been mentioned several times, the American Pharmacists Association Ten City Challenge, and other studies that have been done, that look at the time needed for a pharmacist to actually conduct a good patient assessment interview and advise the patient on appropriate changes to their drug therapy regimens. And we look at those studies and we see that, in fact, it will take more than one or two minutes standing at the counter, in most cases, to be able to make a decision.

Now, in the case of a vaccine, we know that that decision takes about the same amount of time as the process of dispensing a prescription, and there've actually been time and motion studies conducted to prove that. So providing a vaccine to a patient in a pharmacy is likely not going to take any longer than getting a prescription filled.

However, we don't have data that show what the amount of time would be in the case of a statin, for instance, that a pharmacist would need to consult with that patient. And it's expected that if we're going to have pharmacists engaged in this process, that the consumer would have to have an expectation up front, that this is going to be an interaction that may take a little more time, but will be worth your time if you have – if you can get access to a medication that could save your life.

So these are life-changing therapies and again, I think many of the people have mentioned today that we need to look at these things, not necessarily as categories of drugs that would be switched, but as drug products individually that would be switched, and we need to think of careful messaging. It could be that specific messaging needs to be mandated for statins, for instance, that – to communicate to consumers that you might not require for another group of drugs, for instance, a vaccine. You might not require the same messaging.

However, I do think that you're going to have to have some targeted expectation messaging so that consumers understand that you don't just ask your pharmacist for it and they give it to you. There's more to it because currently, that's the problem we have with pseudo-ephedrine. And the manufacturers of pseudo-ephedrine products simply say, "Just ask your pharmacist and you can have it." And that's basically what the advertising says. That's the wrong expectation. I hope that answered your question.

MR. LUTTER: Diane, one more question?

MS. MALONEY: Okay. Just listening to this, I have a question with regard to how do the pharmacists envision the assessments or the consultations might happen because right now, a lot of it is just across the counter. Do you see it varying depending on a particular product? Do you see there being some waiting room? You'll come over here, wait, and then see the pharmacist, so –

MR. HOGUE: I'll answer and then give the others an opportunity as well, but I think that, as I said, our institute believes that one of the key criteria for placement of a product in the BTC category needs to be that use of the product requires typically only patient interview and very limited physical assessment in order for that drug to be considered for BTC status. That's necessary for a lot of different reasons.

But one primary reason is for the time consideration. I do not see a group of patients necessarily in a waiting room. It depends, I guess, on the volume of products that are available in a BTC category. I think of the agency, however, is selective about what goes into this category, has good scientific evidence for placing products into this category, the time demands on a pharmacist are going to be fairly reasonable. And I don't anticipate long lines of waiting or so forth at the pharmacy counter.

I do think that pharmacists can assess a lot of patients' needs by counseling at the counter, and that happens, as you know, now with OTC products very readily, where pharmacists are engaged in doing some limited verbal assessment of the patient to determine appropriate OTC drug therapy. So what you're asking the pharmacist to do is only slightly more complex than what many pharmacists already do in nonprescription drug therapy selection and assisting the patient with self-care decisions.

MR. LUTTER: Thank you, other – Dr. Soller?

MR. SOLLER: I'm just going to comment quickly. With the experience in this Northern California collaborative program that I've talked about earlier in diabetes management, I don't think it's necessarily one size fits all. For disease management, where there is hands-on, the use of the whisker (?) test for foot exams or blood pressure evals or downloading the glucose monitor for 90 day readings, all of that, at least in our program, is occurring in separate consultation rooms off from the main pharmacy that had been set up specially by Raleigh's.

And there're a number of pharmacies that are going through this reconfiguration, but I could see easily another type of BTC product that might have the standard – a separated counter that we see in most pharmacies, and it probably is going to be dependent.

It does bring up an issue that was brought up by another member. I think Dr. Axelrod may have brought it up, and that is, in relation to PHI. And having gotten involved in this program, the Northern California collaborative program, there's no question in my mind that the pharmacy is set up to protect personal health information, to meet clear standards within the state, and that there is a mechanism of transferring this information, not only within the pharmacy to corporate headquarters, but then very easily getting it out to academic sites, or over to Blue Shield, who's also collaborating. So this kind of transfer of very sensitive information is already occurring and being done with approvals of IRBs from research institutions.

MR. LUTTER: Thank you very much. I found this panel very informative. Please join me in thanking them for their presentations. (Applause.) We'll take a 15-minute break and reconvene at 11:00. Thank you very much.

(Break.)

RANDALL LUTTER: In the interest of sticking to our schedule, we'll start in one minute, please.

Charley, are we set? Sandra, I'll start if you're ready, okay?

MS. : Yes. Let me just get my – (off mike).

MR. LUTTER: Okay.

MR. : Some of the panelists – (off mike) – questions before. So we need to –

MR. LUTTER: I told them we'll do this.

MR. : Okay.

MS. : Yes.

MR. LUTTER: Okay. We're doing U.N. rules, okay? And anybody without a nametag can borrow an adjacent one.

Welcome back to – I hope everybody has had a chance to find appropriate caffeine or other relaxation of their choice. I'm delighted to have an opportunity to introduce Ms. Brigitte Zirger from the Health Canada Therapeutic Products Directorate and as a representative of our neighbor and ally across the border. We're giving her 15 minutes to speak. Thank you. And welcome.

BRIGITTE ZIRGER: I'll push this. Thank you very much for inviting me to speak to you on this topic today. The discussion so far has been very interesting, and I really look forward to hearing the discussions this afternoon as well.

I'm the director of the bureau of policy science and international programs in the Therapeutic Products Directorate, and as such I'm responsible for legislation and regulations, policies and guidances that relate to pharmaceuticals and medical devices. However, our program is necessarily horizontal, so our policies also deal with or touch on biologics and sometimes natural health products, which here in the States would be either drugs or dietary substances. Okay.

This morning I'd like to talk about the federal and provincial territorial authorities. It comes to play very much in how we treat behind-the-counter drugs. I'll be talking about prescription versus nonprescription status, which you will hear is Schedule F federally. I'll also talk about some of the factors for listing drugs on Schedule F. The conditions of sale you'll hear is a provincial jurisdiction and territorial jurisdiction, and I'll be dealing with a few of the factors for behind the counter. And the invitation came very late last week so we actually scrambled to get a few comments form our pharmacy regulatory authorities on their perceptions of behind the counter. While it's not comprehensive, they are interesting.

One of the points that I want to make more than "come visit us" and to promote tourism in Canada. (Laughter.) We are a nation of ten provinces and three territories, and this will become relevant later on in the presentation.

The federal and provincial authorities. Now, Health Canada, where I come from, is the federal regulatory authority for drugs, medical devices, biologics and so on, and we determine whether a drug should be prescription or nonprescription. And that's all. The conditions of sale, however, including behind the counter is the responsibility of the provinces and the territories. They may schedule with more restrictions than Health Canada, but never fewer. So for example, a prescription drug federally must always be a prescription drug provincially. However, they can elevate a nonprescription drug to prescription status or even behind-the-counter status. And this will be dealt with a little more.

The Food and Drugs Act is the body of legislation that I deal with most often and to Schedule F, which is that list of prescription drug substances, are to the food and drug regulations, and it lists drugs that require a prescription from a practitioner. We have two parts to that list. Part one is prescription for both human and veterinary use, and part two is prescription for human use, but not veterinary use, if it's so labeled.

The practitioner is defined in the Act to mean a person authorized by the law of a province of Canada to treat patients with any drug listed or described in Schedule F to the regulations. And this is relevant because very recently we've actually got pharmacists that are considered practitioners for the purpose of prescribing. The Province of Alberta, which I won't cover in any detail, but the Province of Alberta has just given pharmacists prescribing rights. We're still looking to see what that means. It was within their competencies. There are certification programs and so on, but it's an interesting development that we will be watching.

I want to talk about control drugs only very briefly to note that they are not on Schedule F, but they have their own schedules. And this will be relevant in a moment as well. The process for listing a drug on Schedule F – and again, this is Health Canada – a recommendation to add or to remove a drug from Schedule F results from a clinical review of a drug's submission. There's roughly ten factors that are considered. I'll deal with these in the next slide. The recommendation is reviewed and finalized by the drug's schedule, status committee, which I can never say. It's an internal committee. It's multi-organizations, so it's the Therapeutic Products Directorate, Biologics, Natural Health Products. It's a horizontal committee within Health Canada.

And once that recommendation is finalized, it comes to my area which is in the policy area, and we undertake a regulatory process to add or delete a drug from Schedule F. Now, Schedule F is a regulatory list. It's not an administrative list. And as such, it requires a regulatory process to update it, and as a result it's about 12 months – we're doing it within a 12 months right at the moment.

Some of the factors – this is certainly not comprehensive, but the website – I give the website address to the document. Some of the factors for listing on Schedule F. Whether or not the drug requires individualized instruction and/or intervention of a practitioner. Is there a narrow margin of safety? What are the side effects at normal therapeutic ranges? What's the toxicity in animals? If there is toxicity in animals but there's not enough long-term clinical use to establish a profile in humans then it would become prescription drug. Threats to – it treats a serious disease that's easily – can it be used to treat a serious disease that would be easily misdiagnosed by the public? It's that self-assessment idea. Can it be used to mask other ailments? Is there a possibility for dependence or misuse? And what is the possibility to develop resistant strains of microorganisms in humans? I noted this morning that a lot of these factors were also addressed by previous speakers.

Now, this is something that would allow us – these are the factors in consideration for adding something to prescription status. But these factors are also considered in reverse, when we remove a drug from Schedule F making it nonprescription status. And I've done something.

There are exceptions to scheduling. Exceptions will be considered for drugs which are needed readily for emergency circumstances. And an example of this would be adrenalin or epinephrine. And we heard the case of auto-injectors this morning. That's actually not scheduled. It's nonprescription in Canada. Something that is rarely used without a practitioner's supervision. An example there would be insulin and nitroglycerin. And then finally, whether or not these could have dangerous interactions with drugs or foods, but effectively labeling can minimize the risk. I don't have an example for that one. So that's what we do federally.

Now we move to the conditions of sale provincially. Now, the provinces have pharmacy regulatory authorities, and one of the comments that we've recent gotten – recently received was, in British Columbia, we've had behind-the-counter status since the 1970s, so therefore, we have for quite some time had the drugs controlled in some way at the provincial level. In 1995, however, the National Association of Pharmacy Regulatory Authorities, and I'll be referring to this as NAPRA hereafter, they endorsed a national drug scheduling model to align the provincial drug schedules so that the condition for sale of drugs would be consistent across Canada. And this horizontality was quite important.

So the model consists of three schedules or four categories of drugs. There's a consistent inclusion factor for each schedule, a standard process for scheduling, and the National Drug Scheduling Advisory Committee, NDSAC, which makes the recommendations to place drugs on the provincial – on one of these schedules. These schedules are referred to or incorporated into legislation provincially so that every province now has a consistent way of referring to the NAPRA schedules.

NAPRA has also developed National Standards of Practice outlining the level of intervention for each schedule. These are the NAPRA schedules. Schedule I. These are the drugs for which a prescription is required. It includes all Schedule F drugs. Remember, those are the federal ones. It includes all the control substances as well, plus provincially scheduled drugs. Again they can go higher, but they can't go lower. The other thing I need to say is all of these schedules are drug substances. None of them contain drug products. Now, these drugs would be available from a pharmacist. The sale is controlled in a regulated environment as defined by the provincial pharmacy legislation.

Schedule II. This is your behind-the-counter drugs. No prescription is required, so federally it is not on Schedule F. The pharmacist intervention is required at the point of sale. There is no public access. So they would be in the dispensing area. Schedule III, again no prescription is required. It's available in the self-selection area of the pharmacy that is under the direct supervision of a pharmacist. It's over the counter. And the forth category – this is why you have three schedules, four categories – is unscheduled so there's no prescription required, there's adequate labeling for self-selection, and it may be sold in any retail outlet. This is the grocery store, the gas station, et cetera, you would have these kinds of products.

Now, what is an NAPRA's scheduling process? The scheduling recommendations, again, this is NDSAC that makes the recommendation, it embodies – I've done it again – it embodies a cascading principle. The drugs are first assessed against Schedule F factors. If insufficient factors are covered to leave it on Schedule I, then the drug is assessed against Schedule III factors and then against Schedule – oops – Schedule II factors, then Schedule III factors. And if the drug does not meet the factors for any of the schedules it becomes an unscheduled drug.

Remember that Schedule I factors are very closely aligned with Health Canada's Schedule F factors. And in fact last night I was putting them side by side on the table to really compare them.

What are some instance – this is behind the counter – what are some of the factors that NAPRA consider or NDSAC considers for Schedule II, behind the counter? The initial identification, the disease or the need for this drug would be initially identified by a physician. It would be chronic or a recurrent therapy to be monitored by a pharmacist. There might be exceptional circumstances when prescriptions are not practical. Again, I'll give you some examples of this. There's evidence of abuse. There's a selection of drug – the selection of a drug requires pharmacists to confirm the self-diagnosis. A drug may mask the symptoms of a serious disease. And then it might be a drug where the pharmacist may wish to reinforce or expand the explanation on its use. This is not an exhaustive list, but the drug schedules and the criteria or the factors are on the website as well.

Examples of Schedule II drugs. Clobetasone. In 2006 we switched it from – Health Canada switched it from prescription to non-prescription. However, when it's sold in a concentration of 0.05 percent, Clobetasone in cream preparations for topical use on the skin is a behind-the-counter drug substance. Epinephrine and its salts in pre-filled syringes for emergency use. This would be the EpiPens, the auto-injectors. They would be behind the counter so you would receive it from a pharmacist, but in all other forms, epinephrine and its salts are listed on Schedule I provincially, even though they are not prescription federally.

Insulin. Because it's needed for daily dosing, once the dosage schedule has been established, diabetics need ready access to that. Federally, insulin is nonprescription. It is behind the counter provincially. Iron and its salts, I can attest to this. You have to go to the pharmacist and ask them for it. In preparations of more than 30 milligrams, element iron, per solid dosage unit or 5 milliliter oral liquid, it would be behind the counter. Again, it would be nonprescription federally.

I'm a lot faster than I expected to be. So I said we engaged the assistance of NAPRA yesterday – or on Friday trying to get them to canvas a membership – now, this would the pharmacy regulatory authorities – just to see what kind of comments we can ascertain on behind-the-counter usage. We got a few comments. They're certainly not comprehensive, or in any depth, but they are interesting nevertheless.

Generally there's strong support from the pharmacists for behind-the-counter status. In British Columbia, for example, the behind-the-counter status has been in place since the 1970s or so, and most pharmacists have never known a system that does not incorporate behind the counter. It facilitates interaction with – between the patient and the pharmacist. And there's been – in Canada there's been a lot more emphasis on ask a pharmacist, signage in the stores saying medication information here. And in Ontario, where I live, there's now a public service campaign to encourage people to seek the advice of a pharmacist when they're taking three or more medications. And those would be covered under the – the cost of counseling would be covered by the province.

According to the comments that we received last week, there's no evidence of a lack of support from physicians or other prescribes. On the other hand, we were asking the pharmacists as well. So there could be other comments there, but there wasn't any evidence last week. Behind the counter is seen as a good transition stage from going – when a drug is moving from prescription to nonprescription.

In terms of patient concerns – again, this came from the drug – the pharmacy regulatory authorities – the patients may be unaware that certain nonprescription drugs may be obtained from the dispensary area and therefore may not be able to locate it. But then lots of people go up to the pharmacist ad ask as well.

The pharmacy of operations may become an issue. Especially in big bulk stores there are situation where the pharmacy component will actually close earlier than the store, and hence the pharmacist would be not available either for dispensing a behind-the-counter drug or in fact giving assistance for over-the-counter drugs. Recall that the Schedule III drugs are in an area supervised by the pharmacist. And I've seen situations – I don't know if you've got Costco here – where even the over-the-counter drugs are locked up because a pharmacist is not on duty.

So those are the comments that I bring to you this morning. And I'll entertain questions.

MR. LUTTER: Thank you very much for the presentation. Do we have questions from the panel? Lisa Bernstein.

MS. BERNSTEIN: Thank you very much for your presentation. I'm curious about the factors that the provinces use. And we heard earlier that we need to have some evidence-based data for some of these decisions with respect to BTC. I'm wondering how much – are you aware of what kind of data is used and what kind of studies are done by the provinces in order to make these decisions?

MS. ZIRGER: I can't speak in any depth on that. I know that the NDSAC members are pharmacists and they're delegated by their regulatory authorities. Health Canada does have a member on that committee for information purposes. I believe they use a lot of post-market data that can be supplied by the manufacturer, or generally post-market data. But I can't really give you any more detail than that.

MR. LUTTER: Other questions from our panel? Dr. – (unintelligible).

DR. : (Off mike) – oh, there it is. When – at the initial scheduling – initial point of determination of whether something will be on Schedule F or not, do sponsors or manufacturers of products come in with a proposal to be on Schedule F or not, or are they – or is it completely – are they not supposed to lobby one way or another?

MS. ZIRGER: For the most part they're new drugs, and I think it's anticipated that the new drugs would be automatically on Schedule F. I haven't seen a situation where a new drug submission would result in a nonprescription scheduling. Most of the time for new drugs the non – the removal from Schedule F would be a submission as well –

MS. : For specific a proposal?

MS. ZIRGER: Specific brand proposal. But for the most part, they go on Schedule F. MS. : Okay. Thank you.

MR. LUTTER: Lisa?

MS. BERNSTEIN: Are you aware how often something may move from Schedule II, the BTC to Schedule III or IV which should be more open, I guess not behind the counter? Do drugs – I guess my question is, is BTC viewed as a transitional or a fixed class or both?

MS. ZIRGER: I actually can't comment on that.

MS. BERNSTEIN: Okay.

MR. LUTTER: Deb Otter (ph) please.

DEB OTTER (PH): Thanks. I'd be interested in hearing a little bit more about the infrastructure that's associated with the BTC products. For example, do the pharmacies in Canada actually have a private consulting room in which a pharmacist can talk to the patient? And I don't know if you know this, but whether you're aware of what happened before the 1970s when the BTC – if I understood you correctly – when the BTC products went into place, whether there was a transitional period, whether there was any additional infrastructure, training, physical structure in the pharmacies that was created to accommodate this new system?

MS. ZIRGER: On your second question, no, I definitely don't date back – I date back a long way, but not that far. (Laughter.) So I don't know how it was actually brought in. In terms of infrastructure, counseling areas, there is supposed to be a quiet area where they can counsel. This was certainly an issue about – in the last couple of years. Whether or not every pharmacy has that, I'm not sure, but they are supposed to have counseling areas.

MS. OTTER: Thank you.

MR. LUTTER: Scott?

MR. DANZAS: I just have a question whether or not – are you aware of any data that would be available on whether or not access and usage of products has increased when it's moved from Schedule I, prescription, to Schedule II, which would be BTC?

MS. ZIRGER: I don't have any data. I know where I would look for it, but I certainly don't have any.

MR. DANZAS: Another question. Canada has a national health insurance system. And is reimbursement for products dependant on the various classes, or schedules I could say?

MS. ZIRGER: I would say yes. Generally reimbursement is not – the formularies will not reimburse for nonprescription drugs. However, this morning I was listening to the conversations and I was trying to figure out, okay, so what happens with the EpiPen? It's definitely reimbursed. Insulin is reimbursed. Some of the other examples that I mentioned are reimbursed, even though federally they are nonprescription. So I would say in general nonprescription drugs are not reimbursed, but I would say that depending on the nature of the Schedule II or the behind-the¬counter product, they may choose to reimburse, but it's not necessary.

MR. LUTTER: Dr. Ganley, one last question. Thank you.

MR. GANLEY: Yes. When Health Canada makes the determination that it's not Schedule F and it could be nonprescription, does that mean that there was enough data to support the safety and the self-diagnosis for a unscheduled – that it could be unscheduled in some of the provinces?

MS. ZIRGER: No. It would be – that would be over the counter. Our assessment is nonprescription to the point where it would be over the counter. We do not – I've been assured we do not take into consideration what NAPRA might do making it behind the counter or unscheduled or whatever. So we go to the point of over the counter.

MR. GANLEY: Right. But there must be some assessment that we have a lot of safety data or we know that people –

MS. ZIRGER: Exactly.

MR. GANLEY: – self-diagnose, that you would be comfortable with being unscheduled also.

MS. ZIRGER: Exactly. We would be comfortable with an over-the-counter usage, not necessarily unscheduled.

MR. GANLEY: So you don't call unscheduled over the counter then?

MS. ZIRGER: No.

MR. GANLEY: That's only limited to pharmacies?

MS. ZIRGER: Yes.

MR. GANLEY: Okay.

MR. LUTTER: Diane.

MS. MALONEY: So I just had a question, if you've noticed the cost of the drugs depending on what schedule they're in, if they're transitioning from Rx to – and then in the provinces Schedule I, II, III or IV?

MS. ZIRGER: Again, I would not have that data.

MR. LUTTER: Thank you very much for the presentation. Please join me in thanking Ms. Brigitte Zirger for her – (applause).

Our next panel – our next group has five speakers, and the first is Ms. Amy Allina from the National Women's Health Network.

AMY ALLINA: Thank you. I'm here speaking on behalf of the National Women's Health Network, which is a nonprofit advocacy organization that works to improve women's health by influencing policy and supporting informed consumer decision-making. And we don't accept any financial support from drug companies or medical device manufacturers or really anyone who has a financial stake in women's healthcare decision- making.

I'm here to express the Network's support for the addition of a BTC category for drugs that can be safely used with some kind of screening or counseling or other intervention that a pharmacist can do as well as another trained provider. And we support this reform because we think it has the potential to offer concrete benefits to women in convenience and cost by eliminating the need to visit a prescriber when having a prescription written is the reason for the appointment.

If the creation of the BTC class of drugs is well executed, it could address some important problem with access and compliance that we face today and it could improve concrete health outcomes. But that potential will only be realized by a deliberate and thoughtful reform, so we appreciate the meeting today and the thought that the FDA is putting into the question. And we want to make the point that keeping the goals of improving access and consumers' ability to take a drug correctly and consistently, keeping those goals foremost needs to be a priority as such a system is set up.

A BTC drug distribution system will have to include a mechanism for reimbursement of drug costs. It will have to establish a clear process that consumers can easily follow to get the BTC products, including the interaction with a pharmacist. And it will be essential to also strengthen and expand the kinds of training that pharmacists receive in order to make the system one that will improve outcomes for women.

Because all of this is somewhat abstract, I though it would be useful to look at an example of a drug that currently requires a prescription but might be safely distributed another way, and I want to consider the case of oral contraceptive pills. Today, there's a great deal of inconsistent OC use and it contributes to a high rate of unintended pregnancy and to poor health outcomes for women. The prescription requirement is a barrier to access and compliance for some women who discontinue pill use because they don't have time or don't get around to scheduling an appointment with the healthcare provider before their prescription runs out. And if there were a mechanism for covering the costs of BTC drugs, the simplified logistics of getting a new pill pack without having to go to a healthcare provider could have important benefits.

On the other hand, a poorly executed BTC system could make existing problems worse or even create new barriers for women. If BTC products aren't covered by insurance, if pharmacies don't establish a way to allow confidential conversations between a woman and a pharmacist, if pharmacists aren't well informed and up to date about the latest research on OCs women's compliance and access could actually be reduced. If you consider what might happen when a new study revealing a health risk associated with pills hits the newspaper as one did last week, I think that becomes clear, women with concerns about the pill that she's taking everyday need to be able to turn to the person who's providing their pills for reliable information about this research and answers to their questions. And if that's not available, many women are going to vote with their feet and stop taking their pills.

I've used the OC example to try to be more concrete about my comments, but I want to make the point that even though I think it is illustrative of the opportunities and pitfalls of making pills available or medications available BTC, we do as an organization think there's a compelling case to be made that pills are an appropriate candidate for a full OTC switch. We're not currently advocating that, and if FDA were to consider it we would raise some of the same concerns that we're raising about BTC there. We think those are problems that would need to be addressed in order to expand access. But in either case, we recognize that the burdens of the current prescription requirement combined with the burdens imposed by insurers who limit duration of pill prescriptions and require frequent renewals are making it harder for women to use OCs effectively.

So what we would say about whether a BTC category improves access or not is that the evaluation for that, for OCs or for any drug, has to include components that gather direct input from consumers. Access can't be measured accurately if we don't ask the people taking the drugs how the new distribution system affects their ability to get and take their medications correctly and consistently.

Finally, I want to give just a note of caution about drawing lessons for the BTC questions from recent experience with emergency contraception. A number of people have mentioned it already this morning. And although emergency contraception is not technically a BTC product, the dual label that FDA imposed on it, continuing the prescription requirement for women 17 and younger while making it OTC for women 18 and older, creates a situation that is in some ways similar to what BTC distribution might look like, albeit without the benefit of a full BTC system to support that. My colleague who's speaking after me from the Reproductive Health Technologies Project is going to address this in greater depth, but I just want to make sure that I take the chance to convey the National Women's Health Network's views.

We saw the agency's decision to make EC available to most women without prescription as an advance for women's health, and yet a limited advance. The benefit of that advance has been undermined by the political compromise of the age restriction that FDA's own scientists and that the medical community at large agree is not necessary for safe and effective use of this product. And if the FDA goes forward with the plan to create a behind-the-counter class of drugs for the United States, it can't be used in that way. Drugs that meet the medical and scientific criteria for OTC distribution should not be restricted to behind-the-counter distribution because of political concerns rather than a science-based assessment of the best outcome for patients.

So those are my comments, and thank you for the chance to give them. I'd be happy to answer any questions.

MR. LUTTER: Thank you very much, Ms. Allina. Our next speaker is Ms. Kirsten Moore from the Reproductive Health Technologies Project.

KIRSTEN MOORE: Hello. My name is Kirsten Moore and I'm with the Reproductive Health Technologies Project. Our mission is to empower women to make decisions about their reproductive health. Similar to the Network, we don't accept any money from any pharmaceutical drug, device manufacturers.

We want to thank the scientists at the FDA for calling this meeting. Clearly, there is a need to transform the U.S. healthcare system. Almost 47 million Americans are uninsured and another 16 million are uninsured, and this means as an earlier speaker noted that families every day have to make considerations of whether they're going to access the healthcare system or meet their food needs. Creating a new class of behind-the¬counter drugs, thus eliminating the need for a costly and time-consuming doctor's visit, may be one way to increase access and convenience to needed medication without compromising quality of care for many Americans. And I do want to just come back to the insurance. In addition to being uninsured, the restrictions that insurance companies seem to be eager to impose on individuals who need to get monthly refills or periodic refills of their drugs means that if it's the third Tuesday of the month and you can't get your pill until the next Thursday but you're traveling, that is another barrier to access.

Rather than discuss a third class in the abstract though, our HTP believes that it would be more useful to identify criteria for the kinds of products to which easier access would improve health outcomes. Some examples include drugs with well-established safety records in the general population that are used to prevent disease, treat a long-term health problem, or for which urgent and timely access is key. Once the criteria have been determined, the question becomes whether and how health outcomes can be improved by a learned intermediary such as a pharmacist or a pharmacist assistant. The role of the intermediary must enhance the ability to, or at the very least not undermine, individuals from accessing necessary drugs, and I want to take this opportunity to speak to the knowledge gained from our experience with the current de facto status, behind-the-counter status of plan B emergency contraception as a case study for both the potential benefits and drawbacks of this kind of approach.

In August of 2006, the FDA approved for over-the-counter access to plan B for consumers aged 18 and over. The good news, access to plan B has increased for many Americans. Before the label changed, women were filling approximately 17,000 plan B prescriptions weekly. Currently, 40,000 units of plan B are sold weekly, of which only 6 or 7,000 are dispensed by prescription. Clearly, removing the unnecessary prescription barrier to this product has improved consumers' ability to obtain the product and potentially improve health outcomes. The bad news, females under the age of 18 are still required to have a prescription, and this is a shame as there is ample medical evidence that the drug is safe and effective for all women of reproductive age.

Also, we know that plan B is more effective the sooner after unprotected or under-protected sex that it is used. As a result, the prescription requirement for these women unnecessarily delays access to this time-sensitive treatment. It's also worth pointing out that the proof of age limits the ability of a woman who is 18 and older but doesn't that necessary documentation to access this drug in a timely manner. Because of its dual- label status, plan B is kept behind the counter rather than on store shelves. In this case, the learned intermediaries' role is solely to check for proof of age. This is not value added for the consumer or for the pharmacist, and it does not enhance individuals' ability to access plan B, and in fact may deter them as reports persist of pharmacist or pharmacy staff using this opportunity to impose their personal viewpoint on consumers by denying them the product. This doesn't happen frequently, but it does happen, and for that consumer that is an experience she's never going to forget.

We believe plan B is a cautionary tale for the agency and we urge the FDA to prioritize improved health outcomes as it considers future such arrangements. The current status of plan B has given consumers more timely access to a second chance to prevent unintended pregnancy, and we think it is critical to explore other strategies, creative strategies that could enhance consumers' ability to access other pregnancy prevention options without compromising quality of care or coverage. And this brings me to my last point.

I realize this is a little bit beyond the scope of the FDA's authority but this question of who pays must be answered as you are considering this new arrangement. If the FDA proceeds down the path of expanding access to some drugs within the confines of the current system, then all we may be doing is improving convenience. Convenience may improve health outcomes for some people, but as has been shown with the plan B experience, it leaves others behind and does not result in the kind of overall public health payoff we should strive for. There has to be a broader commitment to reducing medical care costs in this country. Thank you.

MR. LUTTER: Thank you for your presentation, Ms. Moore. Our next speaker is Mr. Sean Tipton from the American Society for Reproductive Medicine.

SEAN TIPTON: Good morning. I am pleased – you will be pleased to know that I intend to be well under my time limit. In the interest of disclosure, unlike the two previous speakers, the American Society for Reproductive Medicine does have extensive relationships with companies both in the pharmaceutical side and the device side, typical of what you'd find with any medical professional society, so we sell ad space, we sell exhibit space, we get unrestricted educational grants.

The American Society for Reproductive Medicine represents over 8,000 physicians, researchers and nurses and other health professionals dedicated to advancing knowledge and expertise in reproductive medicine and biology. At this time, the society does not support the creation of a category of drugs for behind-the-counter availability. We believe that the current system of classification of drugs as over-the-counter or prescription only is workable and appropriate.

We are concerned that an additional classification for behind-the-counter distribution might result in making reproductive medications even more difficult for our patients to obtain. As we have seen recently in several states, pharmacists may allow their personal feelings and moral beliefs to influence their decisions on whether or not to dispense a particular drug even when that drug has been prescribed by a physician. In an environment where the pharmacists may be given additional power, a physician's medical judgment is at risk of being thwarted at the point of sale with the result that his or her patient will not receive the appropriate treatment.

Pharmacists provide an essential element in patient care in correctly formulating and dispensing medications. They are in an important position to advise patients and protect their health and safety. But pharmacists do not have the training to diagnose illness or disease, and it is not their role to determine the correct drug for a patient or whether or not that patient should receive it. Physician involvement is necessary for many drugs. If a drug is safe enough for an individual to take on his or her own initiative, it should be available over the counter. If it is not, it should be available by prescription only. We appreciate being given the opportunity to share our views on this matter.

MR. LUTTER: Thank you very much, Mr. Tipton. Our next speaker is Ms. Rebecca Burkholder of the National Consumers League.

REBECCA BURKHOLDER: Thank you and good morning. The National Consumers League is a private, nonprofit advocacy group representing consumers on marketplace and workplace issues. We are pleased to be able to comment today on this concept of behind the counter or BTC availability of drugs.

For years, NCL has been in favor of a third class of drugs where certain drugs would be placed behind the counter and only available with the intervention of a pharmacist. NCL believes that this class of drugs could improve access for patients, but we do have numerous concerns about how such a system will work safely and effectively. We will be including those concerns, as well as how BTC could benefit consumers, in our comments today. Our comments are focused around several questions that were posed in the Federal Register.

Question one: should there be BTC availability of certain drug products and why? Historically, NCL has been in favor of a BTC drug class to increase patient access to those medications they can safely use after consultation with the pharmacist to self-treat those conditions they can self-diagnose. Consumers today are taking more active role in their healthcare and self-diagnosing and self-medicating with over-the-counter medications, as well as dietary supplements and herbals. A BTC class would expand the range of conditions that patients can self-treat without spending time or money on a doctor's visit. Quality pharmacy consultation would be critical to ensuring that the appropriate medication is taken safely and appropriately.

While a BTC class would appear to benefit consumers by giving them greater access, questions do remain, such as which drug should be in this class and how will pharmacists counsel patients. Because of the many questions regarding how a BTC class system would actually work, we support the suggestion that will also be put forth by the Consumers Union later today that FDA should first test the BTC concept in one or two states.

The Federal Register also asked: what will the impact of BTC be on patient access and cost? A BTC class would likely increase access to medications for consumers since they would not have to obtain a doctor's prescription for the medication. For the 47 million consumers without health insurance, a BTC class would increase their options for self-treatment without the added expense of a doctor's visit. We also need to remember however, that under-served and rural communities do not always have access to a pharmacy, and thus less access to BTC drugs.

Regarding the cost of BTC drugs for consumers with insurance, a drug switch from prescription to BTC could mean the loss of insurance coverage for that drug. Thus, there could be additional cost for these consumers if they now must pay the entire cost of the drug, but the consumer would also save the cost of a doctor's visit, the co-pay for the medication and the time spent in the waiting room. To ensure that costs are not shifted to the consumers, we suggest that when a drug moves from prescription to BTC, that insurance coverage stays the same.

Concerns about privacy regarding medications may also impact access because most pharmacies do not have private places to talk to a pharmacist. Some patients may not feel comfortable receiving counseling from a pharmacist for a BTC medication such as oral contraception. If counseling is required, some patients may forego the treatment due to embarrassment or feeling uncomfortable receiving counseling in a non- private area from a pharmacist they do not know. For other consumers, access would increase since it would be easier for them to purchase oral contraception at a local drug store without the expense and hassle of a doctor's visit. Establishment of a truly private pharmacy counseling area should be required for a BTC class to ensure that access would increase and not decrease.

Question five from the Federal Register: what is the role of the pharmacist? Clearly the role of the pharmacist is critical to ensuring the safe and effective use of BTC drugs. We know that consumers do not always read the labels of OTC products they purchase, and over a quarter have trouble reading and understanding the label. Thus, the pharmacist should be available to provide one-on-one private counseling to ensure consumers understand the appropriate use of BTC medications. However, pharmacists are not always available for counseling or the line at the pharmacy counter is too long and time is too short. And many times consumers sign away their right to counseling without even knowing what they're signing.

We know from experiences in other countries with a BTC or pharmacy class of drugs that counseling is not always engaged in or complete. A 2004 study of Australian pharmacy counseling found that the majority of time the advice given was poor and questions were not asked to ensure that the medication discussed was appropriate. Also of note was that often the first contact for the consumer was the pharmacy assistant, not the actual pharmacist. In a 2002 study of New Zealand pharmacies, consumers often found it difficult to distinguish between the pharmacist and other assistant staff. Consumers were able to confirm that a pharmacist was definitely involved in counseling in only 46 percent of visits.

In the United States, pharmacists continue to be a trusted source for consumers, and in some neighborhoods more accessible than a primary care physician, but they need to come out from behind the counter. A pharmacist's role includes assisting consumers who have trouble reading English or need that extra help to understand the drugs they are taking. When self-medicating, consumers need assistance with diagnosing because they may not recognize the symptoms of a more serious condition and delay a needed visit to the doctor.

For example, stomach pain, gastrointestinal distress, can be a symptom of a number of medical problems. While consumers may use a proton pump inhibitor such as Prilosec for symptomatic relief, potentially serious GI problems may be missed because a doctor was not consulted. This underlines the need for appropriate pharmacy counseling about when consumers should consult a doctor. For certain chronic conditions, such as high cholesterol, pharmacist should encourage initial physician evaluation and follow-up to assess the progress of the disease, while it may be possible for pharmacists to conduct some follow-up testing and the logistics of this would need to be worked out.

There must be clear pharmacy counseling urging people to check with their doctor before use and continue to have regular visits while taking their medication. A few years ago, with the possible switch of a low dose statin medication to OTC status, NCL was concerned that consumers would not consult their doctor before or during the use of an OTC statin. Based on a survey we commissioned, consumer overwhelmingly demonstrated their willingness to continue to consult with their doctors. If FDA determines that low dose statins are appropriate for a BTC class, how would pharmacists be able to ensure that patients actually visit their physician?

A pharmacist's role would also include providing continuing education on safe and effective use of BTC medications. Even though a drug may be in a BTC class for years and consumers who have been counseled may need less assistance, the consumer who just begins therapy will need active pharmacy counseling. Because consumers often mistakenly believe that more is better, particularly for medications that do not require a prescription, pharmacists will need to continue to check for appropriate dosage, and pharmacists will also need to pay special attention to the risk of interactions between BTC drugs, others prescriptions, OTCs and dietary supplements.

A pharmacist should have access to the patient's full medication list to avoid interactions and double dosing. Since many consumers receive their medications by mail or by Internet, it would be the responsibility of the consumer to maintain an up-to-date medication record to share with their pharmacist. Ideally, an integrated e-prescribing system is needed for a BTC class to be safe and not result in more confusion among multiple prescribers in multiple settings.

Federal Register also asked: Should BTC availability be a temporary status as prescription drugs transition to OTC or a permanent status? While a transition class may be appropriate for some medications in order to determine if they can be used safely and effectively as OTCs, for other medications a permanent BTC class may be more appropriate. This would depend on the safety profile of the drug, including potential side effects and harmful interactions.

Regarding how the FDA determines which drugs are moved into a BTC class, we suggest as Consumers Union does, that rather than respond to random petitions to move a drug to a BTC status, the FDA convene an advisory committee once a year to consider several drugs that FDA staff believe are good candidates for BTC. The issue of whether BTC is a permanent or temporary status raises the question of how the drug is regulated regarding advertising. Can the drug be advertised to consumers as an OTC or as a prescription drug and therefore required to include a summary of risks and benefits? How a drug is advertised will impact consumer perception of its risk and benefits and subsequent use of the medication.

Finally, question 13: what measures would be needed to ensure patient safety? First, establishment of a system that ensures quality pharmacy counseling occurs which would require more than just the consumer's signature. The consumer could be asked to check off and certify that they received counseling in specific areas such as interactions. Second, certain information should be conveyed to consumers through counseling, labeling and any promotional materials. This would include when a doctor should be consulted, common interactions, and a 1-800 number and website for consumers to contact if they have any questions, along with MedWatch contact information to report adverse events.

Lastly, before a drug moves to BTC status, drug manufacturers should be required to conduct a public education campaign for consumers, as well as prescribers and pharmacists, to explain that the drug will be available BTC, that a pharmacist must be consulted to obtain the medication, and any potential risk. Thank you for this opportunity to comment.

MR. LUTTER: Thank you very much, Ms. Burkholder. Our next speaker is Dr. Michael Greene of the American College of Obstetricians and Gynecologists.

MICHAEL GREENE: Thank you very much for giving the college the opportunity to comment at this meeting. We very much appreciate it. My name is Mike Greene. I'm a practicing obstetrician/gynecologist at Massachusetts General Hospital in Boston and I'm a professor at Harvard Medical School. I'm a former chair of the FDA's Advisory Committee on Reproductive Health Drugs and I remain an SGE. I speak here today on behalf of the college which, much like the ASRM, does accept money for advertising space in its journals from drug manufacturers and device companies, and also accepts money as unrestricted educational grants.

The college understands the criteria for over-the-counter status of medications to include the following essential elements: that the patient or consumer must be able to recognize the indication for the use of the drug, that the person must be able to understand how to properly use the drug and must be able to read and understand the label, there must be minimal risk when taken according to direction and there must be a high safety margin for use of the medication, there must minimal to no potential for abuse for the medication, and with rare exceptions, there usually need not be – be no need for continued monitoring or active assessment of the safety or efficacy of the drug.

We understand the potential advantages of over-the-counter status as compared to prescription drugs, and these include expanded access to consumers through several features. First, more competition due to more outlets for sale of medications ,and also in eliminating professional fees for learned intermediaries that would need to prescribe or dispense the medication. The criteria for behind-the-counter status seem somewhat less clear but seem to have evolved de facto from some apparent current examples.

As has been mentioned several times here already today, the flu vaccine seems to present an example of de facto, behind-the-counter prescription where there is some screening for risk factors that's necessary that could place the patient at risk for severe adverse events; specifically a screening for allergy to egg proteins that could place the patient at risk for anaphylaxis given the injection. In this particular case also, the route of administration is not something with which the average layperson is familiar or comfortable or skilled; that is, it must be administered by an intramuscular injection.

The use of the medication is episodic rather than chronic, and in the case of an influenza vaccination it would be, generally speaking, once a year, and it does not require ongoing monitoring for safety or efficacy of the medication because this is a one-time administration and no monitoring is needed to be sure that the patient's condition has not changed in any material way that could affect safe and effective use. Specifically, here we would be concerned about the change in status which is pregnancy or lactation. Interestingly, pregnancy has not been mentioned here yet this morning to the best of my knowledge.

With respect to pseudo-ephedrine which has also been mentioned several times this morning, the seeming only purpose of behind the counter has been to prevent bulk purchases that might indicate an intent to divert the medication for purposes of abuse. The emergency contraception example has also been cited several times. And I was a member of that joint committee that advised the FDA on the status of emergency contraception. The American College of Obstetricians and Gynecologists was very disappointed with the FDA action to effectively place plan B behind the counter, imposing upon the pharmacist the FDA's apparent new role as arbiter of sexual practice. There is no more rationale for emergency contraception behind the counter than other minimal-risk contraceptive measures such as spermicidal foams and jellies and condoms which are now readily available over the counter.

The American College of Obstetricians and Gynecologists has concerns with respect to behind-the-counter status, and these include the potential limit to access both by reducing the number of retail outlets where medications are available as compared to over-the-counter status. We're also concerned about limiting access by the intimidation factor of a patient being required to ask the pharmacist to dispense the medication. We're concerned about what standards pharmacists will be held to with regard to counseling patients regarding the relative risks and benefits of the medications. This responsibility would include assessing the potential for pregnancy, which might significantly change the risk benefit calculation for a medication and in this case, we would think specifically of statins which are demonstrated human teratogens.

How would counseling about possible current or future pregnancy be done in a community pharmacy setting that would protect the patient's privacy? How would this counseling be documented to be sure that the process has been adequate to fully discharge the pharmacist's obligation to a perceived standard of care? Pharmacists may realize that with respect to professional liability and pregnancy they may have grabbed a tiger by the tail. This is a problem, a liability problem that the American College of Obstetricians has been dealing with for decades.

How would that counseling information be stored to protect its confidentiality? What obligation would the pharmacist have for monitoring the patient and the patient's pregnancy status? Would women want to share that information with their pharmacist? What obligation for counseling about appropriate contraception would the pharmacist have? We don't know whether the usual training of a pharmacist includes the didactic and practical clinical experience to equip them to perform the counseling regarding the full range of contraceptive options of drugs and devices.

The College is trying to take a nuanced view of behind-the-counter status, but we do have concerns about the potential impact of behind-the-counter status on women's health. We recognize the potential advantage of increased access compared to prescription status and are concerned about the decreased access compared to over-the-counter status. We do have questions about protection of confidentiality, privacy and the unique risks when women change status from non-pregnant to pregnant. It is well recognized that 50 percent of all pregnancies in the United States are unplanned and many of these pregnancies are not recognized until well into or after organogenesis. This fact must be borne in mind by anyone prescribing, recommending, or dispensing medications to women of childbearing potential. Thank you.

MR. LUTTER: Thank you very much for your remarks. At this point, we have an opportunity to take questions from the FDA panel. And we've developed a new protocol here to be sure we know whose turn it is to ask questions. We're following United Nations rules, so you feel free to raise your nametag to the upright position. Dr. Creeder (ph).

DR. CREEDER: My nametag actually says Dr. Throckmorton. He's not reading. I had a question for Ms. Allina. You made a comment that any such system would have to be – behind-the-counter system would have to be carefully designed because a poorly-designed and executed system would actually limit access. Can you be a little specific about what kinds of things you were thinking of there?

MS. ALLINA: Sure. What I was thinking about was the potential for creating new barriers, or at the same time as you take away one barrier limiting women's access to a source of information that they might need. So one thing that I discussed in the statement was this idea of you're taking oral contraceptive pills and you read in the newspaper one morning that a new study has come out that shows that they increase risk for cardiovascular disease and you're concerned about that. Currently, you would be likely to try to contact the prescriber and ask about it. Do I need to be worried about this? Should I keep taking the pill? How does this affect me? And if you were getting your pills from a pharmacist and that pharmacist was prepared to answer – available and prepared to answer to those questions, it could be a very similar interaction to what you might have with your prescriber. In fact, it might be easier to get that information than to actually get your prescriber on the phone. But if the system wasn't set up to account for that need and if pharmacists didn't know about that study and weren't trained in how to evaluate that research, then a woman with those questions would have nowhere to turn or would have nowhere that she felt confident turning, and that would create a new barrier for her.

MR. LUTTER: Thank you. Other questions from the FDA panel? Deb Otter please.

MS. OTTER: Thank you. I had a question for Ms. Burkholder. I would just be interested in hearing any more details she can provide about the Australian study. You mentioned an Australian study which said that the pharmacists' advice was poor the majority of the time and fraught with some other difficulties. Is there anything else you can tell us about their system or about the findings of that study?

MS. BURKHOLDER: That study was numerous researchers that were disguised as shoppers went into many pharmacies across Australia. And how I understand Australia is that they are required to counsel on certain specific items. I think it may vary by state, but as opposed to some European countries, there are certain specific things they are supposed to counsel on. And what was found was they did not always ask appropriate questions about a patient's medication history and about other medications that they were taking. And there was also this confusion about who the consumer was actually talking too, and I think that's a good point to remember as we discuss BTC drugs and the importance of pharmacy counseling, that the counseling should be done by the actual pharmacist and not by the technician. It was also – I think it was in that study though that there was a certain eagerness on the part of the pharmacists to talk to the consumers as well. The problem was their advice wasn't always right on.

MS. : Thank you.

MR. LUTTER: Other questions?

MS. CREEDER: I actually have a follow-up to that question, and then I also have a question for Ms. Moore. I'm also not familiar with that study. It sounds really interesting. Did they do a comparison looking at the advice that patients got from their physicians?

MS. BURKHOLDER: No, they did not. This was actually a study by Choice, which is Australian Consumer Organization, so I do not think they did a comparison.

MS. CREEDER: Okay. Thank you. Ms. Moore, you had commented about one particular example of a product that's essentially behind the counter now, and I'm not sure if I'm paraphrasing you or you actually said that this system is not value added as it stand – there's no value added for the consumer as it stands. And I'm wondering if you have any thoughts about what would value added be in a behind-the-counter program for any products in general.

MS. MOORE: I think along the lines of what the Network laid out, it's an opportunity for a consumer or a client to get more information, feel more confident about the decisions that they're making about which medications they're using, how it is going to interact with other medications that they're using, that there is something – because we're asking a consumer to interact with a professional, there should be something gained out of that experience or there should be some expectation about what we expect the consumer to gain out of that experience, and that it's going to improve an outcome rather than just in the case of plan B give people something to hide behind.

MS. CREEDER: Thank you.

MR. LUTTER: I sense it may be time for lunch. Please join me in thanking very much this panel for the informative remarks. (Applause.) We'll meet back here at 1:45 p.m. So we'll start the next session at 1:45 p.m. Thank you very much.

(Break.)

MR. LUTTER: Welcome to the afternoon session of our public meeting on behind-the-counter availability of certain drugs. I hope everybody has had a chance to enjoy lunch and get caffeine as appropriate. Our first speaker this afternoon is Ms. Mary Ann Wagner from the National Association of Chain Drug Stores. Each speaker has ten minutes, and then there'll be questions and answers from the – questions from the panel for a period after that. Thank you very much and welcome.

MARY ANN WAGNER: I am Mary Ann Wagner, senior vice president, policy and pharmacy regulatory affairs, with the National Association of Chain Drug Stores.

We applaud the efforts of the Food and Drug Administration to explore the public health benefit of certain drugs being available behind the counter without a prescription, but with the intervention of a pharmacist, and appreciate the opportunity to share our views on this important subject. NACDS represents the nation's leading retail chain pharmacies and suppliers, helping them to better meet the changing needs of patients and customers. Chain pharmacies operate more than 38,000 pharmacies, employ 114,000 pharmacists, fill more than two billion prescriptions yearly, and have annual sales of nearly $700 billion.

Within the correct parameters, NACDS supports a behind the counter class of drugs. We believe pharmacists, already one of the most trusted and accessible healthcare providers and experts in appropriate use of medication, are uniquely qualified to take on this new role. Structured properly, BTC availability of certain medications has the potential to increase access, improve patient compliance, and reduce healthcare cost; however, a flawed structure could result in a group of drugs with limited access, reduced compliance, and lacking in a clear compensation policy for pharmacists, despite the additional clinical and administrative responsibilities that it would impose.

We believe some of the most important components of a successful BTC class of drugs are that it be clinical and not enforcement based, safe, consistent, and predictable, and that it creates fair payment and coverage, liability protections, and is monitored and regulated appropriately. I'll speak about each one of these components.

The fact that it would be clinical and not enforcement based. NACDS strongly believes certain medications should be available BTC if there is a clear clinical profile requiring pharmacist intervention. This class should not be used to enforce age or quantity-based limits on certain medications or otherwise restrict access. For example, the recent requirement that products containing pseudoephedrine be moved behind the counter is not a good example of effective use of BTC status. This move was based on reducing diversion. There is no clinical need and these products do not require additional counseling or other forms of pharmacist intervention. The time of pharmacists is limited as is the space behind a pharmacy counter. Both would be best used by basing decisions on BTC status on clinical profiles.

And then safety we feel is very important. Patient safety is paramount in creating a BTC class of drugs. We feel this class should be structured in a manner that ensures safe products are available to patients, clear clinical protocols that define eligibility for treatment are developed, and any lab tests associated with the class should be appropriate for a pharmacist to administer or monitor. In compliance with appropriate protocols for patient privacy, information about BTC medications should be available for review along with prescription drug history to ensure drug utilization review and continued monitoring. The use of BTC medications should be monitored as part of a patient's entire drug therapy and overall health care needs.

As far as consistency and predictability, NACDS believes a BTC class of drugs should not become the temporary stopping ground for every drug moving from legend to over-the-counter status. If a medication is determined to be appropriate for OTC use, it should be available in this manner immediately. Furthermore, patients, pharmacists, payers, and others need clear guidelines on what types of drugs would qualify for BTC status. Consistency and predictability are needed to train pharmacists and other pharmacy staff to determine formulary placement and reimbursement policy and ensure uninterrupted availability for patients. As a result, NACDS advocates that BTC should be a permanent class for drugs that require special counseling, monitoring, screening, lab testing, or other clinical intervention.

Regarding payment and coverage, while the FDA's role may be limited in determining payment and coverage for BTC medications, this is arguably one of the most important factors in the success of BTC medications. Traditionally, prescription drugs have been covered by payers, while OTC medications have not. It is possible that moving medications from legend to

BTC status would result in both public and private payers ceasing to cover these medications.

Without a question, a BTC class of drugs would provide additional roles and responsibilities for pharmacists. Pharmacy workflow and procedures would change and additional counseling, monitoring, and patient interaction by pharmacists would be required. These additional clinical roles must be appropriately recognized and compensated. NACDS urges health insurers and others to cover BTC medications, include them on formularies, and establish mechanisms for the added reimbursement for clinical services that will associated with this new class.

BTC medications hold great promise in improving patient compliance, expanding access, and aiding in the effort to control prescription drug spending. However, these opportunities will be lost if the move to BTC status results in no coverage for these products and the shifting of all costs directly to patients.

Regarding liability protection, liability protection for pharmacists and pharmacies is also an important component of creating a BTC class of drugs. As medications move from legend to BCT status, we believe it is critical that liability for the safety and effectiveness of these products not be passed down from manufacturers to retail pharmacists and pharmacies. As with OTC medications, manufactures should be required to supply labeling or packaging inserts, adequate directions for use, and warnings. While NACDS recognizes that an expanded clinical role for pharmacists may result in additional liability, it must be managed sufficiently to ensure robust participation by pharmacies.

Monitoring and regulation. Finally, NACDS believes the FDA has the scientific expertise to determine which drugs are appropriate for inclusion in a BTC class. We believe that the FDA should make these determinations and state boards of pharmacy should continue to regulate the practice of pharmacy. Currently state boards already hold the pharmacists responsible for proper patient education and drug regimen review. This partnership between the FDA, state boards of pharmacy, and state licensed pharmacists and pharmacies works well today in regulating other aspects of prescription drug use and pharmacy practice, and we see no reason why BTC medications should not fall into this existing model.

Thank you again for the opportunity to present our views today. We look forward to working with the FDA and other stakeholders to address these issues and other unanswered questions regarding BTC medications. And I'd be happy to answer questions later on after the rest of the panel has spoken. Thank you.

MR. LUTTER: Thank you very much, Ms. Wagner. Our next speaker is Mr. Stephen Giroux from the National Community Pharmacists Association.

STEPHEN GIROUX: Good afternoon. I am Steve Giroux and I'm president of the National Community Pharmacists Association and an actively practicing pharmacist from Middleport, New York, a rural western New York community.

NCPA would like to thank the FDA for holding this public meeting to explore the public health benefit of certain drugs being available without a prescription, but only after the intervention by a pharmacist in the behind-the-counter or BTC class of drugs.

NCPA strongly supports the creation of a BTC class of drugs. We believe it would reduce consumer health costs, increase patient convenience, and provide a vehicle for post-market safety supervision for consumer protection.

NCPA represents the pharmacists, owners, managers, and employees of more than 23,000 independent community pharmacies across the United States. We are community leaders actively involved in community-oriented public health civic and volunteer projects. Many hold local offices. Others service state legislators. Often we serve on hospital boards. The nation's independent pharmacists dispense 1.4 billion prescriptions annually or 41 percent of the retail prescriptions in the United States. This is a huge responsibility, but as the medication expert it is a responsibility that our members readily accept. Not only are pharmacists the most accessible healthcare providers available to patients, pharmacists have the training and knowledge to provide clinical interventions and ensure through specific clinical protocols that patients meet the conditions for specific BTC use.

We are also well qualified to educate patients on appropriate use of the drug product and follow up with the patients to ensure compliance with the medication regimen.

Today we are here for our patients and to support the BTC class of drugs, which is similar to the "pharmacy only" concept in the United Kingdom. Our colleagues in the U.K. have told us that the pharmacy only concept has provided their patients greater access to more medications, leading to improvement in patients' self-care and a decrease in unnecessary visits to the doctor. Independent pharmacists already offer a wide range of patient services, including nutritional counseling, compounding, diabetes education, immunizations, and vaccinations, and smoking cessation clinics. Therefore, additional services such as the counseling of patients on BTC medications should be easily integrated into the workflow in the pharmacy.

In a survey conducted by NCPA on November 2nd of 2007, our members were overwhelmingly positive, 97.1 percent, about the prospect of helping patients by being able to offer a BTC drug after a pharmacist consultation and clinical evaluation of a patient, with no prescription from a physician necessary.

Regarding patient safety, our members regard pharmacist involvement in patient screening, lab testing, additional counseling, follow up, and monitoring as a benefit to patient safety. They were very positive about the potential to enhance patient safety through their participation in these activities. The ePrescribing Initiative that NCPA and NACDS have embarked on through SureScripts, and the EMR, Electronic Medical Record initiatives, will further enable this information exchange.

Many pharmacists responded that through increasing patient contact, they can better ensure the patient gets the right medication at the right dose for the right condition and that they can refer patients to a physician for appropriate care when needed.

NCPA has long held a statement of position in support of a transitional class of drugs called pharmacist legend. So the idea that the BTC class could be transitional was well received by our members. We believe that the vast majority of the medications in the BTC class would be transitioning from Rx to BTC status, therefore, increasing access to these products, not limiting it. However, we do realize that on occasion this could be a two-way street, such as the move of pseudoephedrine products from OTC to BTC. This is actually an extremely good example of why we need a uniform, standardized process in place for handling the BTC class of drugs.

There were many thoughts by our members with regard to benefits and costs to the healthcare system, and for the most part we see great potential to relieve some of the growing burden on emergency rooms and busy medical practices by providing access with oversight from a healthcare professional to medications in the BTC category. Additionally, pharmacists are trained to be medication experts. We undergo a minimum of six intensive years of university training to learn about drugs and their effect on the body. By increasing the pharmacist's involvement with the patient in a formalized process, patients will benefit through an increased understanding and better use of their medications. And our patients agree.

A recent survey of 1,000 consumers aged 18 and older conducted by the Polling Company found 68 percent of Americans strongly or somewhat strongly supported the development of a BTC category. By a greater than two-to-one margin, Americans endorsed a policy that would bring certain medications that are available off the shelf to behind the counter. Nearly two-thirds or 62 percent of Americans would also support allowing pharmacists to dispense specific drugs that currently require a doctor's prescription. These numbers hold especially true for parents.

American with children under the age of 18 in their households were much more inclined than non-parents to support creating a BTC category, 77 percent versus 63 percent, and giving pharmacists the ability to dispense certain medications that now require a doctor's prescription, and moving some medications from OTC to BTC status.

Ultimately, we believe the decisions in this area should put patient care first. The person who walks into a drug store is a customer, but once they reach the pharmacist counter, they are a patient. We need to consider what is best for the patient, rather than what is best for the healthcare system. That's why we're here today. It's all about our patients. And if we get this right, it will benefit the healthcare system as well.

Now, about the logistics associated with BTC drugs, NCPA members were not at all fazed by the logistical questions asked by the FDA. Workflow, inventory, record-keeping, billing, all fundamental to keeping a community pharmacy open and successful, and we will apply these same tactics to the logistical activities associated with BTC drugs when they become available.

As far as where to store BTC medications, our members assume that the first BTC drugs, other than pseudoephedrine of course, would already be behind the counter, and as a prescription – currently as a prescription medication, so they wouldn't really need to make room for it on their shelves. All agreed that there must be a standardized protocol and an electronic platform for dispensing these drugs for patients, as well as practitioner safety and liability.

With regard to reimbursement, pharmacists must be paid for the services provided in conjunction with BTC medication. Health insurers should consider the addition of BTC medications to their formularies as a way to improve patient health care and lower costs. In fact, in our market in western New York fully two-thirds of the plans currently cover OTC Prilosec, as an example, as their preferred proton pump inhibitor, and it is a covered benefit. The New York State Medicaid program, in a cost containment decision, covers over-the-counter medications many times far more cost effectively than other therapies.

This topic deserves much further discussion than this forum is able to provide.

One key point our members made was the need for all BTC protocols to be available in central locations such as computer database or a website, although most felt that a uniform electronic system could also enable tracking and monitoring of patients who go to multiple pharmacies and could potentially increase acceptance and participation by patients, pharmacists, and physicians.

Our members were kind of split, 50-50, regarding who should oversee the BTC program. However, many thought that the FDA and the State Board of Pharmacies should work together to define a process for the BTC class of drugs.

NCPA members feel strongly that a BTC class of drugs belongs solely in a pharmacy where well-trained personnel can ensure appropriate patient care. We believe only a licensed pharmacists, and potentially a pharmacist intern under the supervision of a licensed pharmacist, may provide the clinical intervention necessary for the dispensing of a BTC drug to a patient. This class of drugs should not be available in venues where pharmacists are not available, such as gas stations, convenience stores, or vending machines, as OTC drugs often are.

The training of pharmacists and staff is important, and there were many suggestions encompassing web-based programs, live CE programming, and other types recommended by our members that we would be glad to share in more detail with the FDA in our written comments.

Overall, NCPA members feel that the availability of BTC drugs will have a very positive impact on the practice of pharmacy, on the practice of medicine, and on our patients. In general, the availability of BTC products will build much better relationships between patients and their pharmacists.

NCPA would like to propose the first BTC product be available to patients in the United States as early as 2009, and we pledge our support to work with the FDA to make that happen.

We thank you for the opportunity for allowing NCPA to comment on this incredibly important healthcare issue. Thank you very much.

MR. LUTTER: Thank you very much, Mr. Giroux. Dr. Sidney Wolfe from Public Citizen is our next speaker.

SIDNEY WOLFE: Thank you. We do not have any financial conflicts of interest. We have not ever taken any money from drug companies or device companies, and so forth.

When the FDA makes an important policy decision, the evidence for the benefits and risks of that decision needs to be weighed as carefully as the evidence concerning the benefit risk balance of a drug. In the case of behind-the-counter availability of drugs, heretofore BTC, it is useful to hear the opinions of various parties, including those with obvious financial conflicts of interest, whose opinions can be predicted. This is not the first time this issue has come up, and people working for a certain company say the same thing as a function of what company or organization they work for. But before any decision is reached, particularly because new legislation would probably be needed if behind-the-counter availability of drugs is to be established as a general principle, there needs to be evidence, not currently available as I will discuss, that benefits do outweigh the risks of such a new system.

Thirty three years ago – and Dr. Crout who will talk later this afternoon was there, so he remembers this – spurred in part by pharmacists' desires to restrict certain OTC drugs to pharmacists only or behind-the-counter availability, the FDA stated – this is a Federal Register notice in 1974 – quote, "There is at this time no public health concern that would justify the creation of a third class of drugs to be dispensed only by a pharmacist or in a pharmacy. The third class of drug issue is at this time solely an economic issue. The Commissioner therefore categorically rejects the establishment of a third class of drugs at this time." Now, again this is pressure to regulate over-the-counter drugs more than they had been.

More recently, in 1994, prompted in part by some Congress people's wishes to revive the idea of BTC availability for certain drugs, Congressman Dingell asked the GAO to do a comprehensive study to collect data on the experiences of other countries that had, by then, implemented such systems. The study involved ten countries: Canada, Australia and, eight European countries. It came out in August of '95. The title was "Nonprescription Drugs: Value of a Pharmacist-Controlled Class Has Yet to Be Determined."

I will quote directly from the summary of the study and then go through a couple points in more detail. Quote, "Little evidence supports the establishment of a pharmacy or pharmacist class of drugs in the United States at this time as either a fixed or a transition class. The evidence that is available tends to undermine the contention that major benefits are being obtained in the countries that have such a class. This conclusion is substantiated by six points.

One, reliable and valid studies that examine the effect of different drug distribution systems on overall health and healthcare system costs do not exist; two, while a pharmacy or pharmacist class exists in all ten countries, it is not used with any frequency in any of them to facilitate the movement of drugs to sale outside specialized drug outlets; three, the EU has decided not to impose any particular drug distribution system on its member countries because it has found no evidence of the superiority of one system over another; four, there is no clear pattern of increased or decreased access to drugs as nonprescription products where a pharmacist or pharmacy class exists; five, while a pharmacy or pharmacist class is assumed by some people to improve safeguards against drug misuse and abuse, in the ten countries these safeguards are easily circumvented, and studies show that pharmacist counseling is infrequent and incomplete; six, experience in Florida with a class of drugs similar to pharmacist class – this is a law in Florida allowing pharmacists to dispense some then prescription drugs – has not been successful. Pharmacists have not regularly prescribed these drugs, and record-keeping requirements have not been followed."

The body of the GAO report elaborated on a couple other points. One, cost. Quote, "Our interviews with officials in the study countries indicated that the cost savings from fewer physicians visits may not be as great as expected. They said that many patients do not pay the full price for a prescribed drug. For instance, an insured patient might have only a $5 co-payment for a prescription drug, while having to pay the full price for a nonprescription product. Patients might thus have an incentive to go to doctors for a prescription."

Second issue, pharmacy counseling. And they reviewed a large number of published studies, 16 of which involved, as was suggested earlier, blind approach where you've got trained shoppers going in there and actually recording what was said. Quote, "The results of the studies in the United States are rather similar to those in countries where the sales of at least some nonprescription drugs are restricted to pharmacies. In general, the theory of pharmacy practice diverges from the reality. The advice of pharmacists is often appropriate but not universally given. In addition, it is often incomplete, with little information being given to customers on such items as possible side effects. In other words, what information is given is accurate, but not enough was passed onto consumers. Researchers consistently found a lack of information gathering on the part of pharmacists. For instance, information is often not gathered on symptoms and other medications." That's the end of the quote from the GAO report.

The theory that pharmacists can counsel patients on OTC, prescription, or behind-the-counter drugs diverges, as stated by the GAO, from the reality. Evaluation of this includes the 1990 OBRA law requiring a system of pharmacist information for patients for prescription drugs. That has not worked nearly as well as hoped. In one published study 31 percent of the pharmacists did not make counseling available. And it also includes the above-mentioned elements of the GAO study that looked at counseling by a prescription – by pharmacists for prescription drugs and then the information of behind-the-counter drugs in other countries.

More recently – and these are two studies just published online, and I don't think they're available in print – there are some evaluations, surveys of pharmacists, of the 2004 U.K. decision to make the statin drug, simvastatin, available in a pharmacist-only setting without requiring a doctor's prescription. Some of the findings of these two recent published studies are as follows.

Questionnaires returned by 1,156 community pharmacists, which is 58 percent of those surveyed, 956 respondents or 82.7 percent reported no sales of simvastatin in the previous 14 days; 82, or 7 percent, sold one pack and 4, or 3.5 percent, sold two packs. Health promotion material aimed at reducing cardiovascular risk was on show to customers in just over half of the pharmacies, 52 percent. And again quoting from one of these studies, "This is the first relatively large-scale national study to report community pharmacists' experience of OTC simvastatin in Great Britain." Again, OTC means a pharmacist's there. It's only in a pharmacy and the pharmacist is supposed to be involved. "The majority of respondents had undertaken an array of continuing education, had established sales protocols and expressed confidence in making an appropriate cardiovascular risk assessment in line with the OTC license. Most considered this to be an idea requiring personal input from the pharmacist rather than being delegated to other pharmacy staff. However, very few sales had actually taken place during the study period and there were major concerns relating to the need for full cardiovascular risk assessment, access to full clinical information prior to simvastatin use, and the lack of an evidence base for the licensed dose, 10 milligrams there, and these reflect reservations voiced by the medical profession as well."

This notion of a third class of drugs has been tried, and there is much evidence that it didn't work. A doctor writes a prescription. A pharmacist fills it. If the doctor is removed from the equation, the public could be harmed, as evidenced by the concerns of U.K. pharmacists about simvastatin.

Positions taken on this issue are predictable, as I alluded to earlier. Pharmacists like it. I would like it also if there was evidence that it worked. Doctors oppose it in part because their roles are replaced. Some drug companies like it because they see it, as in the case of the third try to switch a statin to this category, as a way to boost sales. Companies who sell to 7-11s and other markets represented here today by CHPA don't like it because many of their outlets don't have a pharmacist so they couldn't sell these drugs.

Speaking on behalf of pharmacists – I am speaking on behalf of pharmacists – they are well skilled and often know a lot about the drugs they dispense. In practice, when asked to counsel, they often don't because they don't have the time. There's no mechanism to reimburse them for their time. As a policy, it wouldn't work. It would probably take congressional law to make it happen.

Twenty years ago, painkillers ibuprofen and naproxen were only available by prescription. The more we learned about the drugs and their safety, those drugs became over the counter. Pain is an easy self-diagnosis. Thus far, and there are a couple exceptions that we have intervened in successfully and they stopped the switch to over the counter, but thus far the Rx to OTC switch process has worked quite well. Plan B, as mentioned by the people, is not an example of that. Plan B is an example of a drug that should have been available to all women over the counter, and only because of religious, political reasons was it delayed as long as it was and did they have the irrational 18-year cutoff.

The current push for behind-the-counter class was precipitated clearly recently by drug companies who make statins and want to switch them to OTC. In those two hearings, people said, "Well, if we had a third class, then maybe that would be a better decision." I disagree. I've testified twice and I'm going to testify next month for a third time opposing statins becoming OTC.

In summary, there is a lack of comprehensive evidence on this for the last 12 years. In conversations yesterday with the staff of Congressman Dingell, who requested the study in 1994, they seemed very interested in sponsoring and asking GAO to do another study, and I hope that they follow through on that. I believe that they will.

The second point, I've mentioned before that neither Plan B, and I'm not mentioning pseudoephedrine, are example of BTC – the Plan B because it should have been OTC, and pseudoephedrine because of its diversion for possibly making methamphetamine, the quantities were limited. That concludes my remarks and my time available here and I'll be glad to answer questions at the end of this panel. Thank you.

MR. LUTTER: Thank you very much Mr. Wolfe. Our next speaker is Mr. William Vaughan from the Consumers Union.

WILLIAM VAUGHAN: Thank you very much. Consumers Union are the folks who publish "Consumer Reports," and we take no money from industry or outside sources. And we don't just test lead in toys, although that's keeping us very busy, we try to help people with safe and effective prescription drugs through a best buy drug program. And I did have a written statement that I hope you all have. And we thank you for including us and raising this issue.

We agree with the National Consumer League and some others, so I will be pretty brief. We could see places where this could save some money. Our readers tell us that costs – healthcare costs are the number one consumer issue, and CBO last week saying the way we're going, we're going to be at 50 percent of the GDP on health, we need to start looking at some things. And for example, we supported moving OTC on a number of things, the antihistamines, and we thank you for recent action there, but this has to be done right and it has to be done carefully. And we have to take our time because, as Dr. Wolfe said and others have said, there are so many questions. In particular, if it's going to save money for consumers, as NCO has said and others, there has to be insurance coverage of BTC. And if there weren't, if insurers start dropping coverage, boy, I think that would guarantee congressional involvement by Mr. Dingell and others very quickly, so that issue has to be looked at. But one's sense is as we get serious about trying to save money in the healthcare system, that something in this area is coming, is just we feel not ready for prime time, and the questions you raise need to be very carefully answered, and it's worth waiting on technologies that could solve many of these safety issues.

We need, and I think Ms. Wagner talked about this, a system for you all to identify two, three, four drugs a year you think are prime for going OTC or BTC and put them out there for people to comment on. Maybe call one of your advisory committees to vet it and get outside views. And we'd urge you – this is four or five years away, but the thing that former Dr. McClellan (sp) had talked about, Section 905 of the new FDA law that just went into place, where you're going to have massive databases of medical records for routine active – a great use of words – routine active surveillance of their side effects and long-term effects, before you moved something to DTC – OTC or BTC run – do some of that routine active surveillance and make sure there isn't some static out there or some background smoke that we should know about before people start having an easier time of getting those – of those drugs. And we think it's absolutely essential that you have the electronic platforms in place, health information technology, e-prescribing. There's – today there's what, 8 percent it looks like at least of folks who – they've gone to Dr. Smith and Dr. Jones and they've gotten two prescriptions in the same class and they're piling pill on pill. The pharmacist has to know the full range of what a person is taking, and I'm not sure that's possible by 2009.

We got a ways to go here, and the software is a little rocky, but if we don't know what the patients are taking and they wander into one pharmacy or another, we should be promoting for quality purposes a medical home. And this takes us away from home if we're not at all careful.

And I did mention DTC. We like a new and little bill that Mr. Waxman and Kennedy have put in that relates to cold medicines for little kids, that people ought to start warning of the side effects of those in DTC ads, and we would urge that in any OTC, BTC movement.

BTC doesn't have to be for every pharmacy. Why not just those that are certified to be quality and competition, if there's savings there, as Dr. Wolfe questions, but if there's savings – if this is a useful thing – excuse me, I may need a pill – if that's a useful thing, other pharmacies will come along once they meet the certification. And again, given the huge questions that have been raised, we do have a federal system. Why not try it in a couple of states? Roll it out in one or two states, and then we could see if there are savings. We could answer some of these questions rather definitively. So thank you for your time and consideration.

MR. LUTTER: Thank you very much, Mr. Vaughan. Our next speaker is Ms. Laurie Tansman from the Mount Sinai Medical Center.

MS. LAURIE TANSMAN: Let me preface my comments by first of all saying that I am speaking on behalf of myself. I'm sorry. I'm also recuperating from a little throat problems. Let me preface my comments by stating that I am speaking on behalf of myself only, and I thank you for this opportunity. I am a practicing registered dietician, as well as an educator with the Mount Sinai School of Medicine and an adjunct with CUNY.

So why are we so interested in this BTC drug status? Is it because of cost, convenience, and/or safety? A couple of weeks ago, the FDA revealed the results of a study of consumers who purchased drugs over the Internet, and it seemed that bypassing their physician to obtain a prescription was the reason for such a purchase. Dr. Luda stated this is a risky practice, and I don't think he meant solely from the perspective that many of the drugs sold via the Internet may not be what they appear to be.

So what might be another reason? Increasing the availability of drugs intended short-term use, such as antibiotics? I don't think so. Or as some had mentioned here earlier today, maybe decreased access of current OTC drugs. However, I believe that the interest in BTC may be to make more readily available drugs intended for chronic use, whether it be a statin, an ACE inhibitor, or an oral diabetic agent such as Metformin.

In fact, when I spoke out against OTC approval of Mevacor in January 2005, I showed the slide where I raised the concern about increased availability of drugs used for chronic conditions. I unfortunately will not be there next month, but my feelings are the same. They have not changed.

So the next question is, why should we want to make medications for chronic use more readily available? Most distinguished – there are many distinguished, I should say, scientists and physicians who are focused now on prevention versus treatment. So if statins were approved for BTC, then we may be able to reduce the incidence of heart attacks. And if oral diabetic agents are approved for BTC, then many at high risk for diabetes may be able to delay its onset. And if BTC antihypertensives were available, we may be able to reduce the incidence of strokes. But let me tell you, if we are going to get serious about preventing chronic illness, then we need to increase access to nutrition intervention and exercise services. And if we make more drugs more readily available, then that will negative – that could negatively impact on consumer willingness to make necessary lifestyle changes.

In this quote from Dr. Robert Bono, who is a past president of the American Heart Association, he clearly stated his ambivalent feelings about making the statins more readily available. That is, people who ought to be dieting and exercising are going to feel that since they are taking a pill, they can now continue habits that are unhealthy. And in this article that appeared in the "American Journal of Cardiology" in 2004 by Gordon and his colleagues, it was stated that, "however, because of the widespread availability of powerful medications, the value of therapeutic lifestyle changes per se in contemporary medical practice is often discounted by clinicians, health insurers, and patients." And as a registered dietician, I want to emphasize my concerns about the lack of reimbursement by still the majority of the insurance industry for nutrition intervention.

People need help in making lifestyle changes and when they get that help, the results can be amazing. The data from the diabetes prevention program show that lifestyle intervention at 58 percent was more effective than Metformin in reducing the incidence of diabetes in persons at high risk, and those who were on Metformin, it was reduced by only 31 percent.

So if we want to get serious about helping people at risk for chronic disease, then the insurance industry needs to get serious about providing reimbursement for services to help individuals make necessary lifestyle changes, not the FDA making drugs more accessible. And that means insurance coverage as provided by – for nutrition intervention as provided by registered dieticians; likewise, insurance coverage for demonstrated participation at say a gym; and last but not least, improved health care insurance so that all Americans can obtain the medications they need if their physicians determine that need.

In the Federal Register notice announcing today's meeting, the FDA included that variations of a behind-the-counter status are already in effect in a number of countries, including Australia, Canada, New Zealand, and the United Kingdom. These are countries where all their citizens are insured, unlike the United States where it was most recently estimated that approximately 16 percent are uninsured. Increasing the availability of prescription drugs via BTC is not the answer to improving health, but better access to healthcare for all Americans via improved insurance is what needs to be done.

And now, let's project into the future. Pretend you've gone to a health fair, and you didn't eat that morning because you wanted to take advantage of the screenings you were being offered for diabetes and lipid profile testing. The results show that your fasting glucose finger stick was 120, your LDL cholesterol was 120 and your HDL cholesterol was 30. So now what are you going to do? Are you going to maybe increase your gym workout? Are you going to switch to fruit juice instead of sugar-sweetened soda? Not a good idea, that's not going to help the blood sugar. Are you going to stop by the drug store in the way home and try the newly approved BTC statin, an oral diabetes pill, and/or you're going to follow up with your physician? But better yet, forget that this experience happened to you. Pretend that it happened to your 21-1/2 year old daughter away at college. She calls you up and tells you that because of the results of the screening, along with your family history of diabetes and heart disease, that she was going to try those BTC drugs that you recently approved for reduction of heart disease and the other one that's for diabetics. What's your reaction? Are you going to insist that she'd make an appointment with a physician at student health services at her school to be retested and then decide if it's really indicated for her to take these meds? Whatever you would guide your young adult daughter to do is what you should want for every American, and nothing less.

And finally, returning back to that fair, you're hungry since you've been fasting all day and there's a local store at the fair giving away samples of the pictured items bellow. Given the results of the screening you just had, which of these would be the best choice for you, the full fat hard cheese, the fat-free Snackwell cookies, or the chocolate-covered almonds? If you don't know the best answer, then I hope you had easy access to a registered dietician. Thank you.

MR. LUTTER: Thank you, Ms. Tansman. Our next speaker's Dr. Kelly Jones from the National Alliance of State Pharmacy Associations.

DR. KELLY JONES: Yes. Thank you very much, Dr. Lutter. Thank you for the panel. Thanks for allowing me to be here. I know it's been a long day, and I want – I know a lot of things have been presented here. It's very informative. You almost want to respond to a lot of things you hear, but you can't do that obviously because there's so much to stay.

Can I pick the chocolate-covered almonds, Laurie? (Laughter.) Okay, okay, yes.

I do represent the State Pharmacy Associations. There is an alliance of us together, all 50 states. We're pulled together. I'm from South Carolina, as you probably can tell, and I'm the president elect of that association. And I represent myself here today as well.

One thing – I want to just think through some things. A lot has been said today, but I want to just highlight some very specific things that may have been lost in all of the discussion. But we have talked about education here today, and pharmacy is becoming a patient-focused education. It's not just a product-focused education. We're licensed. We're regulated. We have a lot of degree options. We're pharm M.D.s. We now have a doctorate-level degree. Like an M.D. is a doctor of medicine. We're a doctor of pharmacy. It's a clinical-based degree. Some pharmacies or schools are attaching themselves to MBA programs. So you really need to see. We're doing – back in the '80s and '90s, we adopted pharmaceutical. Through CMS we've adopted the medication therapy management. And now we're looking at other options. This behind-the¬counter medication is awesome.

What you see here is, I believe healthcare – and if you can stay with me here and focus on the population of the healthcare is sort of like a funnel, I like to think of it as. And the way I'll describe this is that CT surgeons see a very small amount of the healthcare population, less than maybe a pulmonologist. Pulmonologists may see more patients. Urologist probably sees more patients than a pulmonologist. An internist sees more patients than an urologist or pulmonologist, et cetera. They've become maybe a source of primary care.

Family physicians see more patients than internists. They see even more patients. But we stop there and say that's primary care. Well, it's not necessarily. It is, but there's another level of primary care, and that's self-care. And we need to acknowledge that and remember that. People want to take care of themselves. More people take care of themselves than go to a doctor. So we need to be – pharmacists can be there to be an intermediary, to help patients help themselves. And I think that's the right concept here.

So behind-the-counter medications, one, that's available for consultation and evaluation by a pharmacist with documentation procedures, and I believe increases the referrals to a physician. Others have alluded to that and I would ditto that.

We believe pharmacists can make an informed decision, can actually take patient data and take information from the patient and make an informed decision. And what better place than a pharmacy? A pharmacy is a place of self-care. It is a place where patients have the opportunity, an opportunity not just to get a product, but to discuss, to say things, to discuss something with a pharmacist. Discussion about healthcare can be very healthy. And the thing I want to drive home today that hasn't been really said is there is a pharmacist-patient relationship that develops. It's vital to patient's safety. It's very important. As a doctor-patient relationship, so is a pharmacist-patient relationship, and there's a lot that can go on there that's healthy. And it's not just a product. It's sometimes helping patients to understand what's wrong with them.

Access. We believe that access – that some medications will not go OTC. We've heard today some of that, worrying about things not going OTC, but some products can't go OTC because the labeling may be too difficult or there may be some monitoring.

Behind-the-counter products should only be dismissed after consultation with a pharmacist. And to maximize access, systems cannot be overly burdensome. That's what's happened in Florida, Florida – too many – too many barriers. You had to have a written notice by a physician to actually get a product for smoking cessation. Excuse me.

We believe that if FDA can put a committee together, pharmacists and physicians, to appropriately help patients pick the right drugs – we think safety is important. State boards of pharmacies should regulate the program. We think it's cost effective.

So I want to highlight again some of the same things that have been reiterated today.

So benefits to pharmacy, it allows the pharmacist to help patients help themselves, develop that relationship that's builds trust and loyalty. It creates the opportunity for discussion. It encourages compliance or adherence to all medications. It elevates the practice of pharmacy. Job satisfaction, drug utilization review, it helps a lot of those things and that's beneficial to pharmacy, and it's beneficial to the patient. It's self- focused and therefore convenient. Pharmacists provide oversight and access. They can monitor patients' medications and help with drug interaction potential, therapeutic response, and drug utilization for all medications the patient has. Hopefully they will review all of the medications the patient is taking before they recommend a behind-the-counter medication. And we believe that adverse event reporting is very vital to the pharmacist and the patient for sure.

And I think I skipped a slide, but I just want to mention here, patients have access to more medications, so it's beneficial to healthcare and it becomes an access point in healthcare for those who are not currently being treated. Very important, because it can in a sense because it's a higher form of primary care, it is an opportunity or a gateway, if you will, for patients who aren't otherwise in the medical system for sure.

Pharmacy consultation will likely increase referrals to a physician, as we've mentioned before, and I think that will definitely happen. And we see that it will reduce emergency room visits as well. It can reduce costs there as well.

So those are some comments there. I appreciate it. We'll take some questions. And I tell you, I think – I think I want to do something right quick. I got a minute. Let me – I want to do something real quick. I want to read something. I'm in pharmacy education and I interviewed a young man who put it so well, and I want to read what he said. This is a young man interviewing, and I interviewed Monday.

The small white-haired man lay in the intensive care bed with a peaceful look upon his wrinkled face. A plethora of tubes and wires snaked around his frail body and brightly covered monitors would record the last minutes of his life. I watched from the doorway of his room with a sense of great sadness and feeling of guilt. Only hours earlier I had reassured the hesitant man that his surgery would work out wonderfully and he'd be home in no time. I had become quite close to this gentleman and his family while taking care of him in the days leading to his surgery to repair of his aortic aneurism. The surgery did not go as planned and there was simply nothing else the vascular surgeons could do to save his life. Only hours later, he would become the first patient I witnessed dying in my medical education. The patient would have a profound effect on me for the rest of my third year of medical school. I had learned during the course of his stay in the hospital that no one had really explained to him the need to stop smoking. The county he lived in has very limited medical resources and he rarely was able to visit his physician without having to wait for hours in a crowded waiting room. Eventually he just gave up and hadn't seen a physician in over 15 years prior to admission to our hospital.

Dr. Hogue today said it well. He said patient's access – there's a patient access crisis. So this is a great example. This young man who I interviewed Monday gave us a great example of why this particular process and this program can increase access, hopefully, even simply to reduce smoking succession, and so just a wonderful example of why this is needed. Thank you.

MR. LUTTER: Thank you Mr. Jones. We'll take questions from the FDA panel. Jane?

MS. AXELRAD: I had – my first question, a lot of the speakers on this panel and earlier have talked about the need for an electronic platform, a consistent platform that would form the basis for access to patients records and all of that. I was wondering if Ms. Wagner, Mr. Giroux or Dr. Jones or anyone else, but those three particularly, could comment on where we are today in terms of developing that kind of an electronic platform, and if we aren't very far along with it, what are the steps that it's going to take to get there so that we would have a platform that you could use to support behind-the-counter system, and how long do you think it would take to get there?

MS. WAGNER: As an interim step – that would be nice to have it all in one place – but as an interim step, I think one of the advantages of having drugs behind the counter is that the pharmacist has access to all of the patient's medication histories. They may be going to two or three different doctors, but the pharmacy is one place that has all that information. So there could be a way of documenting it within the store system by way of the pharmacy computer. But to go beyond that, I'll let someone else speak to that as far as a platform. But as an interim step, they do have the pharmacy system now.

MR. GIROUX: And that's what we would envision, is that the pharmacy dispensing system for prescription drugs would be utilized for the BTC class to do that documentation or record-keeping, but I think your question goes beyond that, and I referenced it in my remarks. And I'm very excited to say that yes, it is a bit preliminary, but in conjunction with NACDS, NCPA started several years ago SureScripts, which is an electronic pipeline, if you will, a platform for the communication between healthcare providers, between the prescriber so to speak, the physician and the pharmacy, for the initial purpose of e-prescribing, however, rapidly expanding into refill request authorizations and therefore the exchange potentially of EMR information, lab data, and whatever other clinical data that can be exchanged in an electronic fashion. Pharmacies are the most electronically positioned healthcare provider right now. All of our claims are electronic. There's just no paper any longer other than the actual scribbles of a physician on a piece of paper, which seems to be ironic in and of itself. So that system is in existence and it's growing leaps and bounds every day. I think there are – someone told me just recently – over 300 physicians a day becoming wired for this process of information exchange, and I think – I don't know the numbers. We can get that information to you and will.

But secondly, in the Medicare D environment, we've created something called Marixa (sp) which is a platform – again, a web-based platform for pharmacists for medication therapy management cases in this instance, but also down the road post-market surveillance, phase four clinical trials, and these types of things. The platform – the electronic platform is there to push these cases and to be able to communicate on the part of the pharmacies. It really is in its infant stages. I think in the first year of the mandate with the Medicare Modernization Act I think there were over 100,000 cases presented in '06, '07 so far. I think the numbers that I've heard were upwards of 70,000 thus far in the year that had been worked and actually medication therapy management cases have been delivered in this electronic platform for a population of one D plan, which has 1.2 million lives covered. So the capability is on the cusp very, very ready to explode and that opportunity for that electronic interchange and communication is there and those systems have been developed and put in place.

MR. LUTTER: Dr. Wolfe, did you want to add to the question on electronic platforms?

MR. WOLFE: Well, I think that electronic platforms where everything that happens in the hospital, in the outpatient doctor's office, and the pharmacy are a great idea, but they should not be posited as the only thing that's keeping us from doing behind-the-counter. The enormous improvement in medical care, both in terms of treating, diagnosing, finding out what kinds of occupational exposures might have caused various diseases, is going to leap forth as this gets more complete. But I just – again, I just caution against – were it not for these platforms being completely there, all the other problems that have been raised by many, the GAO, some of my comments would be okay. I just don't think there would be.

MR. LUTTER: Thank you. Do you have a follow up, Jane?

MS. AXELRAD: Yes. I have a follow up because I wasn't sure whether I was hearing you say that you think that basically we're there, that you think that there is enough of an electronic platform that if we decided tomorrow to move drugs behind the counter there would be sufficient methods for doing record-keeping and exchanging information and getting patient information into the system, that we could do it safely. As many people have suggested, that's sort of the paramount concern. And sort of a related question is I think a lot of what people have been saying about how useful it is to have a behind-the-counter system is premised upon the fact that there is this really close personal relationship between the patient and the pharmacist. And I'm wondering in this day where people move around a lot, there's a lot of – people are filling their prescriptions to chain pharmacies, the days where you had a corner drug store and a pharmacist that you'd known all your life are long gone, so I'm wondering how much having a safe behind-the-counter system depends on this kind of continuity of care, which is what I thought I heard a lot of people say.

MR. LUTTER: I think we should have only two people answer this in one minute each. Do you have –

MS. AXELRAD: Okay, that's fine.

MR. LUTTER: Are you targeting your question for a particular individual? Mr. Vaughan?

MR. VAUGHAN: Thank you. It sounds so good in theory, but the reality – maybe set a goal that when the CDC reports less than 1,000 deaths a year from drug interactions, maybe we can trust these systems to be actually working. Because right now you're getting so many drug duplications and if people do pharmacy shop, I – it sounds so good, but be careful of moving before what's out on the street matches the dream.

MR. LUTTER: Ms. Wagner, please.

MS. WAGNER: Yes. If I might speak to – thank you – the pharmacist-patient relationship. We represent the chain pharmacies in America, and I fully support the idea of the pharmacists having a relationship with their patients. I realize here, in busy metropolitan Washington you don't see as much of that as you do in other parts of the country. I also happen to live in Indiana, and I can tell you that happens in chain pharmacies, it happens in independent pharmacies, where the pharmacists do know their patients, the patients do depend on them everyday. They do a lot of triaging just in their normal day, where they interact and see the patient more often than any other healthcare professional. There is a drug store 2.3 miles from everyone in the United States. So there are relationships across the country and people do trust their pharmacist. But I realize here in Washington – and we run into the same problem in Congress. Members of Congress don't see this happening, and I don't know whether is because it's such a large metropolitan area or what the problem is, but across the country there are these relationships.

MR. LUTTER: Thank you. Diane?

MS. MALONEY: So my question goes to – in general I think about pharmacists dispensing drugs, and what I'm wondering is if you see your doctor, the doctor might say you don't need medicine, so it's along the lines of the prevention discussion. What role do you see the pharmacist playing when somebody comes in and there are various options, including one being change in diet and exercise? And that can be to anyone on the panel.

MR. JONES: Well, this is Kelly Jones. I think definitely there is – pharmacists definitely have the opportunity, and it's eluded in my testimony, for that discussion that goes on with the patient is so critical, and the opportunity to decide things. And I think one thing is sometimes to reiterate to a patient that they need to go see a physician. A lot of patients are scared to go to the doctor, and oftentimes from my experience – I work with 35 physicians every day and I know how they think, and sometimes patients are scared to go. And I think pharmacists can help deliver people to the doctor for sure. So that's one comment I had. Anybody wants to make a –

MS. WAGNER: I agree that often pharmacists work in partnership with physicians, and many times in the course of the day, they tell patients they need to see their doctor. This is something that's serious, you need to be concerned about it. So I would see this working very well together with them.

MR. GIROUX: And if I might just add real briefly. The community pharmacy is the hub of the community where often the civics lesson – we're kind of sometimes at the center. Many times we have a coffee hop or whatever, I won't get too aw, shucks on you're here. But the reality of it is we see patients far more frequently than the physician does, and we have the opportunity as a matter of fact – one of my biases is smoking cessation.

And people walk into my store and they've left their burning cigarette out front, I know it. I don't know that they always tell their physician that they smoke. And I don't know that the physician sees them promptly enough to be able to smell that on them as the pharmacist does. So just as a highlight of an example of how we can intervene on a patient's behalf on a wellness issue and really have more interaction and more contact than other healthcare professionals can, and again make the referral potentially to the healthcare system, but really make a life-changing impact. If we wear seatbelts and quit smoking and do those kinds of things and have public sanitation, I think we'd do more than improve the healthcare of people than anything else. So I think we need that intervention.

MR. LUTTER: Thank you, Dr. Creeder.

MS. CREEDER: I want to follow up on that, Mr. Giroux and maybe play the devil's advocate here. One of the – in most cases, it's not 100 percent, but the system that we do have in this country does at least directly make a distinction between the prescriber and who stands to benefit from the sale of a product. And when one puts the pharmacist into the position of taking care of the patient in the community pharmacy setting – the comment was made that, well, we know when it's time for them to be referred to a doctor. But I – some people worry that perhaps chances will be taken that shouldn't be, regardless of how trained well is because there is an opportunity to make a sale. And I have raised the point that there is an inherent conflict of interest between pharmacists selling and dispensing drugs – just dispensing the drugs, and actually some of the things I've heard here seem to be – draw – cause me to question are we talking about asking for something that is behind the counter or actual pharmacy prescribing? And I'd wonder how you might respond to the conflict of interest issue.

MR. GIROUX: Well, first of all, I don't believe that there are any documented cases of what you're talking about. Obviously pharmacists many times intervene on patient's behalf and don't fill prescriptions when there is a conflict, a problem, and so on. And certainly there's not a system currently in place that compensates the pharmacist for not filling a prescription and yet because we are healthcare professionals and we are loyal to what it is that we do, we do often make those interventions and do what's right for the patient because we stand on the side of the patient. And we're there to help them and help them make the best decisions for their healthcare because many times they may not agree with what the physician has done and so on.

I don't want to get into that kind of a discussion, but I clearly – my understanding of this issue is that this is an opportunity for the most part to make what we perceive or what you all perceive as relatively safe products that are previously restricted to prescription only more readily accessible to patients and therefore lower the cost to them. I would much rather have a patient take a $20 drug than a $400 drug. And that's what we see on a regular basis. Maybe that's a little bit extreme because I think the proton pumps inhibitors are probably only about $150 a month versus an over-the-counter prilosec at $20 a month. Same drug, still safe. You'll have to explain to me why there still is a prescription version of that when the opportunity of savings is there.

And in fact the insurance companies, the plans have recognized the savings opportunity of that. But I don't really perceive it as a conflict of interest to the patient. It's not like we're mandating the patient to take things. It's the patient has a need, we're there with an armamentarium of product available to solve that need and we make that available hopefully at a low cost and in a monitored environment where we can follow up with the patient, we can make sure they know how to use it, we can make sure they know what to expect with it, just what pharmacists do I would submit, all the time in terms of prescription drugs, maybe not all the time, but a majority of the time. And I think that paradigm has changed dramatically in the 13 years since the study that Dr. Wolfe has cited.

I think pharmacists are doing that job and we will continue to do that job and we will continue to expand our role to do that job in a better fashion to take care of our patients without conflict of interests.

MR. LUTTER: Thank you. Dr. Ganley?

MR. GANLEY: Yes, this is for Dr. Wolfe. I was struck by your comment that you didn't think the data that was presented earlier regarding the sale of Plan B indicated there was increased access to that medicine simply because it should have been OTC.

MR. WOLFE: No, no. That's not what I – what I said was I don't think it's an example of what people are discussing as a behind-the-counter drug. It's a drug that if everything had gone right it would have been switched from prescription to over the counter and made available to everyone, not just people over the age of 18. Clearly – we heard the data that there was increased access as there sometimes is when drugs are switched from prescription to over the counter. I'm just saying let's not look upon that as an example about what this meeting is about today. That's all.

MR. GANLEY: What kind of data would you be interested in seeing to help define that this would be something that would be worthwhile? I suspect if you conducted another GAO assessment that you're not going to find any other data that really is able to define that these programs are successful. So what kind of data is that you would want to see?

MR. WOLFE: Well, on the benefit side, the whole argument for it is that there is increased access, and whether one's talking about the extremely disappointing, to use their words, lack of acceptance or taking off of the British simvastatin behind the counter, or all the data that were collected 12, 13 years ago by the GAO, there just isn't evidence that there is overall increased access via this class. So you have to ask what is the purpose of it? Is it to lower cost? Again, there were no data from the GAO study that the costs were lower. There were concerns both in that study and in these two studies that have just been electronically published about safety concerns. So like anything else, that's why I started out by saying you would need to evaluate the benefits and the risks. The last time they were comprehensively evaluated, there was no evidence that the benefits were there and that they outweighed any risks which were also there. And that's why I firmly hope that the Congress does order another study.

You just heard that things may be different and probably are in some way, in this country at least, from what they were back 13 years ago. They may be better. They may be worse. They may be about the same in these other countries. So the kinds of variables they measured there, including a review of literature and everything else, I think were very useful. And if the same results occurred after this new study or what I hope will be a new study, we'll just have to say we're not ready for it. Nice idea. Again as I said, pharmacists are in a great position to do this counseling, but if it turns out it's not being done – half of the pharmacies who responded in the U.K. didn't have risk reduction information on diet and exercise, it's just not ready to be worked on.

Again, we have the model which has pretty much worked from prescription to over the counter. And so the evidence is very much the same kind of evidence that they looked for and found 13 years ago repeat because it's much later now.

MR. LUTTER: Thank you. Elizabeth Buck (sp).

ELIZABETH BUCK: We've heard from a lot of people on the panel about the improved access and the decrease in healthcare costs. And what I'm wondering about is how does the person who's not a patient, who isn't going to a pharmacy now, how is BTC – how do you see that helping them? What benefits do they get from that, or would they get from that? And also I'd like to hear how the panel responds to Dr. Wolfe's comments.

MR. LUTTER: Do you want to make clear to whom you're asking the question?

MS. BUCK: Anyone on the panel.

MR. : The panel.

MR. LUTTER: Mr. Vaughan, please.

MR. VAUGHAN: Well, to save on a doctor visit. And some of these things, and again you've got to be so careful what you put BTC, but on some of these things you might answer some of the Institute of Medicine's three-volume study of last year that there's a heck of a lot insured middle class folks going to ER rooms at midnight because they can't find a doctor or anybody else open. And I think a lot of your members stay open till midnight. So there's – there's some savings there that could work through the system, but they're not clear. I think Dr. Wolfe has got some good points that maybe – why not try it in a state or two. You'd probably get some – couple of your members who would love to try it, and let's get a little more hardnosed on the savings and costs. If we don't deal with the safety issues, you could increase costs with adverse events. So you've got to do this right.

MR. GIROUX: I think further, the – I think the point has been made many times this morning. You had someone from the Food Marketing Institute who didn't necessarily take a clear position on this issue, but pharmacies are a very competitive sector and we have the Chain Association which they say they have a store every 2.3 miles. Mary Ann, I live in a community where I serve people that are about 12 miles away from me, so – that's average, okay. I got figured that's what you meant. But you have grocery stores that have drug stores. You have department stores that have pharmacy departments, independent pharmacies, 23,000 strong. So I think the point is made that we are a very readily-accessible and widely-distributed healthcare professional with whom the public comes into contact far more often than any other healthcare professional. And so if there's an opportunity there, as Dr. Wolfe has indicated, for pharmacists to rise that challenge, I think it's worth exploring.

I would submit that we are in fact rising to the challenge in many instances in related types of activities along these lines, so that if we want to improve access to healthcare by the disenfranchised patient who never sees a doctor and doesn't want to see a doctor, and they become aware of it through – and I think the message was delivered this morning, where it's important that we educate people about this process and what it means that these products will be available, and simply that education to the fact that they are available and they don't need a threatening environment of a physician appointment where they have to wait for two hours to see a very busy healthcare professional, where they come in to the pharmacy, potentially get these products and have the clinical services associated with that, which include the triage, the evaluation as to whether or not this patient needs to see another healthcare professional or be referred to the healthcare system in some fashion and maybe be referred to health and wellness ancillary benefits at the same time, I think that's a system that really does make sense and does improve access and does end up saving money, and in fact identifying potential risk factors that we can hopefully minimize over the course of time.

MR. LUTTER: Thank you.

MS. AXELRAD: I just wanted to follow up. We've – I've also heard that people, at least pharmacists would like to be compensated for those services. So I guess I'd like to kind of get a sense from you what the differential is between the price of the doctor visit and the pharmacist. I hear you talking about consumers saving time with a he pharmacist, but in terms of money.

MR. GIROUX: Well, I think part of the disconnect that was referred to earlier too in terms of pharmacists potentially not doing some of these roles, there hasn't been the compensation associated with it. And I think with the compensation comes the behavior change, so I think that has to be looked at and evaluated. I can tell you that on a prescription drug, the average cost to dispense in the country is about $10.63, across the board. That's a national study that was just completed within the last couple of years in regard to Medicare Part D issues and so forth. So that I would presume, and this is only a presumption on my part, that it would be something less than that in terms of a per-transaction cost to provide this service if there wasn't the same – I think there needs to be somewhat similar levels of record-keeping requirements and ongoing maintenance and so forth. So I think that number, if that's a solid number, is significantly less expensive than an office visit and then if you add on the benefit to society in terms of the cost savings and in fact the speed with which patients can get healthy and back to work, because presenteeism is a big thing today with our country's employers. They want their workforce back to work as quickly as they possibly can get them because that saves industry money as well. And I think the access and the long hours and so forth that have been referred to play into that very, very strongly.

MR. LUTTER: Thank you. We have time I think for one more question. Dennis – (unintelligible) – please.

MS. TANSMAN: And can I make a – I'm sorry, but I just have to say this. No offense to you. You can't substitute for a physician's office visit a visit to the pharmacy. You just – we've got to push towards better insurance, and every American should be seeing a physician. It's just unacceptable. There's just no – I'm a firm believer, I'm very straightforward, and you've just got to go to your doctor. We know so much today.

We've made such advances in medical science. And the only way you could screen somebody properly is if you go to a physician. And there is just no excuse not to go to a physician. And we have to make it available to every American.

MR. LUTTER: Thank you.

MS. TANS MAN: That's the bottom line.

MR. LUTTER: Dennis – (unintelligible) – please.

MS. BUSHMAN (?): Yes, I just wanted to get a quick verification from Mr. Giroux. From your presentation, one of the concerns we would have is, if one goes for with this in the future, is making sure people have access to the pharmacists. We always heard today that people go to the pharmacy, and they're not sure who they're talking to. Is it a pharmacist, is it a technician or what? And you said in your presentation, I believe, that the pharmacy intern can be involved in BTC counseling. Is that what I heard?

MR. GIROUX: Yes, we would support that. And as a matter of fact most states – I think all states allow pharmacy interns, which are graduate level fourth and – or third and fourth-year professional students in pharmacy. Those are pharmacy interns that have some advanced training – this is getting feedback – and therefore they are actually pharmacists in training, so to speak. They're very, very close to sitting for their licensure exams. And that would be an area of ancillary professional that would be potentially empowered under the supervision of a pharmacist to participate in these types of activities. Similarly to the state regulations under OBRA 90 which didn't take effect right away in '90 and went on to be implemented by various states and various ways, that pharmacy interns can do those roles under the supervision of a pharmacist as well.

MR. BASHAW: But now you're devolving the pharmacist professional role down to a student, which is merely a professional student. But again the concerns we've had, the classes of drugs people have talked about today as being potentially candidates involving therapeutic monitoring cleotest weight (ph) wave cleotest (ph), et cetera. Is this just going to be a devolving of the responsibility? We've already seen the pseudoephedrine, which I know it's a different issue, but still it's related to it some ways, where it has gone now from the pharmacies to the front cash register where the record and the logbook is kept up there. It seems like it's a step – it's a bit of a step to go from the licensed professional to the quote, unquote "professional in training" operating under the supervision of a pharmacist –

MR. GIROUX: Maybe we're making a misunderstanding. Pharmacist interns are in fact licensed by the states. The State Board of Pharmacies issues intern permits to those students that qualify in the pharmacy program for an intern permit. And it would be under the direct supervision of a pharmacist. But it's – it's just a suggestion. We're not stating anything other than we see – there are some that have raised the issue of busy pharmacists being able to do this and I don't actually see that. In my practice, I think our pharmacists are in fact performing these roles. Our membership tells us that they are and this may be one technique for some that are in their busy practice flow to use ancillary personnel, not technicians, not clerks, but pharmacy interns which are in fact regulated and licensed.

MR. LUTTER: Thank you very much. We have time for one additional question. Jane?

MS. AXELRAD: Yes, I just wanted to follow up on my earlier questions about continuity of care. And since we generally try to be a data-driven agency, I was wondering if there is any data out there about, for example, the length of time a pharmacist stays in one place or the length of time that a particular patient visits the same pharmacy, or how often they move around and change. I was just wondering if there is any data out there and if anyone knows whether there is, they could submit it for the record.

MR. LUTTER: Thank you. Thank you very much. In the interests of time, I'd like to ask the audience to please join me in thanking the speakers for their presentations today.

(Applause.)

We're scheduled for a break at this time and we'll come back, why don't we say at 3:17 since we're running a little bit late. Thank you. We'll see you at 3:17.

(Break.)

MR. LUTTER: Welcome to our final set of presentations for the "Behind the Counter Availability of Certain Drugs Public Meeting." Our next speaker is Dr. Saul Shiffman from Pinney Associates.

DR. SAUL SHIFFMAN: We can put up the presentation. I do want to start with the good news that this is the beginning of the last panel of the day. My name is Saul Shiffman. I'm a professor at the University of Pittsburgh. I also consult to Pinney Associates Consultancy on OTC switches and risk management under whose auspices I appear today. And as you see on the slide, I also consult to the pharmaceutical industry and have other interests.

MR. LUTTER: You'll want to speak a little bit closer to the mike.

DR. SHIFFMAN: Okay, sorry. By way of background, I've been conducting research on health behavior and smoking for a little over 30 years – I don't want to say quite how long, and have been involved in the OTC switch of nicotine replacement products as well as several other complex switches. Now, several speakers have already mentioned nicotine replacement as an example of over-the-counter availability, and in fact, I would like to use the OTC switch of nicotine replacement therapies for smoking cessation to illustrate a few key points.

First, that with a systematic approach to OTC even complex switches can be managed and, in fact, we need to recognize that today we're in the era of the new OTC paradigm, that is, full OTC availability, but supported by a system of consumer guidance and in-market surveillance. Now, OTC uniquely affords consumers access to needed medication and conversely putting medications behind the counter can impair access. In other words, the OTC system is not broken, but BTC may well break it.

The NRT switch is a useful case study of the new OTC paradigm and, in fact, we've been researching the experience with NRT over the last ten years, have recently published a review of those publications and analyses, and those will be the basis for my comments today. But stepping back, OTC switches and the current consideration of BTC status involve balancing two factors. The benefits of increased public access and public health benefit of access to effective medication and concerns that increased access would lead to misuse of medications. And the history of NRT shows that we can successfully manage that balance in an OTC setting.

Starting with the benefits of access. The need for more access to and more use of NRT was then and is now urgent because smoking kills one half of the smokers who don't quit and NRT has known to double the chances that a smoker has to quit. Yet, when NRT was a prescription medication, it was underused and therefore limited in its public health impact. So the aim of the OTC switch was to increase utilization of NRT. Was this successful? The answer yes. The use of NRT increased by 150 percent as a result of the OTC switch, and, in fact, that increase in utilization has been sustained and the benefits are dramatic. It's estimated that OTC NRT has saved over a million lives in the U.S. since the time of the switch. So OTC access can be lifesaving.

Could we have achieved the same results with BTC? The data suggests not. These data come from Australia, which has a BTC category and, in fact, NRT product started – went through a number of regulatory steps, starting being behind the counter going to over the counter, but for sale in pharmacies only and finally, going for OTC sale in a full range of retail outlets, the equivalent of our OTC. And what you can see is that with each step of increased access, utilization and therefore, public health benefit went up, and, in fact, it went up 150 percent, going from BTC to full OTC.

So the benefit of the over-the-counter switch of NRT is clear, but there were certainly many concerns at the time of the switch. It was a groundbreaking switch in many, many ways. It was meant to be used for months, not days. It was to be used for prevention, not for symptom relief, and it was intended to promote behavior change, but without formal counseling with a professional. And after all, it was putting a potentially addicted substance on OTC shelves. So there were concerns that NRT would be abused by youth and non-smokers, that smokers would use it for purposes other than cessation, that users would transfer their addiction to tobacco to NRT and use it for a long time and there were more subtle concerns that taking NRT on prescription would cause physicians to disengage from smoking cessation and that smokers would lose access to behavioral treatment which is considered important for quitting.

The FDA and the sponsors took these concerns very seriously and addressed them programmatically. As formal conditions of approval, NRT was not to be sold to anyone – was not to be sold in convenient stores or vending machines or to anyone under 18 and, in fact, age verification was set up in the retail environment. A consumer 800 number was set up to collect and address consumer concerns and further pharmacists, thousand of pharmacists were trained to help smokers choose the right medications and to help them quit smoking. In fact, I can't help but comment that many of the speakers today have talked about the virtues of counseling by a pharmacist, but in fact, that is available to consumers today in the OTC marketplace. So the issue seems to be more of who's going to fund it which would seem to be a very different issue than that before us today.

Additionally, users of NRT were offered free behavioral treatment through carefully developed clinically meaningful print and web programs, and the marketing was targeted toward adult smokers who are committed to quitting smoking, and importantly the products were not marketed as magic bullets, but rather as aids to cessation. To be sure that over-the-counter NRT was used appropriately, FDA also mandated a thorough program of surveillance. So media reports were monitored for indications of misuse or abuse, a network of school of community officials were regularly polled to watch for any emerging trends of abuse. Population surveys and purchase databases were analyzed to assess patterns of NRT use, and calls to consumer hotlines were analyzed and the surveillance data were regularly reported to FDA.

So with all of this in place, how did things turn out? The results have been very positive and reassuring. There has been no pattern of misuse by youth or non-smokers. In fact, NRT is used by adult smokers for the purpose of quitting smoking. Use of NRT beyond the indicated period actually decreased from that scene in the prescription era and physicians have stayed actively involved in smoking cessation and in OTC treatment. In fact, it's been estimated that physicians make ten million recommendations a year for OTC NRT products, and programs – behavioral support programs developed by – oops – developed by the sponsors demonstrated through randomize clinical trials that effective convenient behavioral intervention could be widely disseminated through OTC channels, using new technology. In other words, all of the concerns about increased access to NRT have been addressed while maintaining open OTC access to these important – (inaudible) – allowing more people to use NRT and saving lives.

In summary then, the experience with NRT shows that concerns about misuse of OTC products can be managed using systematic, programmatic approach with FDA input and sponsor accountability. So would BTC help better manage OTC medications? The GAO's report certainly concluded that this was not the case. As you've already heard, the GAO concluded that putting medicines behind the counter did not add to public health or assist in the management of OTC or non-prescription medications.

So given the public health success of over-the-counter NRT as an example, FDA should think very critically and very carefully about any approach such as BTC that would reduce Americans' access to needed medications as long as things can be managed in an OTC environment. So OTC allows access to needed medications and consumers reap the health benefits. BTC hampers public access to effective medication and without a demonstrated benefit, behind the counter status would be an unnecessary barrier to consumers and potentially an impediment rather than a help to public health.

Thank you for the time and for your attention.

MR. LUTTER: Thank you very much, Dr. Shiffman, for your remarks. Our next speaker is Ms. Ashley McEvoy from McNeil Consumer Healthcare.

ASHLEY MCEVOY: Good afternoon. My name is Ashley McEvoy, and I'm president of McNeil Consumer Healthcare. We are a leading manufacturer of OTC medications in the U.S. and around the globe. In addition to these remarks, we plan to submit expanded written comments to the docket as well. We would like to thank the FDA for opening what we hope will be an ongoing dialogue on the importance of providing consumers with expanded access to products to optimize the healthcare benefit.

Our company believes behind the counter should not be viewed as a way to restrict consumer access to medicine, but rather should be driven by the overarching goal of expanding consumer access to safe, effective and appropriate medications. Products currently OTC, which are already generally recognized as safe and effective, when used according to label directions should not be considered in these discussions, nor should it be an option where an Rx-to-OTC switch would be safe and effective and appropriate without distribution limitations. However, we do recognize that in some cases increasing access to a medicine currently available only by prescription may be best achieved through a model with distribution restrictions as an intermediate or fixed step. It should be the objective of these discussions to combine increased consumer convenience, personal control over one's own healthcare, access to guidance and counseling from a pharmacist or other healthcare professional, all while ensuring broader, safe access to beneficial medications.

We recognize that there may be situations where behind the counter status might be appropriate to optimize the healthcare benefit to the consumer. However, each situation should be evaluated on a case by case basis through the NDA process so it may be done in a data driven manner. A continuum could result for OTC products that would begin with the prescription product and after evaluation of the submitted data. A product could be switched from Rx-to-OTC as we know today; a product could be moved from Rx-to-OTC requiring the interaction of a pharmacist or a healthcare provider as a transitional step; or a product could move to OTC requiring the interaction of a pharmacist or a healthcare provider as the final step. Through the decision-making process, the umbrella goal of expanding access to medications should always be kept top of mind.

In closing, multiple organizations and individuals have a stake in this discussion. Many are here today. The path forward should involve consideration of difficult issues with the stakeholders. The path forward will also involve consideration of new data so the path will be one that is driven by science. Ultimately, the path forward will expand access of medications to increase consumer convenience and control over their own healthcare.

In sum, we are committed to expanding consumer access to safe, effective and appropriate medicines, and we will support the FDA in all of its effort to make that goal a reality. Thank you.

MR. LUTTER: Thank you very much, Ms. McEvoy. Our next speaker is Dr. Richard Crout, former director of Bureau of Drugs at FDA. Welcome.

DR. RICHARD CROUT: Hello. My name is Richard Crout. I am testifying at this hearing as an individual and represent no other party. I served as director of the Bureau of Drugs, now CDER, from 1973-1982. I was intimately involved in both the policy development and implementation of the OTC review during those years.

The OTC drug category has always included a behind the counter subgroup. Pharmacists have the authority to place any OTC drug behind the counter, and until the last half of the 20th century, most drugs both OTC and prescription, were typically dispensed to the patient directly by their pharmacists. This general practice weighed in with the rise of chain store pharmacies and the mass distribution of OTC drugs, but the BTC category remains available today for certain specific drugs or situations. These are: one, insulin, which has always been OTC under the Food, Drug and Cosmetic Act, but is held BTC because it needs refrigeration; pseudophederine, which has recently been placed BTC because it can easily be converted to methamphetamine; third is Plan B, which require certification by the user of her age; and fourth, drug products subject to theft, typical ones are nicotine patches and Prilosec, at least in my neighborhood, but may include any drug at the discretion of the pharmacy.

It is important to note that these BTC drugs are under pharmacist control and that signatures and records keeping may be required for their dispensing, but the decision to dispense is a ministerial one. The pharmacist's duty is to see that certain regulatory product integrity or commercial requirements are met. These are valiant professional duties, but they do not place the pharmacist in the role of a prescriber or learned intermediary.

The question today is whether to go beyond these few examples and establish an expressed category of drugs: pharmacist controlled drugs. This question has been considered twice previously by the FDA. The first of these occasions was at the time of the FDA's landmark review of all OTC drugs began in 1971. The agency was lobbied intensively at that time by both advocates for and opponents of what was then called the third class of drugs. Predictably, the advocates were the APHA for and the AMA against. The Community Pharmacists Association's for and the chain store association's against, with the drug manufactures divided, depending on what each thought was best for its business.

The same arguments presented today were heard then. In the end, those of us responsible for the OTC review were persuaded that customers had to be trusted to make their own decisions on selection of an OTC drug, that manufacturers were obligated to give them truthful and accurate labeling in lay language, that the consumers' self-diagnoses had to govern since no health professional, physician or pharmacist was in a position to diagnose illness in the public setting of a pharmacy and that pharmacists' control of a properly labeled OTC drug was not likely to add to its safe and effective use.

Indeed, if such control were necessary, the Durham-Humphrey standards would require that the drug be a prescription drug rather than OTC drug. We, therefore, rejected the idea of a third class of drugs. This broad policy decision has stood to this day with few exceptions noted previously.

The second occasion for a review of BTC class of drugs occurred in 1995 when Congressman Dingell in the context of his committee oversight asked the GAO to review the evidence for creating such a class. You've heard about the GAO report and what it says and I will not review that further. I would only note that if you have not read the GAO report, I would strongly urge that you do so. It has regrettably a devastating account of foreign experience.

The current thrust for a BTC class of drugs seems to contemplate a new wave of prescription to OTC switches would be aided by a BTC policy. It is useful to examine some of the drugs suggested by some for such a switch. One example, seasonal allergy medications. Since the apparently successful switch of Claritin to OTC status, some have proposed switching the whole class of seasonal allergy medications, including Allergra and Zyrtec to OTC status. This is reasonable proposal from a medical and regulatory point of view, as far as I can tell, but there is no evidence that a BTC category is needed for such a switch. If Claritin can sit safely on a shelf, available to consumers without a prescription, the other drugs in the same class can too. The other drugs in the class are for practical purposes identical and pose no safety or drug selection issues requiring the intervention of a health professional.

Second set of drugs suggested is erectile dysfunction drugs. Some have suggested that this group of drugs can be used safely without a prescription and they certainly meet the test that the consumers able to diagnose the condition. (Laughter.) If switched to OTC, however, it is difficult to imagine what additional information the health professional could impart to the consumer that he has not already seen on television advertising. There may be a case for making them OTC, but there's no rationale for placing them BTC.

Let me turn to cholesterol lowering drugs. This proposal is driven by applications from Bristol-Myers and Merck to switch their respective statins, Pravachol and lovastatin, from Rx to OTC status. Careful consideration of this proposal reveals several important logistical, professional, legal and economic problems that need to be dealt with. To diagnose and manage patients with lipid disorders in a pharmacy setting will require pharmacies to build statin clinics that can assure patient privacy and accommodate physical examinations and blood drawings. Serious questions of professional roles, licensure, records keeping and liability would need to be resolved. A point I don't think that's been emphasized, the regulation of their advertising would move from the Food and Drug Administration to the Federal Trade Commission. On the economic side, consumers with health insurance would soon discover that their out-of-pocket cost were higher.

Finally, if these problems could be overcome and such statin clinics came into being, many patients would find that their particular – that these particular statins did not provide adequate reduction of the LDL levels. In fact, the best such statin clinic could do is pick off the easiest patients to treat, and refer the rest to their consumers elsewhere. There is no other healthcare model in our society that by design is intended to offer suboptimal therapy with obsolete drugs for a potentially life-threatening risk. Once the true character of this proposal is fully understood by the public, I do not think it will pass ethical or political scrutiny, let alone medical common sense.

Other antihyper drugs such as antihypertensive and antibiotics have been proposed – and I will not dwell on the details at the moment, because I'd like to suggest an alternative model. I would suggest that the FDA and others pay attention to the health miniclinics that are now evolving in several major chain store pharmacies, including CVS, Walgreens and Wal-Mart. These miniclinics are typically staffed with a nurse practitioner who sees patients in a private examining room for a limited set of conditions, like common infectious illnesses allergies, skin conditions, vaccine administration of all the standard vaccines and specialty items like camp physicals, pregnancy-testing cholesterol-testing, blood pressure-testing. The nurse practitioner is authorized to prescribe appropriate drugs under standard protocols, including antibiotics for strep throat and urinary tract infections. Patients who present with illnesses beyond this scope are referred elsewhere.

The miniclinic in the chain store pharmacy is just emerging, but it bears watching as a model with many advantages. First, it is a business model in the private sector and some serious business persons must think they have the potential for long-term economic viability. Second, they are solving the logistical problems of facilities, professional roles licensure, liability, records keeping and quality assurance. They are, in fact, small medical clinics of limited scope, but within those limits practice quality medicine. They are operated by health businesses within the premises of a pharmacy, but are not professionally responsible to the pharmacist. These clinics and the pharmacy does enjoy a symbiotic relationship in which each brings in business for the other, but the traditional separation of the drug prescribing health professional from the drug dispensing pharmacist is maintained thereby minimizing the potential for conflict of interest.

Finally, and let us look expansively into a potentially better future. They could, if they expand appropriately, take on the treatment of well- established preventive treatments like cigarette addiction, hyperlipidemia and high blood pressure. They might even make an impact on cardiovascular mortality. That, I submit, is a goal worth thinking about. The best the FDA could do to support the miniclinic movement, I would suggest, is to do no harm.

Thank you.

MR. LUTTER: Thank you, Dr. Crout. Our next speaker is Dr. Stephen Mann, from the Mann Healthcare Ltd.

DR. STEPHEN MANN: Good afternoon. My name is Stephen Mann. I'm an independent pharmaceutical consultant. I was the lead physician on the switch of simvastatin to self-medication status in the U.K. And I'm going to use that case study to illustrate how behind the counter works in the United Kingdom.

Just to remind everybody as well as prescription only medicines, obviously there are two other classes of medicines in the U.K. The P class is the one we're talking about here. This means that the drug has to be sold under supervision of the pharmacist and it is effectively behind the counter. That is the default category for when drugs move to self-medication status in the U.K. It's also transitional class in that some of those medicines in time will shift into more general distribution where they are effectively over-the-counter and self-selection is allowed. An increasing number of the medicines have been doing that recently.

In 2004, simvastatin ten milligrams were switched for the indication to reduce the risk of a heart attack, and I'm going to describe to you how that whole paradigm was developed, what the intention behind it was, and the experience that we've had in terms of actually making it work in pharmacies. Cardiovascular disease is a major problem in the U.K. We come very poorly in the rankings and it's the commonest cause of premature death in both men and women in the United Kingdom. The government sees cardiovascular disease as a major public health priority. And in 2004 when the switch was being considered, it should be remembered that only very high-risk patients were allowed to have statin treatment on the National Health Service. This left a massive population that was at lower levels of risk, but for which there was a clear body of evidence demonstrating that treating moderate risk was a very worthwhile thing to do. So defining a moderate risk population that could then be targeted for self-medication was felt to have enormous potential for improving public health.

To maximize the impacts on public health, in consultation with experts in the agency, it was decided that a very simple model should be developed, that it should rely primarily self-reported risk factors. It assumed a population average in those age groups that are targeted for blood pressure and cholesterol. It removed the need for liver function testing, which was felt to be unnecessary. I'm sorry?

MS. : (Off mike.)

DR. MANN: Okay. I'm sorry.

It removed the need for liver function testing, which was felt to be unnecessary, and somewhat surprisingly even to the company, lipid status testing was felt to be something that should be encouraged, but was not necessarily mandatory before the statin was dispensed on the basis that if you are at sufficient risk to justify statin treatment, then lowering your cholesterol will benefit you no matter what the starting point.

I think you'll agree this is a fairly radical population-based approach for statin use, but it was intended to produce the maximum public health impact. It was also felt that lifestyle modification could be addressed at the same time in pharmacies.

Just very quickly that the model that we ended up with men over 55 qualify, younger men 45 and over, and women 55 and over had to have an additional risk factor. Again, these were all self-reported, so an early – a history of cardiovascular disease, positive smoking status, being overweight, or being of South Asian ethnicity. Those were the only qualifying factors.

And as with all switches to behind the counter in the U.K., a great emphasis is put on pharmacy training. These were the guides that were distributed to every pharmacy in the U.K. There was also online web-based training and a lot of seminars were held around the country. So pharmacists received a huge amount of information to help them understand this category and understand how to appropriately select patients.

Another thing that's frequently used and was certainly used in this case is a questionnaire to aid delivery of the paradigm in the pharmacy. This – you won't be able to read this obviously, but it was designed to be very simple to do. It was piloted and 50 percent of consumers could complete this in less than four minutes, 75 percent could complete it in less than eight minutes, obviously that leaves some others – had a slightly more difficult history to be dealt with.

Well, how do we get on? A mystery shopping exercise was undertaken in both 2004 and 2005 and what this – what's entailed was 180 pharmacy consultations. These were model patients. These were consumers who should definitely qualify for the statin and had no factors that would disqualify them. The chart shows the recommendation received from each type of pharmacy, and overall 62 recommendations were received in 180 calls. And I remind you these were consumers who should have qualified.

So the average conversion, at least in 2005, was only 34 percent. The reason for showing this chart is across the range of pharmacies, you'll see that there's a great variation in how this is delivered. Some of the multiple, such as (boost ?) seemed to have improved considerably, but I'd also draw your attention to the independent group which is the fourth category along where really levels of recommendation have remained very low, and I think may be good reasons for that.

The reasons for non-recommendation are given in this chart, and you can see there're quite a number of them, including basically empathy about the product, but a great majority were directed to the general practitioner and a reasonably large number were given dietary advice, although these were clearly people at moderate risk and would have benefited from a statin.

Redirection to the general practitioner, which we just saw on the other chart is a major factor, has increased between 2004 and 2005. In 2005, the bulk of those were being sent for a cholesterol test and as you saw earlier on the paradigm actually does not mandate a cholesterol test at all, and 17.3 percent pharmacists just basically said they didn't feel they had sufficient knowledge to be able to recommend. In each scenario, referral was not necessarily according to the protocol. When pharmacists used the questionnaire, they were much more likely to recommend. So of the – when the questionnaire was used and it was only used in 27 percent of consultations, about 67 percent of those consultations – 62 percent of those consultations resulted in sale; when it's not used, that conversion rate is much, much lower at 24 percent.

The outcome of the switch, as you've heard from others, has been very disappointing. All of the factors given there are important. Consumer education attitude and general practitioner attitudes may be pretty much unique to the U.K., but pharmacists' behavior is critical. OTC uses produce no new safety issues and the so-called use of base although small is educated, knows and understands the risks and is addressing all the risk factors, including positive lifestyle changes.

So in summary, the POM piece, which is simvastatin, was a bold regulatory move based on signed clinical evidence to address a major public health concern. Pharmacists have adopted a very cautious attitude and in the case of simvastatin have a very low threshold for investigation and/ or referral even when this is not appropriate. Pharmacists show great reluctance to use the questionnaire that was supplied, although using it clearly improves their performance. Possible reasons for that include lack of time or staffing problems and that may be more of the factor in the small independent pharmacies than in the larger chains. There appears to be a lack of confidence to recommend and maybe again this is a time issue because of the requirement to be educated on the paradigm and the condition.

Another factor that should be borne in mind is once a class like this is introduced, then the pharmacist may find him or herself administering multiple protocols and this may involve keeping questionnaires, for example, for – (unintelligible) – emergency contraception, and this produces a considerable administrative burden for busy pharmacies. Interestingly, Internet pharmacy sales as a result seem to be increasing in popularity because they avoid these difficulties.

So, in conclusion, although a behind the counter class may appear to offer benefits for appropriate consumer selection, in practice this is pretty questionable. Consumers are often given a self-selection questionnaire to deliver and the model can be very simple, and so it could be argued that pharmacist consultation could be optional in that process. Experience in the U.K. suggests that pharmacist intervention often leads to consumers being inappropriately denied access to medicines. In other words, the pharmacist, far from acting as a facilitator, may in many cases act as a barrier. The barriers of behind the counter status may, therefore, considerably blunt any public health impacts which drove the innovative switch in the first place.

Thank you for your attention.

DR. LUTTER: Thank you very much, Dr. Mann. Our next speaker is Mr. Steven Francesco of Francesco International. Let me caution you to speak very closely to the mike because more so at this end of the room than in the back, there appears to be an audible disturbance that's competing with you for our attention. (Laughter.)

STEVEN FRANCESCO: Oh, we also lost our slide champion. All right. Good. Okay. Good, good.

Thank you very much. It's a pleasure to be here, and to speak over the alarms in the garage. My name is Steve Francesco. In the interest of full disclosure, I drove here, I paid for the hotel, and bought myself lunch. (Laughter.) So my opinions are strictly all my own and I'm a very interested citizen. I have about 15 years of experience on switch in the U.S. and international markets, as both a former employee of Schering Plough, Sterling Drug, Sandoz, and also 13 years as a consultation with my own business. And I'm here today to talk about the behind the counter proposal.

Now, in putting this together and frankly, you may have been in this many switch meetings as many of us in this room have been. I've had to really reflect on what it is we're talking about, and in my view with switch we always run into a collision between a public health model and a business model, and a lot of discussion today has been around financing the switch, the role of the pharmacist, will it improve distribution and broaden access. So, in fact, underlying a lot of what's going on in discussions today, in my view, are the collision of two models. There's a public health model and there is a business model. And one can honestly say that in recent history, the last seven or eight years – that's nice – the last seven or eight years, many of the rejections of switch in this room are at – with the FDA have been because of the collision of business models and public health models, and in many cases, the business models have been too grandiose and they've gone for the homerun as opposed to a single.

So, in my view, the central premise of today's meeting, at least for me, is number one BTC is not a third class of drugs. BTC is an extension of self-medication, it's in partnership with OTC, and I believe that if we really look at the prescription categories, we have numerous categories – I'm simply listing one, the black box – but non-prescription, we're talking about OTC – and now – and I applaud the FDA's initiative. We're also talking about BTC. It's an alternative form of non-prescription.

So, in my view, and I'm being very, very pragmatic, having been at many, many meetings, I feel that we need to first perhaps, at least in my view, set as a default that this is an extension of non-prescription and not a separate class of drugs. Therefore, there is no need for new and cumbersome legislation, which as we all know can take a heck of a long time, and your concern as is the concern of everyone here is enhancing public health, and it's not going to be a lot of action for a heck of a long time if we have to get legislation, especially with all the constituencies, maybe even in gridlock. Expanding self-medication is the way to go, so existing laws are sufficient in my view.

I think that the third class of drugs runs into the territory of Europe, and we've talked about the GAO analysis of the European pharmacist role. It's important to remember that the European countries developed one by one. Many of the classification came in after World War II in the late '60s and late '70s, and many of the pharmacies, in fact, were extensions of the government. So, for example, in a place like France, you have seven classifications of drugs. I really don't think you need that kind of a bureaucracy and you will get that as you do a third class of drugs and then decide: Do you need to have a poster in the window or is a poster allowed? Can you use print advertising? Can you use TV? In my view, the challenge here for quick action is to say as a default, this is an extension of self-medication and non-prescription.

In this chart, which is from the PAGB 2005 Annual Report, the U.K. third class is somewhat transitional as would be one in the U.S. The goal is not necessarily to transit to OTC, although we do want that. What we're saying is the BTC group has the potential to transfer to OTC, but in fact, it's an alternative to Rx for broader distribution. So a comparison to OTC volumes is not necessarily relevant for certain groups.

The other point to mention as well is that in terms of profit – and there has been a big issue here about paying the pharmacist. In the U.K., when they established their POM and P status, they provided a guaranteed profit margin for that pharmacist because they wanted to keep pharmacists spread out through the country. So one of the issues we're talking about here is the time –

in other words, the U.K. pharmacist has time. How is he paid? He had a guaranteed profit margin on the products that were on POM.

We're at the risk of being a little bit too strong. What we have in the United States – and I don't mean this in a negative way – is we fall off a cliff after the physician. And in a sense, we go to the lowest common denominator at the moment, and we have to do that. Actual use, trials, and various other efforts must demonstrate that the public is capable of being involved in self-medicating without the learned intermediary. What we're talking about here is filling that gap, and I think we can successfully, without a lot of legislation via the pharmacist – and, as one of the other speakers mentioned, with the miniclinics, I think, as in the U.K., you have other healthcare professionals who can also handle the responsibility of certain categories if they use certain protocols similar to the U.K.

So here's what I consider to be practical. Really we're talking about OTC with all the same rights and privileges of OTC, at least that's what I'm talking about: advertising, OTC labeling, actual use. You may, in fact, be able to, as a thought, redesign actual use to come as a BTC alternative or an OTC alternative. In fact, if you go back to the nonsedating antihistamine discussions in 2001, I think it was, where I testified the arguments by the pharma companies to prevent the switch of nonsedating antihistamines were, I think, we all kind of agree disingenuous at best. If there had been a BTC alternative, there was an alternative for the FDA and that is test. Give me the information that says it should not be available without a prescription via the BTC route, because you wouldn't have lost the entire learned intermediary role, you would have had a pharmacist who's an eligible player on this. So I think a BTC has a wonderful future for those types of issues and that it also says it doesn't give the FDA the right to force a switch. It will be done commercially.

What we're talking about here today, as well, is as the switch panorama has moved, you can see that on the left we have short-term acute use, chronic recurrent in the middle, and long-term use on the right, at the top you have self-diagnosis, and at the bottom, you have doctor consultation. As you move across this grid, what we're focusing on today is discussing how to manage most of the lower right-hand corner. Those are all very challenging switches. There's a lot of public health to be improved, using – looking at those, I'm convinced that BTC is a way to do it, and, in fact, as you'll see, BTC really should be a transitional class.

Now, let's be honest about the commercial issues that are here. Why haven't we had much switch in the last few years? Here I have a chart that talks about the pharma type, the attitude and the fear. What we're seeing here is that really big pharma Rx and OTC are very much negative towards switch, and that's because of lowered volume. Rx only are very negative because of lost reimbursement. That's also true for Rx and OTC. OTC only is very negative because of increased competition and liability. However, if you do provide an environment for BTC – and I have some suggestions on this – you'll have a new competitive environment. I'm convinced that with the right incentives, you'll have private equity who would be positive towards BTC because they're interested in cash flow. Venture capital would be positive because they're interested in product portfolio. Entrepreneurs because – they're positive because of the interest in opportunity. Private enterprise, we know where the best candidates are and we'll go after them, if there's an opportunity to do it. So I think BTC provides a very interesting competitive dynamic, which we need to put into the equation.

Some ideas for commercial incentives. Number one, without question expand use of Waxman-Hatch to BTC, possibly to up to five years. Allow the reuse of Waxman-Hatch to go OTC and make it a true transition class and answer those questions which were not resolved earlier. Allow reduced clinical programs if only interested in BTC status that would save money and speed approval. Reward pharmacists for its involvement via pricing. Again, with Waxman-Hatch. It has exclusivity. The pharmacist deserves to make some money. You gain valuable proprietary knowledge from the pharmacist hopefully if data is requested, and of course, go beyond pharmacy via protocols, which was mentioned by one of the previous speakers.

What we have an opportunity to get is a whole lot more data, and what I'm particularly interested in personally is, as you remember the switch of the vaginal – (unintelligible) – back in the early '90s, there was something called an initial medical diagnosis, which allowed an identification and afterward the sufferer was, in fact, found to be as effective in diagnosing their malady as effective as the doctor. I would like to return to being able to use the initial medical diagnosis and I believe that would be a very good environment for a drug in BTC.

So, in conclusion, I believe that this is a promising enhancement of non-prescription. I don't think the third class of drugs. I think you'd have a business model, which is remodified, and I think that a lot of the questions that have been discussed today in terms of software, location of the pharmacy space, the indications that are going to be discussed, you must resolve the financing. You must address the financing, and I think in this country which is very competitive and very enterprising, I think a lot of the issues will get resolved.

Thank you.

DR. LUTTER: Thank you very much for your presentation. Our next speaker is Mr. George Quesnelle from GlaxoSmithKline Consumer Healthcare.

GEORGE QUESNELLE: Good afternoon. My name is George Quesnelle. I'm president of GlaxoSmithKline Consumer Healthcare in North America. I'm here today to speak in support of the current two-class system of drugs: prescription or over the counter.

As one of the leading Rx OTC switch companies, GCK has had a great deal of experience with particularly difficult switches. These are first-in¬class switches like Nicorette, for example, the first OTC smoking cessation therapy, and Alli for weight control, products where there may be unique issues and/or a need for programs to help consumers change behavior. I was involved with both these switches, and I can tell you from experience we do not need a third class of drugs. FDA and industry can work together using regulation already in place to design unique innovative programs to help consumers safely and appropriately use these OTC medications.

Not only can we do this under our current system, we're doing it now. For appropriate products, OTC access maximizes consumer access. Greater consumer access can result in significant public health benefit, and responsible companies working closely with FDA can develop conditions for approval to allow safe and effective OTC access. I'll go quickly to the next two slides because they've been talked about several times today and that is that FDA has looked at this issue several times, as has the GAO, and in each of these cases, it's been determined that we do not need a third class of drugs, that the current system works well.

And if that's the case, what do we do when these particularly challenging situations are talked about? And for answers, I'll turn it to examples. The switch of Nicorette from Rx OTC has led to significant public health benefit. Back in the mid-1990s, however, it was considered quite challenging for a number of reasons. Its active ingredient is nicotine and nicotine is an addicting substance. There was concern about potential for misuse and abuse, especially by teens, possibly using it as an entry way to smoking. Concern that lack of intervention by healthcare professionals would result in lower quit rates, and concern about marketing based on the advertising and marketing practices of cigarette companies in the past.

But with all those challenges, working together with FDA, GSK's predecessor company designed a series of pre-approval research studies and innovative post-approval marketing commitments to educate, guide and support consumers in safely and effectively using the product. We also committed to end market monitoring to ensure that our programs were doing what they were supposed to do. And as a result, Nicorette was approved for OTC use in January 1996. The approval for requirements for Nicorette included the GSK had to conform to labeling which included use only by adults 18 years and older. We had to restrict sale of Nicorette to locations where it was feasible to obtain proof of age at the register. And I'll remind you that in those days, not all retail outlets were equipped to handle age verification as they are today.

We also agreed to conduct monitoring to ensure that the product was not being abused by teens, and there were also a number of restrictions on the way the product could be marketed. GSK lived up to all of those commitments and filed reports with FDA every quarter. In 2002, because no signs or signals emerged on any of these issues, these measures were no longer deemed necessary by FDA. So here's the case where a challenging first-in-class switch was accomplished. And I want to look now at the benefit to the consumer.

We know for a fact that OTC access makes a difference. It increases use of nicotine replacement therapy. These are data showing a number of quit attempts made by people using Nicorette gum and all brands of nicotine patches between 1993 and 1998. There was a two to three fold increase in quit attempts after these products became available over the counter. From clinical studies, we know that using an NRT product doubles a person's chances quitting versus going cold turkey, and that is true whether the product is Rx or OTC.

Based on these facts, Dr. Shiffman, who smoked – who spoke earlier, of the University of Pittsburgh – he has never smoked, I can tell you that – (laughter) – has estimated that 7.6 million smokers have successfully quit smoking using an NR therapy over the counter. This is significantly more than the number of people who quit when the products were only Rx.

Now, let's turn our attention to Alli and weight loss. There were also a number of concerns surrounding the OTC switch of Alli. Alli is a lower dose form of Xenical. They're prescription product, which has been marketed Rx since 1999. We knew that Alli was not a magic pill. It would provide significantly more weight loss than diet alone, but a low-fat diet is not – is a necessary part of the program. Similar to smoking cessation, our first concern was whether we could help consumers to change their behavior without medical professional intervention. There was also concern about potential for teenage misuse and abuse, especially by bulimics and anorexics, and whether proper consumer – whether the proper consumer in the right range of overweight could select the product. As with NRT, there were questions about how the program would be marketed, primarily given the outlandish claims we see from many supplement and herbal products that are on the market today.

Again, working with FDA, we developed careful pre-submission clinical and post-marketing programs to answer these tough but legitimate questions, resulting in OTC approval in February of this year. And even though, it's early in the marketing of the product, we've already seen the impact of increased consumer access. This chart shows the number of people who've made weight loss attempts using Alli since the product first reached retail shelves in June through the month of September this year. The same date are shown for the comparable period in 2006 when the product was only available by prescription. The number of users went from 96,000 when the product was Rx to two million after OTC availability.

And although we don't yet have the outcome estimates we have with nicotine replacement therapy, we've had a great deal of contact with consumers. And while these comments you see here are admittedly anecdotal, they're typical of many of the comments we receive. While this is anecdotal information, it shows evidence that people are engaged with Alli and are changing their behavior, and if you'd like to see more comments, both good and bad, I urge you to go online to myalli.com and look at our message boards.

So what would happen if instead of being OTC, Alli and NRT were placed behind the counter? Well, we can't know for sure. We do have information on nicotine replacement therapy that provides an indication. This information is from one of the nation's largest retailers. In some areas, because of concern over theft, retailers have put NRT products behind the counter. What we see there is a 30 percent drop in unit sales when these products are BTC instead of OTC. In some areas, it's as high as 57 percent. If adopted nationally, BTC declines could be even more significant, given consumers hesitancy to discuss private health concerns in a public pharmacy setting.

I want to take you back to the estimated 7.6 million people that have quit due to OTC smoking cessation products being available. Let's assume that instead of OTC, nicotine replacement therapy had been placed BTC from launch. Based on the evidence I've just showed you, we would have seen 30 percent fewer consumers who would have quit smoking using these products. That means that 2.3 million people would not have quit smoking; 2.3 million people would not have been able to quit because a safe and effective product was not readily available when they wanted to purchase it, and they would still be exposed to the tars, toxins and carcinogens of cigarette smoke. Two million three hundred thousand people is equal to the entire population of the city of Philadelphia.

I conclude where I began. The current two-class system of Rx or OTC is a system that works well. OTC status can maximize consumer access and consumer access can result in significant public health benefit. FDA can demand that companies working in this area of first-in-class switch with unique issues provide the appropriate education, support consumer guidance and, if necessary, monitoring to ensure the consumers use these products safely and appropriately in the OTC marketplace so that consumers can derive the maximum benefit from these products.

Thank you for the opportunity to present.

DR. LUTTER: Thank you very much, Mr. Quesnelle. We have time for questions from the panel. We'll continue following the United Nations protocol of raising flags vertically when you have a question that you'd like to ask. Jane?

MS. : I'd like to ask Mr. Francesco. He described a business model that might be helpful that might work for behind the counter, but we've had several speakers that have said that the existing prescription over-the-counter system works perfectly well, even for complex products that make it difficult to switch. So do you see – or why do you see, if you do, a need for a behind the counter system, when we have two systems that seem to be working?

MR. FRANCESCO: The question is why do we need an alternative to existing OTC? I think there's abundant evidence to show that a number of drugs either have not been presented to the FDA or have been presented to the FDA and been rejected. And the standard for OTC switch – there are three standards: safety, safety and safety. So that you know that the drug is effective, but usually it's an issue of safety and you've seen that really in the lipid-lowerings where the vote – the first vote was always, yes, we know it lowers lipids, but the second question was we don't think you provided evidence that this is going to be suitable in an OTC environment without a learned intermediary.

My contention using that as an example is that let's take an initial medical diagnosis approach that I mentioned. If you had an initial medical diagnosis and testing of the level of cholesterol, if diagnosed that you need it, the first prescription is, let's say, reimburse written by the doctor, then you get the rest at the pharmacy, the physician can be reconnected by the pharmacist, if he chooses to, but in my view, you would have plenty of opportunity to have interaction between the pharmacist, the patient, and the doctor. So I think in lipid lowering, you would both have had more clear sailing because of that second vote. I think there are other drugs that would fit that category and they are on my chart that are in the lower right-hand corner.

MR. LUTTER: Other questions from the panel? Vicky Babb?

VICKY BABB (PH): Hi, I'd like to direct my question to Dr. Mann. And I apologize for my lack of knowledge about U.K.'s regulatory framework, but of the three categories that you described, do you have – does the U.K. have direct to consumer advertising, and if you do, have regulatory authority over there, are there differences in the categories in how they're advertised?

DR. MANN: Well, the three categories, prescription only cannot be direct to consumer advertised anywhere in Europe, but the P category and the GSL category can be advertised direct to consumers. That advertising is regulated by an industry body, but the government obviously also keeps a very close eye on that and can take companies to task if they feel the advertising oversteps any boundaries. The one exception – the one difference is that when you've got a new switch, such as was the case with simvastatin, the agency, the MHRA will directly vet all advertising, all promotion, all websites for the first typically six to nine months, which was a major task in this case because there was extensive consumer education.

MR. LUTTER : Jane? Ilisa Bernstein?

ILISA BERNSTEIN: My question – many people have mentioned the GAO study and I think there's some good representatives on this panel to discuss some foreign experience. When – I've also read that GAO studying come to some different conclusions because the authors themselves recognize that the practice of pharmacy, the practice of medicine, infrastructure are very different in the United States than other countries and it's – in some ways, you're comparing apples to oranges. And I'm wondering if you could comment on that because we've heard that the GAO study said that it won't work here and, if you're comparing different things then how can you use that to predict how it might work in the United States? Any – any thoughts here?

MR. QUESNELLE: Yeah, I'd like to take a shot at it. I think the GAO study was a noble attempt to do a benchmark type of study. But as we all recognize, OTC is local. It's country-driven. The pharmacy lobbies, the pharmacy unions, the pharmacy organizations were all developed indigenously. In Europe, in country has its own, and to this day, you have multiple pharmacy organizations in countries like Canada and Australia, where there's an overlap.

My feeling is that the GAO study clearly said in some markets outside the U.S., we don't like what's going on and I think that's perfectly valid, while as you look at the U.S. market, we don't have that structure here yet. And we have the right and the privilege to design our own structure to our own standards and not to their standards. So I consider the GAO study interesting background, but I don't think their conclusions in terms of application to the U.S. is correct. So I'd agree with you.

DR. LUTTER: Other comments on the GAO study? Dr. Mann?

DR. MANN: Yes. Not on the study specifically, but on real comment that the systems are very different, so how can – are we comparing apples with pears? As I said, in the U.K. and actually throughout Europe, the default classification for when a product is switched is pharmacy only. The result is the pharmacist is meant to consult on a huge array of medicines. In other words, they're being set up to fail, particularly when you have a series of complex – relatively complex switches, where they're expected to administer questionnaires, et cetera. So you know, the system becomes complex because of the sheer volume. And interestingly in the U.K., we've seen an increasing shift from pharmacy to GSL and that trend's continued because people recognized that when that happens suddenly access goes up.

DR. SHIFFMAN: Certainly, the GAO report remarked that it was more an absence of evidence that a pharmacy only status provided a public health and regulatory benefit, but I think that's very serious because the issue is where is the burden of proof. What we've heard, it seems to me is a lot of speculation and very hopeful ideas about how it might work, but given that we have models in other countries that apparently haven't worked, that doesn't prove it couldn't work here, but it certainly creates, I think, a steep slope that we have to climb to make a database decision, that there just isn't data that is helpful; there are some data that is harmful in terms of diminishing access. So it doesn't prove that it would not be helpful, but it certainly suggests that we need better evidence than hopeful thinking.

DR. LUTTER: Thank you.

MR. GANLEY (?): Yes. This is for Dr. Shiffman. You presented one slide which was the nicotine experience in Australia and your baseline was really the behind the counter. Was that originally prescription?

DR. SHIFFMAN: The complication, as I've discovered trying to figure this out, is the – they didn't switch NRT as a class, different product forms were switched at different times. So, in fact, the data – the product on which the data clears never was prescription. It started behind the counter, and then went to these other classes. If you look more broadly and it's hard to do because the switch just took place at different times and other market conditions change, it does look like there's an increase in utilization going from Rx to behind the counter, but it's very hard to sort out because you –

literally, in one case, you had one dose of a product switching with the other staying Rx.

MR. GANLEY: Another follow-up question.

DR. LUTTER: Sure.

MR. GANLEY: I guess one of the issues for behind the counter class would be in situations where even conducting numerous label comprehension (actually use ?) studies were unable to get self-selection correct – we're able – unable to get use correct. And so the alternative is that switch does not occur, and so would behind the counter not play some role in that situation?

DR. SHIFFMAN: I think it might. As you know, these decisions have to be made on a case by case basis. But it seems to me that the pressure on sponsors to work hard to make something understandable by consumers leads to valuable innovations that allow the products to be in more widespread use, and I share Dr. Brass's concern that it's going to be very easy to default to the unsubstantiated comfort of having the medications in the BTC category with an assumption that that improves either self-selection or access.

MS. AXELRAD: If we were to conclude, to agree with many of the speakers today that a behind the counter program would substantially expand access to consumers – actually I'm addressing this to Ms. McEvoy – she's listening, but I just want to give her a heads up that I'm going to – that I'm asking her to answer this. If we were to find that the systems were in place, the support of behind the counter system, and if we were to find that it would provide substantial benefits in terms of increased access, should FDA have authority to force a switch to behind the counter status – if a company doesn't bring a proposal in themselves to do it or a whole class of drugs, for example?

MS. MCEVOY: Yeah, I think that what we shared today was, you know, clearly McNeil favors expanded access and I think that it has to be done on a case by case basis. We've heard today different discussions around different models that exist out there, where OTC status is clearly the most appropriate and then there's a potential possibility where BTC could provide expanded access for certain drugs, and I think where we're at right now is heavy in the exploratory phase of developing what those models can potentially look like and we would clearly be working with the FDA to advance those working hypothesis of where those models, those n-state models land.

MS. AXELRAD: And follow-up with that, when you say "expanded models" or "models for expanded use" and that others were saying that "we need to look at this on a case by case basis," which you said as well, I'm wondering how – if you do look at this as a case by case basis and you do have some sort of model or various models, to what extent can you as, I guess, manufacture – you can answer this as well, I guess – standardize that process so that there is less confusion out there for pharmacists and consumers in order to get that product, if it is in some BTC way? Does that – do you get my question? Is there a benefit to standardizing the approach, or do you really need to do it on a case by case, which could create some confusion out there?

MR. QUESNELLE: First point I would make is that I don't think the evidence supports that BTC increases access. I think what we've seen today is where we do have evidence, it shows the opposite that actually access can decrease. But as far as every switch goes, everyone is very individual. To think that we could have developed a kind of a paradigm that would work for smoking control that will also work for weight control, I don't think is correct. I think you have to look at each situation because the consumer population is usually different. There may be some similarities, but there are differences. You have to adapt the programs to meet the needs of that particular consumer. Again, working closely with FDA to determine what those conditions should be, not for moving it BTC, but for moving it OTC.

DR. LUTTER: Other questions from the FDA panel? Please join me in thanking – expressing our thanks to this last group of speakers.

(Applause.)

At this point on the agenda, we have an opportunity for an open microphone from – starting at 4:30. Are there other members of the audience who haven't yet had a chance to speak who would like to take advantage of this opportunity to offer oral comments to us about behind the counter access and availability? I do remind people that if they're intimidated by standing between this group at dinner or going home, there are, of course, opportunities to express comments to us in writing at the open docket, which will remain open until the 28th of November. But notwithstanding that, I welcome anyone who wishes to speak here.

Hearing no interest, I'm going to move beyond the open microphone section of our public meeting today and go to closing remarks. Let me first say that I've, by allowing my own name to be put next to closing remarks, I've accepted a somewhat daunting task, which is try and summarize an intrinsically diverse set of comments from a multiplicity of viewpoints. But let me being by first expressing simply my thanks, and the thanks of all of us at FDA to you, the people who care about this issue and the people who care about public health for your comments and your remarks and your insights, and especially for those of you who have been subjected to our questioning for the answers that you provided to our questions. We're grateful for that.

Secondly, I'd like to express my thanks to the members of the FDA team that have put this meeting together, and I think they've done so splendidly, especially Ilisa Bernstein to my left who has done so much to organize this session, and I'm also indebted to Eric Medler (sp) who's not only helped work the IT system, but has successfully defused false alarms in neighboring parts of the building without too much consternation or disruption to people here.

But I'd like to go on and say that I welcome very much the opportunity to hear from everybody here. I found the comments from the public open and informative, educational, insightful, and generally what's remarkable is that they appeared very much to share a goal that – of improving public health and that was reassuring from us, for us also to hear. They reflected a very diverse set of opinions. We've heard from pharmacists, medical societies representing MDs, OTC drug makers, National Association of Boards of Pharmacy, retail pharmacies, pharmacy schools and a collection of recognized experts and consultants.

We heard a need for and interest in a clear identification of goals for behind the counter availability and then a demonstration of benefits behind the counter availability prior to FDA action. We also heard a whole collection of informative accounts from earlier experiences with drugs being sold behind the counter. These included a statin in the United Kingdom, emergency contraception in the United States, smoking cessation products here, experiences in Canada and Australia. We also heard concern expressed about the adequacy of behind the counter access and the appropriateness of behind the counter access generally. We've heard views expressed, on the one hand, the existing laws are sufficient, and we also heard pharmacists and their representatives note that behind the counter for some drugs could increase access safely for some products.

Our goal generally at FDA is to – and our mission is to protect and promote public health, increase behind the counter access may by some accounts – and I stress the "by some accounts" here increase safe use of medically appropriate drug products, where additional action at this point is appropriate is something that we'll address after our review of these comments and also any written comments that you or other members of the public submit to our open docket which closes on November 28th.

So I thank, on behalf of FDA, all of you for coming. I thank you for your interest in this issue, for your shared commitment to public health and very much also for your continued presence here throughout the day. So thank you very much and I hope we have another chance to meet soon.

CHAPTER SOURCES

The following chapters have been previously published:

Chapter 1 – This is an edited, reformatted and augmented version of a United States Government Accountability Office publication, Report GAO-09-245, dated February 2009.

Chapter 2 – These remarks were delivered as testimony given on November 14, 2007, Randall Lutter, Deputy Commissioner for policy, Food and Drug Administration and Douglas Throckmorton, Deputy Director, Center for Drug Evaluation Research. before United States Department of Health and Human Services, United States Food and Drug Administration.

INDEX

B

C

D

E

F

G

H

I

J

L

M

N

O

P

Q

R

S

T

U

V

W